When We Listen:
A Devotional Commentary on Mark

"In his book Pastor William Robertson invites the reader to slow down, wait, and listen for the voice of God. Through his own waiting to hear God's voice through the Gospel of Mark, Robertson shares his insights in these devotions. The format is intended to help the reader to open their hearts and minds to what God may be saying to them. I would encourage you to take the time to allow this book to discover what God has to teach you through the Gospel of Mark."

Dr. David Graves
General Superintendent
Global Ministry Center
Church of the Nazarene

"Will Robertson's thoughtful work "When We Listen: A Devotional Commentary on Mark" is a verse-by-verse journey through the second Gospel that will take you deeper in your appreciation and understanding of Mark's special message. The author's "Read with me, Listen with me, Pray with me" format allows the Word to speak, provides fresh insights, and turns our hearts toward the Lord in prayer. Well worth the read for Sunday School Teachers, Small Group Leaders, Pastors, and anyone who wants to grow in their walk with the Lord."

Dr. Stan Reeder
Superintendent
Oregon Pacific District
Church of the Nazarene

WHEN
WE
LISTEN

A DEVOTIONAL COMMENTARY ON
MARK

WILLIAM S. ROBERTSON

Also by William S. Robertson

A Boy and His Tree

When We Listen: A Devotional Commentary on Mark
© 2017 William S. Robertson

Unless otherwise noted, all Scripture quotations are taken from the Christian Standard Bible ®, Copyright © 2017 by Holman Bible Publishers. Used by permission. Christian Standard Bible ® and CSB ® are federally registered trademarks of Holman Bible Publishers.

Library of Congress Cataloging in-Publication Data

Robertson, William S.
When We Listen: A Devotional Commentary on Mark
Includes bibliographical references
ISBN 13: 978-0000000000 (hardcover)
ISBN 13: 978-0000000000 (paperback)
ISBN 10: 978-0000000000 (ebook)

Printed in the United States of America

10   9   8   7   6   5   4   3   2   1

To Sharla
Who encouraged me to listen,
and to share with others what I heard.

And to Will Jr.
Without whose expertise and encouragement
this book would not exist.

WHEN WE LISTEN

A DEVOTIONAL COMMENTARY ON
MARK

READ THIS FIRST

Why This Book Exists

God still speaks!

But only those with their spiritual ears open are able to hear and understand what He is saying.

This book is an invitation to slow down, to make some time to just sit and listen to the Lord on purpose through the words of Scripture.

Lots of people read the words of the Bible. Some do it as a spiritual discipline. Some do it to meet a goal of reading through the Bible in a year. Some do it out of curiosity. But I invite you to read the words of the Bible in order to hear God's voice.

Each of these devotions is the fruit of pausing and meditating on short chunks of Scripture, slowing down and really letting the words marinate in my heart until I hear what the Lord is trying to teach me through them. Sometimes insights have come quickly; other times it has taken a little more time before I started to understand. Sometimes the Lord used the words to remind me of things that I already knew; other times He used them to open the door to a facet of His word that I had never seen before. Sometimes the words of the passage carry their own rich imagery to my heart; other times the Lord brings to mind other Scriptures that expand and enrich the meaning of that particular passage.

I always meditate on Scripture with a pen in my hand. And as the insights begin to come, I capture them in the pages of my journal, so that I can continue to meditate on them in the days to come, and so that I can share them with others. As you read, I encourage you to do the same. Don't just read what the Lord has shown me, but listen yourself to His voice. Come to the your devotional time with pen in hand, and your journal open to one side, ready to write down any insights that that Lord speaks to your heart.

Each devotional entry consists of three parts:

Read with me – This section is simply the words of Scripture. I have chosen the Christian Standard Bible (CSB) published by Holman Bible Publishers because of its accuracy, its simplicity, and its clarity. Before I begin reading, I put myself consciously in the presence of the Lord by praying the lines from Psalm 119:18: *Open my eyes so that I may contemplate wondrous things from your instruction.* I recommend that you read the whole passage slowly and, if possible, aloud, and with expression. Then read it a second time, picturing the scene in your mind as vividly as possible. Finally, read it a third time, letting the words settle into your heart, alert for any part of the passage that seems to stand out. Let the Lord use these words to direct your thoughts.

Listen with me – These are the insights that I received from my time with each of these sections of Scripture. Many of them include additional Scripture references that should be looked up for the fullest understanding of the passage. Use my insights, not as the last word on the meaning of a passage, but as a springboard for your own conversation with the Lord. As you read with your spiritual ears wide open, capture any insights that the Lord speaks to you in your journal.

Pray with me – This prayer is inspired by the insights captured in the devotional. Each prayer begins with a wide view, often using the pronoun "we." But the latter part of the prayer, where the focus is on application, becomes intensely personal, usually switching to the pronoun "I." As you read the words of these prayers, personalize them, and make them your own prayer, your own confession, your own commitment.

The Gospel According to Mark

There has been much conjecture as to when Mark composed his gospel, and where in the order of composition it stands among the other "synoptic" gospels (Matthew, Mark, and Luke). But it is enough to know that Mark wrote within the generation of those who had heard the words of Jesus directly from His lips, and had seen the miracles that He did first-hand.

Mark is usually identified with "John Mark," the cousin of Barnabas (Colossians 4:10) in whose house the Church met and prayed (Acts 12:12), and who accompanied Paul and Barnabas on their first missionary journey, but who left them part way through (Acts 13:5, 13; 15:37-39). Church tradition tells us that Mark became a close companion of the apostle Peter, and that his gospel is actually composed of the details of Jesus' life and ministry that were frequently told by Peter, which, according to Papias and Eusebius, he captured and wrote down accurately, although not in strict chronological order.

Mark's gospel is the shortest of the gospels, only sixteen chapters. It is written in a rather breathless style, moving quickly from one scene to another, from one miracle to the next. One of his most frequently-used words in Greek is "euthus," which means "immediately" or "at once". Whereas the other gospels give a significant amount of space to the teachings and discourses of Jesus, Mark includes much shorter snippets of these, preferring to emphasize Jesus' miracles, and His power over physical forces (like storms on the Sea of Galilee) and spiritual forces (like demons, which he casts out with a single command).

MARK 1:1-4

Read with me:

The beginning of the gospel of Jesus Christ, the Son of God. It is written in Isaiah the prophet: **See, I am sending my messenger ahead of you; he will prepare your way a voice of one crying out in the wilderness: Prepare the way for the Lord, make his paths straight.** *John came baptizing in the wilderness and proclaiming a baptism of repentance for the forgiveness of sins.*

Listen with me:

Mark simply assumed that when God made a promise through the prophets ("It is written…"), that He would fulfill it to the letter ("John came…"). His is the kind of faith that God wants in all of His people; the kind of faith that opens the door for His miraculous intervention.

John's job was to do exactly what Malachi (3:1) and Isaiah (40:3) had foretold in their respective prophesies. John was God's messenger, destined from the moment of His birth to announce the imminent approach of the Messiah. He would come from the wilderness, where he had spent years living in God's presence, learning to recognize His voice, and learning to trust Him implicitly as He provided for his every need. By the time God called John forth from the wilderness, he had been molded and shaped by God, into an instrument fit precisely to His hand. John's only desire was to do God's will with all of his heart, even when that meant that his own popularity would decrease so that Jesus' could increase (John 3:22-30).

But John was to do more than merely announce the coming of Jesus. He was to actively prepare the way for him - filling every valley, bringing low every mountain and hill, straightening every crooked road, and smoothing out every rough place (Luke 3:4-6). In the five hundred or so years that had elapsed since God's people had returned from Babylon, the majority of them had grown lax and careless in their relationship with Him. But God Himself was coming to visit them in the person of Jesus, the Messiah, to work an even greater deliverance for them: the deliverance from sin and death. And the people needed to be prepared; to have their hearts convicted and turned back to God; to allow the process of repentance to so soften their hard hearts that they would receive Jesus when the time for His revealing had fully come.

Of course, not everyone responded to John's call for repentance. Not everyone was willing to have their hearts prepared for God's coming by such a man as John was. But many did come. And from those prepared people, Jesus formed His initial following, that grew, and grew, and grew.

Pray with me:

Father, it is amazing to see all that you can do through even one faithful man - a man who was willing to follow You and obey You no matter what. Even though he never performed a miracle (John 10:41), John was still filled with Your Holy Spirit from birth (Luke 1:15), and he had the same power to be a witness that You promised to give us (Acts 1:8). Help me, Lord, to be as powerful as John in my witness, and as faithful to my own divine mission (Matthew 28:18-20) as he was to his. Amen.

MARK 1:5-8

Read with me:

The whole Judean countryside and all the people of Jerusalem were going out to him, and they were baptized by him in the Jordan River, confessing their sins. John wore a camel-hair garment, with a leather belt around his waist and ate locusts and wild honey.

He proclaimed, "One who is more powerful than I am is coming after me. I am not worthy to stoop down and untie the strap of his sandals. I baptize you with water, but he will baptize you with the Holy Spirit."

Listen with me:

The coming of Jesus marked a qualitative change in the way that God interacted with His people. John himself was filled with the Holy Spirit from birth (Luke 1:15), but it was very rare for people to experience the Holy Spirit's presence in their lives at all. Mary was "overshadowed" by the Holy Spirit (Luke 1:35) as the means of initiating her pregnancy, but even she was not "baptized" with the Holy Spirit at that time.

In the days before Pentecost, the Holy Spirit would usually "come upon" someone temporarily to enable them to prophecy or do mighty acts. And then He would go away. The people longed for intimacy with God, as well as the practical holiness that His Spirit living in them would bring; an intimacy and holiness that was promised by the prophets (Ezekiel 36:24-27). But up to that time, no mechanism had yet appeared to make those promises a reality. A few people still experienced the Holy Spirit's presence for a time and a purpose, but the long-awaited "baptism" had yet to appear.

But when Jesus was revealed by John's pronouncement, the mechanism was also revealed. Jesus did not baptize with the Holy Spirit in the same way that John baptized with water. In order to bring the Holy Spirit on all of God's people, Jesus first had to suffer and die to pay the death penalty for sins; He had to rise again to proclaim victory over death and hell; and then He had to ascend to the right hand of God the Father. It was from there that He finally poured out the Holy Spirit on the gathered disciples at Pentecost, and a short time later on the three thousand that believed in Jesus because of their testimony (Acts 2). Later that same "baptism" was even experienced by Gentiles (Acts 10). Being filled with the Holy Spirit immediately became the hallmark of the Christian experience.

All of that had been planned and promised long before it became a reality. But with the coming of Jesus, the relationship between God and His people took a quantum leap forward, because now He can guide and direct us, even communicate directly with us, from within our own hearts.

Pray with me:

Father, I don't think that many of us really appreciate how amazing the presence of Your Holy Spirit in our lives really is! Thank You for this massive gift, for Your very presence in my life, and for Jesus, through whom it all became possible. Amen.

MARK 1:9-11

Read with me:

In those days Jesus came from Nazareth in Galilee and was baptized in the Jordan by John. As soon as he came up out of the water, he saw the heavens being torn open and the Spirit descending on him like a dove. And a voice came from heaven: "You are my beloved Son; with you I am well pleased."

Listen with me:

God is constantly at work in the world, bringing His full plan of salvation into effect, and has been since the day that Adam and Eve rebelled against Him in the Garden of Eden. And in God's plan, everything must be done at exactly the right time. Nothing will be allowed to happen before the appointed time. God will not be rushed, and the people that He picks to fill key roles are those who will not delay in doing their part.

Even though some people who have been key parts of God's plan have tried to force His hand, to make things that He promised happen in their own strength (such as Abraham and Sarah, trying to produce the son of the promise through Sarah's maid, Hagar - Genesis 16:1-16), their actions have never actually advanced God's plan by a single second (and they ultimately lead to complications later on!). God brings together all of the pieces of His plan at exactly the time that fits best with the overall plan.

John the Baptist spent years in the wilderness waiting for God's call (Luke 1:80). But when the exact moment came for him to begin his work of preparing God's people for the appearance of Jesus, the call came, and he immediately responded (Luke 3:1-3). John had no idea when Jesus would actually show up, except that it would be at exactly the right time. John simply focused whole-heartedly on the job that God had given Him to do, secure in the understanding that everything would unfold under God's guidance at exactly the right time.

Then, on precisely the right day, at exactly the right time, Jesus came. John baptized Him on the spot (despite a moment of hesitation because of his feeling unworthy of the privilege - Matthew 3:14-15), and God expressed His pleasure straight from heaven. His plan was continuing to move forward, not too early, not a second too late, but precisely on time, with the cooperation of those whom He had chosen as key players.

Pray with me:

Father, Your plan is still moving forward today as we, Your people, tell those around us about Jesus and bring them into the kingdom. Help me to be as faithful as John and Jesus, always on the job, ready to respond immediately, so the I can faithfully do all that You have called me to do, and move Your plan forward, right on time. Amen.

MARK 1:12-13

Read with me:

Immediately the Spirit drove him into the wilderness. He was in the wilderness forty days, being tempted by Satan. He was with the wild animals, and the angels were serving him.

Listen with me:

Jesus' temptation was not some weird occurrence that surprised either Him or the Father. It was all part of the plan. The Holy Spirit personally led Him out into the wilderness to be put to the test.

Jesus started His ordeal with a 40-day fast, just like Moses underwent on Mt. Sinai (Deuteronomy 9:9). This made Him hungry, of course, but He didn't merely fast for those 40 days. Like Moses, He was with the Father for that whole time - hearing His voice, experiencing His presence and His power, and receiving instructions for His public ministry that He would soon begin. So when the enemy approached Jesus, he did not find a weak and vulnerable man who would leap at his tempting offers of food, prestige, and power. He did not find someone who was so desperate to succeed that the means to that end didn't matter. Instead, he found a man who was strong and powerful, a man from whom the presence of God radiated, and out of whom the strength of God flowed. So all of Satan's best temptations merely bounced off!

There was a special symbolic element in these temptations as well. The first Adam, though lacking nothing and well-fed, had buckled under Satan's temptations, causing massive damage to the whole created order. Jesus, as the second Adam (1 Corinthians 15:45-49), the harbinger of a new era in man's relationship with God, resisted the temptations completely, and began a whole new economy in which mankind would no longer have to exist as prisoners of sin and depravity, but in which we, too, could live in obedience to God's commands, serving God in holiness and righteousness all of our days (Luke 1:74-75).

Pray with me:

Father, thank You for the victory of Jesus over the devil, and for the hope that His victory gives us. Thank You that in Him I am no longer doomed to be snared by the enemy's temptations, but that I can be more than conqueror through Him (Romans 8:37). Amen.

MARK 1:14-15

Read with me:

After John was arrested, Jesus went to Galilee, proclaiming the good news of God: "The time is fulfilled, and the kingdom of God has come near. Repent and believe the good news!"

Listen with me:

After John the Baptist went into prison, Jesus began to preach the same message that John had been preaching: "The time is fulfilled, and the kingdom of God is near. Repent and believe the good news!" (Matthew 3:1-2) This was the first declaration of what became known as the gospel (from an Old English word that means "good news.").

The gospel and the here-and-now reality of the kingdom of God have always been intimately related. These days, many people associate the good news solely with the death and resurrection of Jesus, and they push back the reality of the kingdom of God to some indefinite time in the future - after death when people go to heaven, or after the return of Jesus. So the promise of the kingdom ends up separated from the gospel in many believers' minds.

But Jesus was very clear that in Him the kingdom of God had already become a reality (Luke 11:20). And in the vast majority of His parables, the kingdom of God is spoken of in the present tense. Jesus even promised His gathered disciples that some of them (not all of them) would still be alive when the kingdom of God came in power (Mark 9:1), and that they would see it. Some teach that this powerful coming of the kingdom of God was the Transfiguration, which happened six days later. But that would not fit Jesus' prophecy, since ALL of those standing with Jesus were still alive when that happened, and only Peter, James, and John witnessed it. Jesus was actually looking forward to the day of Pentecost, just a few months in the future. On that day, when the kingdom of God was inaugurated among Jesus' followers by the outpouring of the Holy Spirit, Judas was no longer alive, having hanged himself six weeks before. And all of the rest of those who had been standing with Jesus when He had made the prophecy were present to experience it.

Up to the day of Pentecost, the disciples experienced the kingdom of God, its joy, its power, its fellowship, and its miracles through Jesus' physical presence. From time to time Jesus even gave the disciples power and authority to heal diseases and cast out demons themselves (Matthew 10:1), sort of a foretaste of what was coming for them. But on the day of Pentecost, all of the gathered disciples received the poured-out Holy Spirit, and from that time forward they lived in the kingdom of God as a here-and-now reality. They experienced its joy, its power, its fellowship, and even its miracles as the Holy Spirit changed them, moved them, and flowed through them to change lives everywhere they were.

At its root, the gospel message is still "repent and believe the good news." It is still, at its heart about the reality of the kingdom of God. But now the kingdom of God is not only near, it is here! And millions of people all over the world are living in it as a here-and-now reality, enjoying its joy, its power, its fellowship, and even its miracles as the Holy Spirit changes them, moves them, and flows through them to change lives everywhere they are.

Pray with me:

Father, this is good news indeed! Thank You that I and the rest of Your people all get to live in Your kingdom as a here-and-now reality. Thank You for Your Holy Spirit, and for the life-changing, miracle-working power that moves in and through me because of His presence in my life. Amen.

MARK 1:16-20

Read with me:

As he passed along the Sea of Galilee, he saw Simon and Andrew, Simon's brother, casting a net into the sea – for they were fishermen. "Follow me," Jesus told them, "and I will make you fish for people." Immediately they left their nets and followed him. Going on a little farther, he saw James the son of Zebedee and his brother John in a boat putting their nets in order. Immediately he called them, and they left their father Zebedee in the boat with the hired men and followed him.

Listen with me:

Like all of God's promises, Jesus' promise to make Simon, Andrew, James, and John into fishers of men was conditional; that is, it had a condition that had to be met in order to receive the promise. In this case, that condition was that they had to follow Jesus.

Following Jesus meant way more than simply believing in Him, believing His teachings, or reading about what He did. To follow Jesus meant to actually leave their old life behind, and to take up a brand new "with Jesus" life. It meant going wherever Jesus went; being actively engaged in what He was doing; and staying focused, even on the way between activities, as He taught. (And you never knew when a new opportunity or challenge would suddenly present itself on the way!) It meant watching Him closely as He worked, as He prayed, and as He taught, so that they could become just like Him in all of those areas. And it meant putting aside self-sufficiency, and becoming completely dependent on God to provide what was necessary for each day.

These men knew all of this. So when Jesus called them, they immediately walked away from their boats and nets and began the process of following Jesus. And the commitment that they were making to follow Him was not for a year, or two, or three. It turned out to be a commitment to follow Him every day, all the rest of their lives. Even after Jesus' death, resurrection, and ascension, through the presence of the Holy Spirit, they continued to follow Jesus' lead, continued to work where Jesus was working, and continuing to be molded and shaped by His presence and His teaching. And as they followed Him, they really did become fishers of men.

Today the call to follow Jesus is the same. It is not merely a call to believe in Him, learn His teachings, or read about what He did. It is a call to discipleship, to leave our old lives behind, and be made into new creations, taking up a whole new "with Jesus" life. It means going wherever Jesus leads, being actively engaged in what He is doing, and staying focused, even between activities. It means staying sensitive to His leading, and consciously submitting ourselves to the molding, shaping, sanctifying work of the Holy Spirit, so that we can become just like Jesus in how we live, work, pray, and teach. And it means putting aside all self-sufficiency, and becoming completely dependent on God for our daily bread, and for all that we need to fulfill His calling on our lives.

And, for all of us who are willing to follow Jesus, we find not only salvation, but joy, peace, power, and an effectiveness in prayer and ministry that most can only dream about. We too get to become bold and effective fishers of men.

Pray with me:

Father, these are great promises, and the conditions for receiving them are clear. Help me, Lord, to really follow Jesus every day, in every area of my life, so that I really can bring You glory by becoming an effective fisher of men. Amen.

MARK 1:21-28

Read with me:

They went into Capernaum, and right away he entered the synagogue on the Sabbath and began to teach. They were astonished at his teaching because he was teaching them as one who had authority, and not like the scribes.

Just then a man with an unclean spirit was in their synagogue. He cried out, "What do have to do with us, Jesus of Nazareth? Have you come to destroy us? I know who you are--the Holy One of God!"

Jesus rebuked him saying, "Be silent and come out of him!" And the unclean spirit threw him into convulsions, shouted with a loud voice, and came out of him.

They were all amazed, and so they began to ask each other, "What is this? A new teaching with authority! He commands even the unclean spirits, and they obey him." At once the news about him spread through-out the entire vicinity of Galilee.

Listen with me:

There never was a fair fight between Jesus and demons, no matter how many, no matter how strong. Jesus had authority over them which they instantly recognized, and it completely freaked them out. When Jesus walked into a place, every demon in the area immediately started eyeing the exits.

This "unclean spirit" in the synagogue at Capernaum is a perfect example. The demon held his peace while Jesus taught, but finally he could hold it in no longer, and cried out in fear, *"What do have to do with us, Jesus of Nazareth? Have you come to destroy us?"* This was no idle concern. Jesus was God in the flesh, and could destroy demons, torture them, or even send them into the abyss. (Luke 8:28, 31.) There was never any fight, never any resistance, never any threats from the demons in Jesus' presence; only fear and trembling, and pleading. In Jesus' presence, demons were instantly reduced to begging for their very existence.

Some teach that when the demon said, *"I know who you are--the Holy One of God!"* that it was the demon's attempt to exercise some control in the situation, or to try to manipulate Jesus. But it was actually all part of the same terrified cry. Even if nobody else in the room knew who Jesus was, the demon did! And that knowledge filled it with mortal fear.

Notice the lack of "ceremony" when Jesus cast out the demon. There was no holy water, no anointing oil, no candles, or bells, or chanting. None of that was necessary. Jesus had absolute authority over the demon. One command, *"Be silent,"* stopped the wailing. Another, *"Come out of him,"* evicted the spirit in an instant. And the people in the synagogue noticed this. Jesus taught like no other teacher they knew. He never referred to the great teachers and rabbis of the past, but taught from His heart with an authority that could not be denied. And He cast out demons like no other exorcist they knew; He never used rituals and tools, but simply issued orders to the demons that they could not defy.

When Jesus sent out His disciples to minister, He *"gave them authority over unclean spirits, to drive them out and to heal every disease and sickness"* (Matthew 10:1), the same authority that He Himself had. And the disciples were amazed that the demons submitted to them in Jesus' name, just as they did to Him. (Luke 10:17) We see the same dynamics in the book of Acts, with evil spirits being unceremoniously cast out by Christians (Acts 5:23), and Paul ordering a spirit out of a slave girl (Acts 16:16-18). In all of these cases (and many more in the gospels and the book of Acts), there were no ceremonies or rituals. And there was no resistance from the demons. There was no battle, no collateral damage. There was simply a command given in Jesus name, with his authority and the power of the Holy Spirit, and the evil spirits, trembling in mortal fear, complied on the spot! However, it was not the formula "in the name of Jesus" that gave His followers that authority (witness the unfortunate story of the seven sons of Sceva in Acts 19:13-16!); it was the very presence of Jesus living in His followers through the presence of the Holy Spirit.

Today many Christians fear demons, and worry about what they would do if they ever came across one. Books have been written about proper techniques, words, and rituals to cast them out. But if Jesus lives in our hearts, none of those are necessary. And if He doesn't live in our hearts, none of them are effective. Jesus still has all authority in heaven and on earth (Matthew 28:18). And when He lives in the heart of a Christian, He still exercises that authority, even over demons, through us.

Pray with me:

Father, help me to live in Your presence every moment, so that You can work freely through me to bring light to the darkest places, to transform the most lost souls, and even to cast out demons, all in the powerful name and authority of the Jesus who lives in my heart, so that Your name is glorified, and Your kingdom grows. Amen.

WHEN WE LISTEN

MARK 1:29-34

Read with me:

As soon as they left the synagogue, they went into Simon and Andrew's house with James and John. Simon's mother-in-law was lying in bed with a fever, and they told him about her at once. So he went to her, took her by the hand and raised her up. The fever left her and she began to serve them.

When evening came, after the sun had set, they brought to him all those who were sick and demon-possessed. The whole town was assembled at the door, and he healed many who were sick with various diseases and drove out many demons. And he would not permit the demons to speak because they knew him.

Listen with me:

It never mattered what the problem was when people came to Jesus to be healed. He never had to diagnose the illness in order to cure it. Whether it was a fever, like Simon's mother-in-law had, or simply the "various diseases" that the people had when they were brought to Him that evening, it didn't matter at all. Jesus simply healed them.

The reason that it didn't matter what the people had was that when Jesus touched them or spoke the word of healing to them He didn't use some kind of magical incantation or spell that had to be tailored to the specific disease. He simply brought His wholeness into contact with whatever un-wholeness existed in the person, and the wholeness that was working and flowing through Him repaired whatever damage was being done by the disease or demons. Fevers left, lameness was repaired, even leprosy was driven out, replaced by health and wholeness.

And Jesus never had to worry about catching whatever disease the person had, because His wholeness was not a static thing that would drain out of Him, leaving Him open and vulnerable.

MARK 1

Wholeness flowed through Him, like streams of living water, washing clean whatever He touched. He could touch lepers with impunity, knowing that they would become clean without ever making Him unclean. The very wholeness of God working through Him simply made them whole in an instant.

We see the same dynamic working through Jesus' disciples and apostles. They spent little, if any, time diagnosing the problem. They simply saw a need for healing (a fever, lameness, even death!), and brought God's wholeness flowing through them into contact with the brokenness and damage through a word or a touch, and it was healed on the spot. Of course they realized that they did not have any of this wholeness in themselves to heal people. It was only available to them because God's Holy Spirit dwelt in them. But when confronted by brokenness, and prompted by God's leading, they did not hesitate to act, and pronounce wholeness on the spot. And people were healed.

Pray with me:

Father, thank You for this truth. Forgive us for allowing ourselves to get wrapped around the axle, thinking that we have to have so much information before we can follow Your promptings to bring healing and wholeness to broken and diseased bodies, minds, and souls; feeling that some things are beyond Your ability or willingness to heal. (If even death was able to be healed by Jesus and His followers, nothing should be too hard!) Father, help me to stay closely connected to You, obedient and faithful in every way, so that Your wholeness, Your healing power, can flow through me into the sick and broken lives all around me. Use me to continue Your work of healing bodies, minds, hearts, and souls in the world today. Amen.

WHEN WE LISTEN

MARK 1:35-39

Read with me:

Very early in the morning, while it was still dark, he got up, went out, and made his way to a deserted place, and there he was praying. Simon and his companions searched for him, and when they found him, they said: "Everyone is looking for you!"

And he said to them, "Let's go on to the neighboring villages so that I may preach there too. This is why I have come." He went into all of Galilee, preaching in their synagogues and driving out demons.

Listen with me:

Jesus was very popular in Capernaum, and very much in demand by all of those in the area who had friends or family members who were sick or demon possessed. And there were lots of them! If He had wanted to, He could easily have set up shop right there in town and ridden the wave of popularity for years.

But Jesus had not been sent merely to heal the sick and cast out demons, no matter how much the people clamored for more of that kind of thing. He had a job to do, a message to bring. Even though the miracles were an important part of both the job and the message, opening the door for people to pay attention to His words, as soon as the miracles became the main thing to the people, Jesus chose to go elsewhere. The people in Capernaum no longer wanted to listen to what He was telling them; they just wanted to see more amazing healings. That was why they were looking for Him. It was time to go.

Jesus faced this problem frequently throughout His ministry. That was why He sometimes told people whom He had healed, especially those whom He had healed from "incurable conditions," not to tell anybody. He knew that the news would just spawn a whole new frenzy in people who cared nothing about His teachings about God's kingdom, but were only drawn by the prospect of experiencing a mighty miracle.

Some wonder why Jesus even bothered with miracles since they led to this kind of problem. But the very nature of the kingdom of God brings healing, wholeness, and freedom to everyone it comes into contact with in our broken world. It can't do otherwise. And at that time, Jesus was the focal point, the literal embodiment, of the kingdom of God. Where there was sickness and brokenness, He brought healing with His touch. Where there was bondage to demonic power, He set the people free. But when those things became the focus of the people, He left until things cooled down a bit. The message was the vital thing.

Pray with me:

Father, it is easy to see how signs and wonders and miracles can become a double-edged sword, opening the door for our testimony, but also having the potential to blind eyes to anything except the miracles. In this, as in every area, give me wisdom and discernment, and help me to never choose the easy road of popularity (even when that popularity is gained by Your mighty miracles) over the more vital path of clearly preaching Your message of salvation. Amen.

WHEN WE LISTEN

MARK 1:40-45

Read with me:

Then a man with leprosy came to him and, on his knees, begged him: "If you are willing, you can make me clean." Moved with compassion, Jesus reached out his hand and touched him. "I am willing," he told him. "Be made clean." Immediately the leprosy left him, and he was made clean. Then he sternly warned him and sent him away at once, telling him, "See that you say nothing to anyone, but go and show yourself to the priest, and offer what Moses commanded for your cleansing, as a testimony to them." Yet he went out and began to proclaim it widely and to spread the news, with the result that Jesus could no longer enter a town openly. But he was out in deserted places, and they came to him from everywhere.

Listen with me:

Leprosy was a terrible disease, in large part because it isolated people so thoroughly. Anyone who had it was required to stay outside the towns, away from non-infected people. They had to cover their faces, and if anyone approached, they had to cry out "unclean!" to warn them away, so that the others wouldn't catch it, too. Lepers were desperately lonely people, isolated from family and friends, and with no hope. Even though God put a ceremony in the law for someone cleansed of leprosy, cures were rare. Medicine wasn't available for the disease. Only a miracle would work.

This leper had reached the point of desperation. He had heard about Jesus' ability to do miracles of healing, so he searched Him out. And in his desperation to be healed, he broke all the rules. He actually approached Jesus, although he stayed a few paces away. Instead of announcing his uncleanness (which anyone with eyes could see at that distance) to warn Jesus away, he cried out to Him to draw Him closer: "If You are willing, You can make me clean."

MARK 1

This man expected that, if Jesus was even willing to help him at all, He would probably wave His hand or speak a word of healing. He did not expect at all what Jesus actually did. With a look of incredible compassion on His face (instead of the look of revulsion that the leper usually saw on people's faces), Jesus said, "I am willing." He stepped forward, closing the distance between them so quickly that the leper didn't have time to react or pull back. And then He reached out and did the unthinkable: He touched the leper and said simply, "Be made clean." In that moment the wholeness of the kingdom of God overwhelmed the uncleanness in the leper's body, and he was healed, just like that.

Jesus' stern warning not to tell anyone who it was that had healed him sailed right past the former leper's ears. He went to the High Priest to be declared officially clean from the disease. But when the High Priest asked how he had been made clean, the man couldn't keep it to himself. "Jesus touched me, and I was made clean by His touch!" In his joy, he told everybody. The words just flowed out of him. Jesus had given him his life back! With a single touch He had smashed the man's isolation and hopelessness, and had replaced them with hope and a future!

Pray with me:

Father, I know that, even though it complicated Jesus' ministry for a while, He really understood that this man who had received so much from Him really would not be able to keep it to himself. His overflowing joy transformed him into an evangelist, sharing the way that he himself had received a whole new life, and urging others to the same source: Jesus. May I do the same. You have given me eternal life! Open my lips so that, with the same joy and gladness that this man showed, I can go out and share You, the source of my life, with everyone. Amen.

WHEN WE LISTEN

MARK 2:1-2

Read with me:

When he entered Capernaum again after some days, it was reported that he was at home. So many people gathered together that there was no more room, not even in the doorway, and he was speaking the word to them.

Listen with me:

Jesus was very popular, there was no doubt about that! Dozens of people showed up at Simon's house, filling the room, hanging in at the doors and windows, and even filling the narrow street outside the house. Jesus had made a huge impression on these people, teaching with authority, healing bodies and minds, and casting out demons with a word. Even those who didn't need to be healed themselves wanted to be around Him - who knew what was going to happen next!

And while Jesus did heal and cast out demons, that was a secondary focus; merely a sign of who He was. His main focus was always preaching the word and teaching the people. John had begun the process of preparing the people for Jesus and the work He would do, helping to turn roving hearts back fully to God. He had confronted the hypocrisy of the Pharisees and tried to get them to repent (Matthew 3:7-12). And he had baptized Jesus in obedience to God. He had even identified Jesus clearly as the Lamb of God who came to take away the sins of the world. Finally, he steered some of his own disciples to follow Jesus (John 1:29-37). But John had been thrown into prison by King Herod, and wouldn't be coming back out again. There was still a lot of heart preparation work to be done, and Jesus was the one to do it.

So Jesus' key focus at this stage of His ministry was to continue the work of heart preparation that John had started. So many of the people had been given a wrong focus by their teachers that would make it difficult for them to receive Jesus for who He truly was - more than a mere prophet; the divine Son of God. They had a national pride that would make it difficult for them to receive God's calling, instead of merely basking in the glory of being "God's chosen people." They needed to catch God's vision of reaching outside of their culture to those who didn't yet belong to God, and growing God's kingdom by leading those others in. So many of them had been given a false idea of what it took to be a child of God. They thought that it was enough to be born of a particular line, without realizing that God could raise up children of Abraham from a pile of rocks if He wanted to. (Matthew 3:9). Instead, being one of God's people meant loving God with all that is in you, and loving your neighbor as yourself. (Mark 12:28-31) So Jesus preached the word to them, in ways that they had never heard before. And when the people clamored more for the miracles than for God's word, He moved on.

Pray with me:

Father, we kind of get this wrong, even today. I hear people say that we need to focus on "need meeting ministries" in order to get the right to tell people about Jesus. But when the need is met, all too often the people leave without our ever telling them about Him. And we comfort ourselves with the idea that we have done some good, and maybe next time they will ask about Jesus. How different from Jesus' emphasis, and that of His first disciples! For them, the message was always central, and they didn't wait to be asked. Anything else that they did, helping, healing, casting out demons, was far secondary, and primarily used to open people's hearts to receive the gospel. Help me, Lord, to turn my ministry back right side up, and to keep the message about Jesus and Your kingdom front and center always. Amen.

WHEN WE LISTEN

MARK 2:3-5

Read with me:

They came to him bringing a paralytic, carried by four of them. Since they were not able to bring him to Jesus because of the crowd, they removed the roof above him, and after digging through it, they lowered the mat on which the paralytic was lying. Seeing their faith, Jesus told the paralytic, "Son, your sins are forgiven."

Listen with me:

"Seeing their faith..." Some have read those words and determined that it was the faith of the friends that compelled Jesus to pronounce forgiveness to this man. But the man lying on the mat before Jesus had faith in Him as well. He was not a bystander in this situation. He was a paralytic, but that only meant that his body didn't work well. He wasn't unconscious or unaware. He himself seems to have had faith that Jesus could heal him.

When those people, the man and his family members and friends, heard about the miracles that Jesus was doing during His earlier stay in Capernaum, their hearts leaped up. Maybe Jesus could heal what no doctor had been able to fix. But then Jesus had left, and their hearts sank. They had missed their chance! But a few days later they heard that He was back in town, and they determined that they weren't going to miss their chance this time.

They carried him through the narrow streets of the city. They could tell when they were getting close to the house where Jesus was teaching and healing because of the masses of people crowding around the place. They pushed and shoved their way closer, but it quickly became clear to them that there was no way that they were going to get inside the house. That's when one of them, out of sheer desperation, came up with the idea of letting him

MARK 2

down through the roof. They dug through and lowered him down right in front of where Jesus sat teaching. When the people inside saw what was happening (and after the laughter died down), they reached up and helped lower his mat down to the ground. Jesus looked up into the expectant faces of those family members and friends, and heard their pleas: "Jesus, we know that you can heal him!" Then he looked down into the expectant and hopeful eyes of the man lying on the floor in front of him in the middle of that crowd. But in that man's eyes he also saw something else: a sense of guilt and shame that frequently arose in people in the presence of Jesus' own holiness.

As Jesus just kept looking at the paralyzed man, not saying a word as He evaluated where this man's heart was, the room grew silent. So silent that nobody missed His words when He spoke: "Son, your sins are forgiven." The room broke out in gasps as people realized the full impact of what Jesus had just said. But Jesus' eyes never left the man lying on the mat. The bodily healing would come - both the man and those who had gone to such great lengths to get him to Jesus had a faith that would not be denied. But Jesus had come to do much more than just restore broken bodies. He had come to heal the relationship between sinners and a holy God through the forgiveness of sin. And that forgiveness, given right where it was needed most, opened the door to every other blessing that He had come to give.

Pray with me:

Father, it is easy to see that a healed body containing a sin-broken soul will result in WAY less than the complete restoration that Jesus came to make possible. But when our hearts are brought to wholeness through Your forgiveness, everything else becomes possible. Thank You for Your forgiveness in my own life that changed everything. Amen.

WHEN WE LISTEN

MARK 2:5-12

Read with me:

Seeing their faith, Jesus told the paralytic, "Son, your sins are forgiven."

But some of the scribes were sitting there, questioning in their hearts: "Why does he speak like this? He's blaspheming! Who can forgive sins but God alone?"

Right away Jesus perceived in his spirit that they were thinking like this within themselves and said to them, "Why are you thinking these things in your hearts? Which is easier: to say to the paralytic, 'Your sins are forgiven,' or to say, 'Get up, take your mat, and walk'? But so that you may know that the Son of Man has authority on earth to forgive sins"—he told the paralytic, "I tell you, get up, take your mat, and go home."

Immediately he got up, took the mat, and went out in front of everyone. As a result, they were all astounded and gave glory to God, saying, "We have never seen anything like this!"

Listen with me:

The scribes in the room, teachers of the law, were actually on the right track in their thinking. But they and those in the crowd who heard Jesus say, "Son, your sins are forgiven" stopped short of reaching the correct conclusion. Their starting premise was that only God can forgive sins, which is totally correct. The conclusion that they should have reached by the end of this event was: since Jesus can apparently forgive sins, then he must be God.

Of course, to get them there, Jesus had to demonstrate that He really did have authority to forgive the sins of this man. His technique to do this was perfect. The easy thing to do in the face of paralysis, which no doctors then could hope to cure, would be to tell the man that his sins were forgiven. This would imply, correctly, that being forgiven was more important than being physically healed. But this forgiveness would not be visible to those gathered around. It was a "safe" declaration that couldn't really be countered by anyone sitting there. Jesus couldn't prove that the man was now forgiven, and those witnessing it couldn't prove that he was not.

But Jesus wasn't into logical games. He was there to bear witness to the Father, and to declare the advent of God's kingdom. His challenge was, "If I do the thing that will be perfectly evident to everyone if I succeed (or if I fail), telling this man to take up his mat and walk, then you will have to admit that it is possible for Me to succeed in declaring this man's sins forgiven." And so Jesus told the paralyzed man, "Get up, take your mat, and go home." He never touched the man. He didn't pray over him or anoint him with oil. He just gave a command, and the man instantly obeyed.

Again, this should have led people, especially the teachers of the law, to construct the following logical proof:

- Only God can forgive sins.
- Jesus can forgive sins.
- Therefore, Jesus is God.

But their prejudices and their closed system of logic, believing that God was in heaven and would never show up as a real human being, kept them from accepting the logical conclusion and falling at Jesus' feet in worship and total surrender. Instead, they were left shaking their heads, trying to make sense of it all, and saying, "We have never seen anything like this!"

Pray with me:

Father, even today those same kinds of prejudices and closed logic systems cause people to overlook the obvious about Jesus. Many people accept Him as a prophet, or a good man, or a great teacher, but are unwilling to accept Him as God in the flesh. But Jesus, by both very clear statements and actions, declared Himself to be God,

WHEN WE LISTEN

and I must accept Him as such, or I cannot be saved. Thank You for Your clear word, and all of the wonders that it contains. Amen.

MARK 2:13-14

Read with me:

Jesus went out again beside the sea. The whole crowd was coming to him, and he was teaching them. Then, passing by, he saw Levi the son of Alphaeus sitting at the toll booth, and he said to him, "Follow me," and he got up and followed him.

Listen with me:

There aren't too many details about the calling of Levi/Matthew in any of the gospels, because it was a very simple affair. Jesus was teaching a large crowd of people near the Sea of Galilee outside of Capernaum when He passed the tax collector's booth where Levi was working. Jesus' words were simple: "Follow me." And Levi's response was just as simple: he got up and followed Him. Just like Peter, Andrew, James, and John before him, Levi simply walked away from his old life (and his old livelihood!) and became a disciple of Jesus.

Levi had heard about Jesus, about the wonders and miracles He had been doing, but he had no real aspirations to be one of His disciples. After all, Jesus was a holy man, and he was despised by all of his fellow Jews, held to be a sinner, and virtually an outcast. The money was good, but the alienation from those around him, the sneering that went on whenever he showed up, was terrible.

But here came Jesus, walking along at the center of a large crowd, every one of them hanging on His every word. As they got near enough so that he could begin to hear Jesus clearly, Levi found himself caught up in Jesus' words as well. He actually forgot what he was doing and just locked his whole attention on this man who spoke so passionately about God and His kingdom that one could imagine being in it right now.

WHEN WE LISTEN

When Jesus drew near the booth, his eyes caught those of Levi. Levi felt a sudden burst of shame, like that of a child discovered where he shouldn't be, listening in on a conversation he had no right to listen to. But though he could feel the sudden rising of blood into his cheeks, Levi found that he simply could not tear his eyes and ears away from this man. Then he saw Jesus smile slightly. He stopped talking in mid-sentence, and held out His hand to Levi, palm up, as if He wanted Levi to give Him something. And then a fraction of a second later He swept that hand forward in a beckoning gesture and clearly spoke those simple words: "Follow Me." It had only been a momentary gesture, scarcely noticed by the others crowding around Jesus. But in that brief flash of time, a spark of understanding had flashed between the two men. And in that moment Levi had placed his whole life, his hope, his entire future into that open hand of Jesus. And he followed.

Pray with me:

Father, the call Levi received is the same as Jesus' call to me: the call to lay down everything, my entire old life, and to follow Him into a new life, a whole new way of living. I know that Levi never regretted his decision to follow, and neither have I. Thank You for opening a door into Your kingdom through Jesus to all of us poor sinners, and for giving me a whole new future in You. Amen.

MARK 2:15-17

Read with me:

While he was reclining at the table in Levi's house, many tax collectors and sinners were eating with Jesus and his disciples, for there were many who were following him. When the scribes who were Pharisees saw that he was eating with sinners and tax collectors, they asked his disciples, "Why does he eat with tax collectors and sinners?"

When Jesus heard this, he told them, "It is not those who are well who need a doctor, but those who are sick. I didn't come to call the righteous, but sinners."

Listen with me:

Jesus scandalized the "good church folks" of His day by intentionally associating with tax collectors and sinners, people with whom no "decent" person would ever be seen. The pious people who hung around Jesus believed that those foul people were spiritually unclean, and that their uncleanness could rub off on them - a kind of "spiritual cooties." So they shunned such people, avoiding any physical contact, or even social contact.

But here was Jesus, arguably a holy man, perhaps even a prophet, and here He was actually in the house of one of them - a house that was now full to the rafters with sinners! And He was eating with them, talking with them, even laughing with them as if they were regular people! They couldn't believe it.

Jesus had many people who followed Him. A lot of them were His regular disciples. A few were occasional followers or thrill seekers, who mostly wanted to be where the action was. But they were all now in and around Levi's house, eating and drinking, and listening to Jesus.

WHEN WE LISTEN

This was all more than some of these scribes could stand. There was no way that they were going to contaminate themselves by actually going into Levi's house to confront Jesus about this unseemly behavior. But some of His disciples were hanging around outside, so they buttonholed a couple of them: "Why does he eat with tax collectors and sinners? He's supposed to be holy! Doesn't He realize that hanging out with those people could corrupt Him? He needs to keep His distance, and just let those people sink from their own weight without letting them drag Him down with them!"

They didn't realize how loud they had gotten, or how good Jesus' ears were. He heard them and turned toward the door where His disciples were trying to figure out how to answer these men. His answer was short, but directly to the point: "It is not those who are well who need a doctor, but those who are sick. I didn't come to call the righteous, but sinners."

That's it precisely! Jesus hung out with sinners not because He craved their company, or, as some people teach, because He found them more "genuine and real" than the Pharisees. He hung out with them because they were the ones who needed the forgiveness, the salvation, the wholeness of heart and soul that He had come to bring. These "sinners" did not respond to His teaching with hostility and accusations. Instead, they drank in everything that He said like cool water of life, gratefully listening and responding. There was no use preaching salvation to those who believed themselves to be holy; there was nothing in them that would respond positively to Jesus' teachings. So He went as a physician to those who were sin-sick, and they received what He brought them with great joy.

Even today many of God's people stay away from those who need the good news the most. Statistics say that within 5 years of becoming a Christian, the vast majority of us have no close non-Christian friends that we spend lots of time with. But even though we have a lot in common with people who are already saved, they are not the ones who are most in need of the gospel that we know, and have experienced, and can share.

MARK 2

Pray with me:

Father, I agree. It is sad how little sharing of the good news we do with those most in need of it. We share our story, our answered prayers, our insights into Scripture, and our testimonies with those who have already been forgiven, when all around us are those sin-sick souls who need so badly the healing balm of the gospel. Help me, Lord, to follow Jesus in this, too. Help me to prefer the company of sinners in order to lead them in the way of salvation, to purposefully spend time with those who need forgiveness so that I can show them where to find it. Then, when we all get together as Your Church, we will really have something to celebrate! Amen.

WHEN WE LISTEN

MARK 2:18-20

Read with me:

Now John's disciples and the Pharisees were fasting. People came and asked him, "Why do John's disciples and the Pharisees' disciples fast, but your disciples do not fast?"

Jesus said to them, "The wedding guests cannot fast while the groom is with them, can they? As long as they have the groom with them, they cannot fast. But the time will come when the groom will be taken away from them, and then they will fast on that day."

Listen with me:

It was taken for granted that the truly pious would observe all of the traditional fast days. God had only established one period of fasting, the Day of Atonement, but people had added many more to it. Many of the Pharisees fasted twice a week (Luke 18:12), and some people still fasted in memory of the fall of Jerusalem at the time of the Babylonian Captivity. To these people it seemed strange, and even heretical, for Jesus and His disciples to not fast.

But Jesus always drew a hard line between the laws that God had actually put into place and "supplemental rules" that were created by man. Jesus and His disciples obeyed God's laws, but felt no need to conform to the expectations of people, or to religiously follow their rules. So when Jesus was confronted over His seeming disregard for "the rules" that even John's disciples obeyed, it didn't faze Him at all.

Jesus pointed out that fasting, as frequently practiced, was a sign of repentance or sadness. But the reality was that Jesus, the long-awaited Messiah had finally come, so sadness and self-denial were out of place. Instead everyone, including the Pharisees (who were waiting for the Messiah as much as anyone) should have been celebrating, not fasting. The Pharisees and those of John's disciples who would not follow Jesus refused to join in this celebration. Instead, they continued to place their focus on keeping traditions, showing that they did not accept Him as their own Messiah.

But even at this early stage of His ministry, Jesus knew where His path led. He pointed to the dark day in the future when He would be arrested, tried, executed, and buried, wrested from His disciples. On that day they would indeed fast, not because of tradition, but because of grief.

In all of this it is important to draw a clear distinction, just as Jesus did, between God's real commandments and those things that are merely man-made rules. Jesus never pooh-poohed God's laws. But He never considered Himself bound by the rules of man. As He demonstrated so ably, true righteousness is not holding to man-made traditions, but living in the ways that God has set forth for His people.

Pray with me:

Father, it is easier than it seems to get caught up in man-made rules, and to judge ourselves as righteous because of our adherence to them, while at the same time disregarding the commandments that you have actually given. Forgive me, Lord, and teach me anew to live by Your word; to follow Jesus' example in this as in everything else. Amen.

WHEN WE LISTEN

MARK 2:21-22

Read with me:

"No one sews a patch of unshrunk cloth on an old garment. Otherwise, the new patch pulls away from the old cloth, and a worse tear is made. And no one puts new wine into old wineskins. Otherwise, the wine will burst the skins, and the wine is lost as well as the skins. No, new wine is put into fresh wineskins."

Listen with me:

Some take this passage as license to completely throw out the traditions of the Church, and some even take it so far as to believe that Jesus is giving them clear grounds for antinomianism, disregarding the laws of God like the Ten Commandments. These ignore Jesus' clear statement that He did not come to abolish the law and the prophets (God's word in what we call the Old Testament), but to fulfill them (Matthew 5:17). And fulfill doesn't mean get rid of. Jesus followed up this statement by saying that until heaven and earth disappear, not the smallest letter, not the least stroke of a pen, will by any means disappear from the law until everything is accomplished (Matthew 5:18). Some take the "until everything is accomplished" to mean until Jesus' death and resurrection. But it would be odd for Jesus to anticipate the requirements of the law going away in less than two years, and preceding that statement with "until heaven and earth disappear"!

Jesus' death and resurrection was the key event in the history of the world, the hinge-point on which everything else turns. But the end is not yet, because everything is not yet accomplished. Jesus Himself said that before the end comes the gospel must be preached to the whole world as a testimony to all nations (Matthew 24:14). There are still billions who have never heard the gospel even once. Millions in America alone! That was why Jesus sent

MARK 2

ALL of His followers out to make disciples of all nations (Matthew 28:18-20), to preach the good news to all creation (Mark 16:15, Luke 24:46-47). Until everything is accomplished, God's people are still expected to live lives of obedience that glorify Him and that serve as a testimony to those around us.

So if Jesus isn't talking about getting rid of the law here, what is He talking about? The context of this saying, in both gospels that include it, is specifically the tradition of fasting that many of the Jewish people participated in. It was believed that those who fasted twice a week were better people, more holy than those who only fasted once a week, who were in turn better people, more holy than those who fasted rarely or never. And those who fasted in remembrance of the captivity in Babylon were expected to get extra blessings from God because of their piety in remembering the sadness of those days. But God did not set up those fasts; they were not part of His law or His commands. Jesus was all about obeying the actual commands that God had set in place, living a genuinely holy life in God's sight, and leaving the mere traditions of men alone, no matter what men thought of Him.

But this new emphasis, this new focus on simply following the actual commands of God, could not be contained within the structures and traditions that had grown up and strangled it in the first place. If Jesus had tried to accommodate all of those traditions, it would only shatter and tear to pieces the old forms, and do damage to the lives of those trying to live with the new focus.

From time to time in the Church, forms and traditions have succeeded in nearly smothering the actual relationship with God that results from real faith. And, at those times, God's people are right in throwing off those forms and traditions. But when we do that, we need to make sure that we don't throw off at the same time the actual righteous requirements of God's law.

Pray with me:

Father, it is sometimes easier than it seems to lose the baby while throwing out the bath water! Only a solid understanding of Your word and the clear leading of Your Spirit can help me to differentiate between Your righteous requirements for me and the traditions of men that are allowed to grow up into them, sometimes even supplanting them altogether. Give me a discerning heart and mind at all times. Amen.

MARK 2:23-28

Read with me:

On the Sabbath he was going through the grainfields, and his disciples began to make their way, picking some heads of grain. The Pharisees said to him, "Look, why are they doing what is not lawful on the Sabbath?"

He said to them, "Have you never read what David and those who were with him did when he was in need and hungry—how he entered the house of God in the time of Abiathar the high priest and ate the bread of the Presence—which is not lawful for anyone to eat except the priests—and also gave some to his companions?" Then he told them, "The Sabbath was made for man and not man for the Sabbath. So then, the Son of Man is Lord even of the Sabbath."

Listen with me:

It is very easy for people to get so caught up in the rules, and by their own supplements to God's rules, that they completely miss the point. In this case, the Sabbath rules are the focus. God's rule for the Sabbath was very straightforward and simple: *"Remember the Sabbath day to keep it holy. You are to labor six days and do all your work, but the seventh day is a Sabbath to the Lord your God. You must not do any work—you, your son or daughter, your male or female servant, your livestock, or the resident alien who is within your city gates. For the Lord made the heavens and the earth, the sea, and everything in them in six days; then he rested on the seventh day. Therefore the Lord blessed the Sabbath day and declared it holy."* (Exodus 20:8-11)

The Sabbath law is unique among the commandments because it is not merely about a moral or religious requirement. As God pointed out right in the commandment itself, it was a rhythm that was embedded into the very fabric of creation from the beginning. God created mankind with that same rhythm of six days of work and one of rest embedded right into our souls. The Sabbath was designed to be a blessing; a time for us to set aside the tools of our trades and our concerns over our livelihood, rest, and put our whole focus fully on our God and Savior for a full twenty-four hours each week.

But people complicated the whole thing, adding requirements, "clarifying" this simple rule that God gave us, until the Sabbath had become an incredible burden to the very people it was designed to bless. They were now told how many steps they could walk before walking became "work," what items they could carry on the Sabbath (which varied from person to person, depending on their occupation), and a thousand and one other things that were not part of the commandment, or in God's mind when He gave it.

On this particular Sabbath, the concern of the Pharisees was not the supposed stealing of grain as some believe. Picking grain to munch on while passing along or through a field is expressly allowed in the law (Deuteronomy 23:25). Instead, they saw Jesus' disciples sinning in three different ways: they saw picking the ripe heads of grain as harvesting, they saw rubbing off and blowing away the chaff as winnowing, and they saw chewing the grain as grinding flour, all of which was forbidden under their additions to the law. But what the hungry disciples were really doing was eating to satisfy their hunger, which is NOT forbidden by God's rules.

Jesus' illustration from Jewish history (1 Samuel 21:1-6) was not to show the Pharisees that God's commandments were unimportant, but that there is more flexibility in the application of them in times of true need than the Pharisees were willing to see. In this case Ahimelech, the priest (and father of Abiathar), understood that the loaves of the presence were sacred, set apart for the use of the priests. But he also saw that David and his men were really in need of food and, with no other source of food anywhere around, was willing to give it to them, provided that they were at least ceremonially clean.

Jesus' final statement does not get rid of the Sabbath as some claim, but it refocuses it back to its original intentions. The Sabbath was made for people as a blessing, for our benefit in being able to rest for one full day out of seven. Mankind was not made for the

Sabbath, to be bound in iron bands of thousands of additional rules made by people, so that its coming was anticipated with dread. The actual rule is simple: take one day in seven off from our work and from the concerns of providing for ourselves and our families. Leave those concerns in God's hands for the day as we receive the blessing of resting ourselves and focusing on Him and His blessings.

Pray with me:

Father, thank You for Your Sabbath rest - a real true blessing. And thank You for every other blessing that comes to me when I live my life in ways that are pleasing to You. Amen.

MARK 3:1-6

Read with me:

Jesus entered the synagogue again, and a man was there who had a shriveled hand. In order to accuse him, they were watching him closely to see whether he would heal him on the Sabbath. He told the man with the shriveled hand, "Stand before us." Then he said to them, "Is it lawful to do good on the Sabbath or to do evil, to save life or to kill?" But they were silent. After looking around at them with anger, he was grieved at the hardness of their hearts and told the man, "Stretch out your hand." So he stretched it out, and his hand was restored. Immediately the Pharisees went out and started plotting with the Herodians against him, how they might kill him.

Listen with me:

These Pharisees who were watching Jesus so closely are some of the saddest cases in the whole gospel story. To begin with, when they went to the synagogue that Sabbath morning, their focus was not on God, on worshiping Him, or on submitting themselves to His agenda. Instead, they went in order to see if they could catch Jesus doing something that they could charge Him with. That morning their hearts were so turned against God that He could have spoken to them through a million loudspeakers and they wouldn't have heard or understood His voice. So, of course, when He spoke to them through Jesus, they missed it entirely.

Jesus knew exactly what was going on in their minds. So rather than doing something in secret, He called a man with a shriveled, paralyzed hand to the front so that everyone could see and hear what was going on. *"Is it lawful to do good on the Sabbath* (as Jesus would do when He healed this man) *or to do evil* (as these men were plotting right then), *to save life* (as Jesus was trying to do by confronting the evil prejudices of those schemers) *or to kill* (as those men were already plotting to do)? This question should have been a no-brainer. Of course it was not lawful for God's people to do evil on the Sabbath (or any other day)! Of course it was not lawful for them to plot murder on the Sabbath (or on any other day)! The answer was so simple that a child could have given it. But their evil hearts sealed their lips. Jesus had put His finger right on the pulse of the issue: the Pharisees, who believed themselves to be so righteous as to stand as judges over Jesus' actions, were now confronted with their own vileness and unlawfulness. But they shut their mouths, hardened their hearts, and plunged themselves deeper into the darkness.

When Jesus healed the man with the shriveled hand, He actually did it in such a way that nobody but God could be pointed to as the healer! Jesus didn't touch the man; He spoke no words of healing. He simply told the man to stretch out his hand, and when the man obeyed, the healing took place. This angered the plotters even more. Even in the face of a clear Sabbath healing they had been robbed of anything that they could reasonably hang on Jesus in a criminal court! And so they left in a rage, and joined together with the Herodians to figure out how they could kill Jesus. What they had intended to be a life or death test for Jesus ended up being a test of their own righteousness or wickedness. And they had failed miserably.

Pray with me:

Father, it is really easy to see bad motives and hidden agendas in others. Help me to keep my eyes open to my own motives and agendas, to keep my heart soft before You, so that I never fall into the same trap, the same condemnation as those self-righteous Pharisees. Amen.

WHEN WE LISTEN

MARK 3:7-12

Read with me:

Jesus departed with his disciples to the sea, and a large crowd followed from Galilee, and a large crowd followed from Judea, Jerusalem, Idumea, beyond the Jordan, and around Tyre and Sidon. The large crowd came to him because they heard about everything he was doing. Then he told his disciples to have a small boat ready for him, so that the crowd wouldn't crush him. Since he had healed many, all who had diseases were pressing toward him to touch him. Whenever the unclean spirits saw him, they fell down before him and cried out, "You are the Son of God." And he would strongly warn them not to make him known.

Listen with me:

At this stage of His ministry, Jesus found it very easy to draw a crowd, but most of those coming to Him were coming for the wrong reasons. Some of them were sick, or brought friends or loved ones who were. They came to get in on the healing power that flowed through Jesus. Others were beset by demons, and knew that Jesus could free them. Still others came out of curiosity or thrill-seeking; they wanted to see a miracle happen.

These people came from a vast area. The people from Galilee were from the northern region of the country. Those from Jerusalem and Judea were from the center part of the country. Idumea was the extreme south. But people also came from the predominantly gentile areas east of the Jordan, and from the far northern Mediterranean coastal towns of Tyre and Sidon in Phoenecia. In other words, they came from pretty much everywhere! Jesus sometimes used a boat to put a little distance between Him and those huge crowds that would press and crowd Him right into the water, trying to touch Him to receive healing.

Of course, Jesus did heal the people. He did free those beset by demons. His demonstration of the reality of God's kingdom was vitally important. But He also taught them from the shore and from the boat about God's reality, His kingdom, and His longing for a relationship with the people He had created. Without that clear teaching, those people whom He had made whole, would simply go back and continue to live the same kinds of lives apart from God that they had been living, and would end up in a worse place later. So Jesus healed and He taught. He freed and He taught. And he urged the people to turn to God with all of their hearts so that their wholeness, their freedom, could be permanent.

Sometimes when Jesus was casting out demons they would yell out, "You are the Son of God" before they left. What they were saying was a fact, but Jesus would shut them up with a word. It wasn't that Jesus was afraid of them, or ashamed of who He was. But the people were not ready for this truth yet. They still had much to learn about the God who loved them and who wanted to save them. They still needed to understand who they were in their relationship with God before they would be willing to see who Jesus was in His relationship to God. All of that would come out, but Jesus knew that, for it to be effective, it needed to come out at the right time.

Pray with me:

Father, we are so privileged to know so much more about You and Your kingdom than the people of Jesus' day! But even knowing who He really is, even having experienced His redeeming power and His presence in my life, it is still tempting to come to Him with my wants and needs as my first thought; to crowd in on Him for a touch, and then not stay close enough and quiet enough to learn from Him. Even the demons fell at His feet and recognized Him as Your Son. I should not do less any time I come. Help me, Lord. Amen.

WHEN WE LISTEN

MARK 3:13-19

Read with me:

Jesus went up the mountain and summoned those he wanted, and they came to him. He appointed twelve, whom he also named apostles, to be with him, to send them out to preach, and to have authority to drive out demons. He appointed the twelve: To Simon, he gave the name Peter; and to James the son of Zebedee, and to his brother John, he gave the name "Boanerges" (that is, "Sons of Thunder"); Andrew; Philip and Bartholomew; Matthew and Thomas; James the son of Alphaeus, and Thaddaeus; Simon the Zealot, and Judas Iscariot, who also betrayed him.

Listen with me:

Jesus had entered the next stage of His earthly ministry. The crowds were too numerous, and there were simply too many places remaining for Him to go for Him to be able to do it all Himself. After spending the whole night in prayer up on the mountainside (Luke 6:12), Jesus called twelve of His disciples, and appointed them to take the next steps alongside Him. Their job would be to be with Him, that is, to officially leave everything behind and live their lives with Him, and to be sent out to preach in the many places that Jesus had not yet gotten to. Jesus also gave them authority over demons so that they could drive them out. (This demonstration of God's power working through the disciples of Jesus would be the hallmark of the early Church after Jesus' ascension. See Acts 1:9, as well as the whole book of Acts.)

The twelve that Jesus chose for the next step are, in some cases, counterintuitive. Peter, James, and John (and sometimes Peter's brother, Andrew) are usually accepted as good choices because of the prominent role they played in Jesus' ministry, and later in the early Church. But Jesus didn't choose them because they were great men; they became great men because Jesus chose them and brought them into intimate relationship with Himself. The same can be said of the rest as well.

Judas is the one who usually raises eyebrows. Why would Jesus pick Judas out of all of His other followers (which surely measured in the hundreds at least) to be one of His most intimate companions? Why not hold him at arm's length, let him follow at a distance if he had to follow at all? Some believe that Jesus didn't know that Judas would be His betrayer, but He knew (John 2:24-25). Some think it was an effort to win Judas over to Him and prevent the betrayal. But Jesus already knew where His future lay, and who would play all of the key roles. No, in bringing Judas close to Himself, inviting Him into intimate fellowship with Him, providing for him, and showing him all of the wonders of God's kingdom, even though He knew that he would betray Him one day soon, Jesus was showing all humanity God's love and His grace.

It is God who causes His sun to rise on the evil and the good, even though the evil will never acknowledge it, and would spit in His face if He showed up in person. It is God who sends rain on the righteous and the unrighteous (Matthew 5:45), even though the unrighteous will claim that the rain that moistens the ground and causes their food to grow is just a natural phenomenon, and will never give Him thanks for it. And it is God in Jesus who called Judas into intimate fellowship with Himself, allowing him the unimaginable opportunity to associate directly with God's one and only Son, even though He knew that Judas would ultimately use that opportunity to betray Him into hands of sinners to be killed.

Pray with me:

Father, it seems amazing that Jesus is so loving and so full of grace that He would choose Judas. But He also chose Peter, knowing that one day he would deny Him. He also chose Thomas, knowing that he would doubt His resurrection. And today, he calls people to Himself, inviting them into intimate fellowship with Himself, even though some of them will ignore Him, others will spurn Him directly, and still others will follow for a while and then turn away to follow their own agendas. But for those of us who accept His invitation wholeheartedly, who choose to follow Him all the way, who remain steadfast through thick and thin, the blessings are inconceivable! Amen.

MARK 3:20-22

Read with me:

Jesus entered a house, and the crowds gathered again so that they were not even able to eat. When his family heard this, they set out to restrain him, because they said, "He's out of his mind."

The scribes who had come down from Jerusalem said, "He is possessed by Beelzebul," and, "He drives out demons by the ruler of the demons."

Listen with me:

Two different groups of people, two different mindsets, two different slants on the same conclusion. Jesus was gaining rapidly in popularity during this phase of His ministry; so much so that He and His disciples could hardly find time to eat. The crowds were constant and so demanding.

Jesus' mother and brothers had heard about all that was going on. They had watched Jesus' amazing rise to popularity over the preceding months. They had heard about the miracles He was doing, and the fact that He had dozens, sometimes hundreds of people following Him from place to place. And now He was too busy to even eat! Their feeling was, "This is getting out of hand! He must have lost His mind! We've got to do something or He's going to work Himself to death!" Their motive was not primarily disbelief; it was love and concern for Jesus.

But their focus on the physical side of Jesus, their son and brother, clouded their ability to see the divine side of what He was doing. They, much like Jesus' own disciples at this stage, couldn't understand His "food to eat that you don't know about" (John 4:32), and the fact that He was receiving a constant supply of strength and energy directly from God.

WHEN WE LISTEN

The other group was the scribes, the teachers of the law. These men had seen Jesus work, healing the sick, casting out demons. They had also heard Him teach, and felt that His teaching was unorthodox at best, heretical at worst. His teachings on the Sabbath, that all of the thousands of rules that the teachers of the law had surrounded God's law with could be completely disregarded, and didn't rise to the level of God's law, put Him entirely at odds with them. He even taught that it was fine to heal people and cast out demons on the Sabbath! Their conclusion was, "This man must be out of His mind, or even possessed by a demon! In fact, He must be possessed by Beelzebul himself to have that kind of authority over demons! We've got to do something or He's going to mislead thousands and do irreparable damage to our religion!"

They, too, were focused on Jesus the man. The only "supernatural" conclusion that they reached was that Jesus' powers could only come from satan, since they themselves were "righteous" men and couldn't do the things Jesus was doing. The theological stronghold they had built for themselves could not allow for Jesus' divinity, for the possibility that Jesus was absolutely correct, and that it was their theological understanding that was wrong.

Both of these groups came at the issue of Jesus from two entirely different mindsets, two opposite motives. But because both groups could only see the human side of Jesus, they reached the same conclusion: Jesus had to be stopped. He was doing the wrong thing, and they had to make Him see things their way.

Pray with me:

Father, it's amazing how terribly far off we can get when we miss the divine part of who Jesus is. Help me, Lord, to always understand that He is not only very man, but very God as well. When I do that, everything stays in focus, and I won't end up with a lot of things that I must "interpret" or explain away! Amen.

MARK 3:23-27

Read with me:

So He summoned them and spoke to them in parables: "How can Satan drive out Satan? If a kingdom is divided against itself, that kingdom cannot stand. If a house is divided against itself, that house cannot stand. And if Satan opposes himself and is divided, he cannot stand but is finished. But no one can enter a strong man's house and plunder his possessions unless he first ties up the strong man. Then he can plunder his house."

Listen with me:

The teachers of the law were exactly wrong in their assessment of the source of Jesus' ability to cast out demons. Their reasoning went like this: All demons are subservient to the king of demons. The demons are subservient to Jesus. Therefore, Jesus must be possessed by the king of demons.

But Jesus pointed out the glaring flaw in their reasoning. If the king of demons was working through Jesus to cast out demons, then he was intentionally tearing apart his own kingdom brick by brick, setting his own slaves free, and even giving God glory in the process. Jesus knew (and so did the scribes, really) that Satan was too smart to ever cut his own legs out from under himself on purpose. So their conclusion, no matter how logical it might seem from a human standpoint, was deeply flawed.

The better, more accurate (and ultimately more logically satisfying) answer was that Jesus was simply more powerful than any demon, even the prince of demons. He could only take back Satan's slaves because He had overpowered and outmastered the "strong man" on his own territory. His power was not a demonstration of satan working against his own self-interest, but of God's overwhelming mastery over a being that mere humans had no ability to fight against on their own.

Luke included a final statement of Jesus in his gospel account of this encounter: "If I drive out demons by the finger of God, then the kingdom of God has come upon you." (Luke 11:20) Jesus' effortless victory over Satan and his demons showed clearly the victory that the people of the kingdom can have over Satan and his forces in the new economy that Jesus made real by His death, resurrection, and ascension. No longer would God's people have to be victimized by this powerful, unseen enemy. Unfathomable power and complete victory can be theirs in Christ!

Pray with me:

Father, thank You for this victory that you came to make real for all of Your people. It is real in my own life, and I see it working powerfully in the lives of so many of Your people. Help us all to become Satan's worst nightmare because we live constantly in the victory that You have purchased and made real for us. Amen.

MARK 3:28-30

Read with me:

"Truly I tell you, people will be forgiven for all sins and whatever blasphemies they utter. But whoever blasphemes against the Holy Spirit never has forgiveness, but is guilty of an eternal sin." -- because they were saying, "He has an unclean spirit."

Listen with me:

People could (and did!) say anything about Jesus they wanted to, and He usually just let it roll right off his back. His critics believed that he was just a man, because they were blinded by the enemy so that they couldn't recognize who He really was. That misapprehension could sometimes be rectified when people were given more information. It could then be confessed and repented of, and God would forgive them.

But there was a much deeper issue in many of Jesus' critics that was surfacing in this event. The critics themselves had grown so far from God, had allowed such hardness to settle into their hearts, that they could no longer differentiate between God's Holy Spirit and the spirit of a demon! There was nothing in them that resonated with God's Spirit, that would help them to recognize the holiness of what was going on in and through Jesus. They could clearly see amazing healings taking place right before their eyes; they could see demons being cast out; they could hear Jesus teaching like no one else; and after all of that, they could still believe that the power operating in and through Jesus was demonic in nature.

At this point, the sin of those teachers of the law was unforgivable. It was unforgivable because it was a sign that their hearts had grown so hard and cold and distant from God that they would never feel guilt or remorse for believing such things, so they would never repent. It was unforgivable because they had grown so corrupt that they called the Holy Spirit an unclean, evil thing, and His works unclean and evil as well. They had become so self-righteous that they could no longer recognize real righteousness when it was standing mere feet in front of them. They had blinded themselves and plugged their ears so that God's call to them could no longer be heard (John 12:37-41).

Many today focus on the "unforgivable sin" as if it was a single action that will condemn a person forever. But the eternal sin has at its core a hard, stony, cold heart that refuses to bow to God's will; a heart so cold that it sees God and His work as evil. When a person has fallen to that level, they will never be forgiven because they will never admit their sin, will never repent, will never ask for forgiveness.

Pray with me:

Father, help me to always keep my eyes and our ears open to You every moment. Keep my heart soft and responsive to You and Your leading. Help me to never grow self-righteous like these scribes, but to always see that it is by Your righteousness in me that I stand. If I stay that close to you always, I will never have to worry about accidentally committing the "unforgiveable sin." Amen.

MARK 3:31-35

Read with me:

His mother and his brothers came, and standing outside, they sent word to him and called him. A crowd was sitting around him and told him, "Look, your mother, your brothers, and your sisters are outside asking for you."

He replied to them, "Who are my mother and my brothers?" Looking at those sitting in a circle around him, he said, "Here are my mother and my brothers! Whoever does the will of God is my brother and sister and mother."

Listen with me:

Some people think that Jesus is being cruel in His statement here, perhaps even disowning His own mother and brothers in favor of those who were following Him and learning from Him. But the reality is deeper than that.

Jesus, as usual, was talking in terms of God's kingdom. The kingdom of God has always been composed of those who have completely committed themselves to loving and serving God. No one gets to be a member of God's kingdom by being a family member of someone in the kingdom, or by joining a certain church, giving a certain amount of money, or adopting a certain set of beliefs. The only way to enter God's kingdom is through faith in Jesus, through being born again in Him.

At this point in His ministry, Jesus had quite a few people, both men and women, who had left all, jobs, families, and property, to become one of His followers. They had staked all that they had and all that they were on who they believed Jesus to be. They were becoming active members of God's kingdom as it was being initiated through Jesus ministry.

WHEN WE LISTEN

As members of God's kingdom, they were already being built into one people, united around the same Messiah, the same priorities, the same overarching worldview. And, as such, they began to have much more in common with those who were also in the kingdom than they did with those who were merely related to them by blood. (Some say that blood is thicker than water, but the water of life is thicker than blood!) This is the reality to which Jesus was pointing. Those who had joined Him in the here-and-now reality of God's kingdom were the ones he had the most in common with, the ones to whom he could easily speak about the things that were most important. They had become His brothers, His sisters, even His mother.

When Jesus was pointing out this powerful relational aspect of God's kingdom, He was not excluding His earthly family members. The door was open wide to them, too. And, thankfully, many of His earthly family did become members of the kingdom through faith in Him. For some, like His earthly brothers, it took His rising from the dead to overcome the contempt of Him that was based on their familiarity (John 7:3-5), the same contempt expressed by the people of His hometown (Mark 6:2-3).

Those who have become members of God's kingdom can easily relate to Jesus' insight. Others who have trusted in Jesus for their own salvation, who have walked the same path from sin through the cross to salvation, often become closer than blood family. And that experience underscores the real unity that is ours as we live together, work together, laugh together, cry together, suffer together, and rejoice together, as members of the family of God.

Pray with me:

Father, this is a glorious reality that has been underscored many times in my own life. Thank You for bringing together all of Your people and forming them into one community, one body, one family. And thank You for grafting my life into that family. Amen.

MARK 4:1-2A

Read with me:

Again he began to teach by the sea, and a very large crowd gathered around him. So he got into a boat on the sea and sat down, while the whole crowd was by the sea on the shore. He taught them many things in parables...

Listen with me:

Jesus' teaching the people in parables was more powerful than just trying to teach them straight theology. The people who came to Him for healing and miracles were not those who had studied in the seminaries of His day. That's not to say that they were biblically ignorant. The vast majority of them were observant Jews who were in the synagogue on the Sabbath where they listened carefully to the rabbi's teachings, who made the necessary trips to Jerusalem for festivals, and who did their best to obey the righteous requirements of the law.

Nevertheless, they were not theologians, but simple working people whose jobs and responsibilities did not leave them a lot of time or energy for pondering the deep things of God. For such people the pictures that Jesus painted in His parables were perfect. Rather than trying to explain theological principles, Jesus told stories that illustrated them. Rather than speaking in the specialized language of the rabbis and theologians, He got them involved in the stories of ordinary people, people just like themselves, participating in activities just like they were involved in, or at least that they were familiar with. In crafting just the right story to illustrate His point, Jesus showed that he was no "ivory tower" theologian, but a man who knew the people to whom He was talking (John 2:24-25); a man who had lived in the real world, and who now drew upon that experience to relate to His listeners with a depth that the teachers of the law could not approach.

WHEN WE LISTEN

But there was always more to a parable than met the ear. The stories were told on three distinct levels. They are much like tide pools. When we first bend over a tide pool and look into it, especially on a sunny day, mostly what we see is a reflection of ourselves and the sky above us. That is much like the first level of a parable, the story itself - simple and charming enough that even children can enjoy it, as any Sunday School teacher can testify. Even if we don't fully understand it, we can see that there is something in it that relates to us. Sometimes the simplicity of the stories causes people to scoff at them, but that's because they are only seeing the surface.

The second level of tide pool gazing comes when we shift our eyes away from the surface and look deeper. At that point we begin to see some of the rocks at the bottom of the pool, a few sea anemones, a starfish or two, and maybe even a hermit crab sidling along, towing its shell after it. When we take the time to look beneath the surface of the parable (with God's help, of course, since all spiritual truth is spiritually discerned [1 Corinthians 2:14], and those who fail to seek God's wisdom in these stories will never truly get below the surface.), we begin to see the truth in it. Most of the parables have one main point that they are making about God, about His kingdom, or about His relationship with us human beings. Often, when someone sees this point, when it resonates in their heart, they are excited and rejoice over the truth that they have discovered.

When we look into a tide pool and see the rocks, and the anemones, and the starfish, and the crabs, it is tempting to move on to the next pool to "see what's in that one." But if we pause for a bit, focus gently below the surface, and just kind of meditate for a few minutes, kind of slow ourselves down, we enter the third level of the pool. Suddenly our eyes will be attracted to movement and, when we look, we will see that the water of the pool is teeming with life. There are tiny fish flitting here and there, water bugs, both on and below the surface, even smaller crabs than the ones we have seen before, and all kinds of tiny life moving around in the depths. We wonder how we could have missed them when we first looked, because now we can see them everywhere. The temptation is to think that maybe they were hiding, and have now grown bold enough to come out. But the truth is that they were always there - it is us who have slowed down enough to really see what is there under the surface, beyond that which is easily noticed. Not the big, slow things that can be seen by any who really take a second or two to look under the surface, but the small, faster moving things that, when we see them, actually change our view of the very nature of that tide pool.

It's the same with Jesus' parables. There is a third level to each one that can only be seen when we are willing to stop for a while, willing to resist the temptation to just move on to the next story, and instead just meditate for a bit. To those who are willing to wait in God's presence, to meditate and chew over the pictures and concepts that they have seen in the parable so far, God can begin to show wonders below the surface, treasures of insight, understanding, and application that we will wonder why we didn't see before. And the more patiently we wait before Him, the deeper we look, the more He will show us.

Pray with me:

Father, I agree that the parables are absolutely marvelous. It seems that we can never fully see all that is in them. Every time I look, every time I pause for a while with You, You are able to point out new wonders and deeper mysteries that have always been hidden there in the depths, waiting to show me the wonders of Your kingdom in ways that I couldn't imagine. Thank You! Amen.

WHEN WE LISTEN

MARK 4:3-4, 13-15

Read with me:

"Listen! Consider the sower who went out to sow. As he sowed, some seed fell along the path, and the birds came and devoured it..."

Then he said to them, "Don't you understand this parable? How then will you understand all of the parables? The sower sows the word. Some are like the word sown on the path. When they hear, immediately Satan comes and takes away the word sown in them."

Listen with me:

This is one of only a handful of parables that Jesus clearly explained to His disciples because they asked (Mark 4:10). The things of the Spirit are spiritually discerned (1 Corinthians 2:14), and Jesus knew before He even told a parable that only those with ears to hear would understand what He was telling them about God's kingdom.

In this parable, the farmer sowing seed represents the one who sows God's word. At this stage of the game, the farmer was Jesus. Later, the picture of the farmer would include the disciples, and eventually would include all of Jesus' followers as the ripples spread outward.

In those days farmers spread seed using a technique called broadcasting, in which he would take a handful of seed and throw it onto the prepared ground in an arc, using his hand to release the seed evenly. He would then grab another handful of seed, repeating the process as he moved over the plot of ground. The benefit of this technique was that it was quick, and was very effective, especially for crops like grains. The disadvantage, especially when working near the edges of the prepared soil, was that some of the seed would be wasted by landing on soil that had not been prepared to receive it.

MARK 4

In this case, the unprepared soil was the hard-packed pathway along the edge of the field. The seed couldn't penetrate this hard soil, so it just lay on the path until the birds came along and ate it up. A good example of this kind of hard-soil in Jesus' day were the Pharisees, Sadducees, and scribes. Many of them were in the crowds to whom Jesus preached each day. A few of them, it must be said, were sincere seekers of the truth. But many had hard hearts that were impervious to the seed that Jesus was broadcasting. Some of their hearts were hardened by self-righteousness, which closed their eyes to their need for a savior. Some were hardened by jealousy of Jesus, who was amassing followers at an incredible pace, and who could do mighty miracles that they, even with all of their piety, could not. Even when they had gone to John the Baptist months earlier (John 1:19-27), a man whose specific job was to prepare the hearts of the people to receive the seed of the gospel (Luke 1:76-79), they hardened their hearts in advance, and ended up merely interrogating John to see where he fit into their theology.

Those people with hearts packed hard by suspicion, jealousy, and self-righteousness were in the crowds when Jesus was sowing seeds of eternal life through His miracles, His deliverances from demons, and His teachings. But the seeds couldn't penetrate their hearts, and just lay on the surface until they were swept away by the enemy. These men stood in the presence of the Light of the World with their eyes firmly closed, and then shrugged and walked off unconvinced. They listened to the voice of Truth itself with their fingers firmly in their ears, then left, testifying that they had heard nothing special.

The wonderful thing about this illustration is that, while hard-packed soil can't receive the seed that is thrown on it, that soil can be made receptive if the farmer works it. It can be broken up with a plow, mulched, moistened, and worked over for a season. Then it, too, can be planted and will be able to produce a crop. If any of those with hard hearts had been willing to surrender themselves to God, He could have reworked the hard, barren soil of their hearts, making it fertile and good, and able to produce a crop for eternal life.

WHEN WE LISTEN

Pray with me:

Father, this underscores how important it is for us to work with You in the area of evangelism - not only so that we can see where the good soil is, but also in praying for those we love who have hard-packed hearts, so that Your Spirit can begin to break up that soil, moisten it, and loosen it with good mulch, so that they can then receive the seeds of the gospel that we long to plant in them. I know that I had such a hardened heart for a long time, until the prayers of those who loved me broke up the hardness so that your seed could get in and grow. Thank you for your powerful love! Amen.

MARK 4:3, 5-6, 16-17

Read with me:

"Listen! Consider the sower who went out to sow...Other seed fell on rocky ground where it didn't have much soil, and it grew up quickly, since the soil wasn't deep. When the sun came up, it was scorched, and since it had no root, it withered away...And others are like seed sown on rocky ground. When they hear the word, immediately they receive it with joy. But they have no root; they are short-lived. When distress or persecution comes because of the word, they immediately fall away."

Listen with me:

As the sower sowed his seed in this parable, some of it fell onto rocky ground. This was not soil with rocks in it, but a thin layer of soil over a base of rock or hardpan. It was not the packed soil of the pathway where the seed could not even penetrate, but it was a part of the property that had not yet been worked and prepared for the seed.

Since there was a thin layer of loose soil, the seeds that fell there by chance soon sprouted and began to grow. But the hard layer just below the surface kept the plants from developing a good root system. As long as the plants received frequent water from the spring rains, they were fine, and looked good, maybe even encouraging the hopes of the farmer, who would think that maybe he would be able to gather an additional crop from ground that he hadn't even worked. But as the harvest season approached and the rains stopped, the plants, unable to find any moisture in their shallow soil, dried up and died.

Jesus likened those plants to people who make a commitment to Him impulsively, based on an emotional response, but without adequately counting the cost of becoming a disciple. Like an infatuated lover, they come with stars in their eyes, certain that the rush of excitement that they feel will last forever. But when the feelings start to fade into the everyday living out of their first love, their commitment fades along with it. When the inevitable times of trial, testing, and persecution come (and there are warnings about the certainty of this for all of Jesus' disciples in Mark 10:29-30; 1 Thessalonians 3:2-4; 2 Timothy 3:12; and many others places), their faith quickly dries up because their commitment is shallow and has no strong root. And so they fall away.

Some are quick to write off those who seem to fall away because of a shallow commitment. But when the good farmer wants to expand his cropland, he doesn't look at the shallow soil area and say, "Some stuff grew there once and didn't do well, but I'll just throw some more seed on the ground there and see how it does this time." Nor does he say, "Some seed fell there by accident once and it didn't do well when the rain stopped, so I'll never plant there again." Instead, he understands that the reason those chance seeds didn't do well the first time was because the soil had not yet been properly worked. So he will take the time to plow the soil deeply to break up the hardpan, to break up and nourish the newly exposed soil. It takes a lot of time and effort, but the good farmer knows that it will be worth it, because that ground that didn't do well the first time will now be productive and yield good crops for years to come.

To break up the shallow ground of a person's heart takes just as much focus and hard work. It takes persistent prayer, consistent love, and a clear explanation, not just of the gospel, but of the cost involved in becoming a follower of Jesus (See Luke 14:25-33). It takes a lot of time, a lot of effort, and a lot of personal contact to prepare shallow hearts to receive the gospel. But the good disciple knows that it will be worth it all, because that person will now be productive, and will himself bring even more people into the kingdom of God for years to come.

MARK 4

Pray with me:

Father, I have seen these shallow-hearted souls respond to the gospel and then fall away before long. This seems to be especially prevalent when we use emotional appeals to convince people to come to Jesus. And, all too often, I have seen Christians either write those people off, or try to convince themselves that, despite no apparent signs of life, they are "still saved." How much better it would be for us to see that there is something there that is responsive to the gospel, and then do the hard (and time-consuming) work of deepening the soil of their hearts, so that the next seed we sow there will grow strong, deep, healthy, and fruitful. Amen.

WHEN WE LISTEN

MARK 4:3, 7, 18-19

Read with me:

"Listen! Consider the sower who went out to sow...Other seed fell among thorns, and the thorns came up and choked it, and it didn't produce fruit...Others are like seed sown among thorns; these are the ones who hear the word, but the worries of this age, the deceitfulness of wealth, and the desires for other things enter in and choke the word, and it becomes unfruitful."

Listen with me:

Like the seeds that fell on the hard path and the shallow soil, the seed that fell on the thorny soil fell there unintentionally. In the crowds that surrounded Jesus, there were definitely those whose hearts were plowed, moist, fertile, and ready to take His words of life deeply into themselves where they would produce a crop. But there were others whose hearts had been hardened and tamped down by their own self-righteousness, so that Jesus' words could not take root. There were others who were there for the emotional rush of being where the action was. They came for the miracles, and to see this famous rabbi that everyone was talking about. Jesus' words impacted them, but they had no depth to their commitment, so when the emotions wore off, or when hard times came, their faith dried up and they fell away.

Other seeds in the parable fell on thorny soil, or, as it has sometimes been called, weedy or crowded soil. Although it hadn't been plowed up or worked well, this was actually good soil, full of nutrients, and with enough depth to allow for good root systems. But there was already lots of stuff growing there. So when the newly planted seeds grew up, the other plants that already had a good root system in place drew off all of the nutrients and water for themselves, leaving the new plant stunted and fruitless.

MARK 4

One characteristic of good, fertile soil is that things will grow on it. If you simply clear a patch of good ground and leave it alone, it won't be long before all kinds of things are growing there. And if you want good seed to grow on that good ground, it is necessary to clear out and root up every plant that is already growing, so that the good seed has no competition for root-space or water. Then the farmer must ensure that any weeds that do spring up after the good seeds are planted are ruthlessly pulled out before they can gain a toehold.

This is one of the reasons for some of Jesus' statements that sound harsh to our ears. For example:

- *"The one who loves a father or mother more than me is not worthy of me; the one who loves a son or daughter more than me is not worthy of me. And whoever doesn't take up his cross and follow me is not worthy of me. Anyone who finds his life will lose it, and anyone who loses his life because of me will find it."* (Matthew 10:37-39)
- Then Jesus said to his disciples, *"If anyone wants to follow after me, let him deny himself, take up his cross, and follow me. For whoever wants to save his life will lose it, but whoever loses his life because of me will find it."* (Matthew 16:24-25)
- *Looking at him* (the rich young ruler), *Jesus loved him and said to him, "You lack one thing: Go, sell all you have and give to the poor, and you will have treasure in heaven. Then come, follow me."* (Mark 10:21)

Unless a person is so determined to follow Jesus that they are willing to lay down everything else that they hold dear, to turn away from all that is important to them, to take up their cross and die to their old life every single day, those other things will grow up, and not only compete with Jesus for first place in that person's life, but will use up the time, energy, and attention that the full-fledged disciple must give to the work of the kingdom, and will strangle that person's faith and make them unfruitful. In the end, even good soil (perhaps *especially* good soil) must be tended carefully, continually, and ruthlessly in the life of a disciple if their faith is going to be fruitful and productive for God's kingdom.

Pray with me:

Father, this is a good warning. It is so easy to let the things of this world and the day-in day-out routines of life crowd out our single-hearted devotion to You. Help me today to be ruthless in my devotion to You, and to have the courage and strength I need to root out of my life all that competes with You, and that draws my time and attention away from Your agenda. Amen.

MARK 4:3, 8, 20

Read with me:

"Listen! Consider the sower who went out to sow...Still other seed fell on good ground and it grew up, producing fruit that increased thirty, sixty, and a hundred times...And those like seed sown on good ground hear the word, welcome it, and produce a fruit thirty, sixty, and a hundred times what was sown."

Listen with me:

The good soil in this parable is the soil that the farmer was aiming at as he sowed His precious seed. The soil had been broken up, plowed deeply, mulched, fertilized, and cleared of other plants so that it would provide the best possible environment for the seed that was thrown there. And after the seed was planted, the farmer would spend lots of time tending the field to make sure that the plants received adequate water and nutrients, and that no weeds were allowed to grow up and stunt their growth, or damage their fruitfulness.

The goal of all of this preparation and work was to multiply the original seed that was sown. When you plant a crop of wheat, each "seed" is actually a kernel of wheat. That kernel could be kept and ground into flour and eaten, but that would be the end of it. So out of each harvest, the farmer holds back some of the precious grain to replant. With good soil and proper care, each grain of wheat will produce a vigorous plant that will head out, ripen, and produce abundant new kernels in each head - enough new wheat to provide food and still leave kernels to plant the next year's crop. But for that to happen, each seed planted in good soil must produce many more seeds just like the one that was planted.

WHEN WE LISTEN

In the same way, those whose hearts have been prepared for the gospel, in whose hearts that seed takes root and grows into eternal life, and who are carefully discipled, will reproduce themselves many times over through sowing the overflow of their own lives into the hearts of their family, friends, neighbors, and coworkers. The new life that is given to God's people is actually designed to multiply itself many times over, just like a grain of wheat, resulting in them bringing into the kingdom thirty, sixty, or even a hundred new believers or more. (The actual number of new births that can be facilitated by each of God's people is unlimited.)

But far too few of God's people are actually involved in reproducing themselves by sharing the good news with others and leading them into His kingdom. Many will live their whole life worshiping God, but never help a single person to be reconciled with Him. Many more will lead one or two people to the Lord - hardly an excellent return on the seed that was planted in them. While some of these people are unfruitful (non-reproducing) due to having too much competition in their crowded lives, many more have been taught that it is not their job to bring other people into God's kingdom. (Which, of course, completely disregards the imperative of the Great Commission!)

The simple truth is that God's expectation, indeed, His commandment, for each of His people is to make disciples of those around us. He has planted in each of our lives the best seed imaginable, engineered to give the highest possible yield. If we are willing, He will work in each of our hearts to keep them soft, moist, fertile, and weed-free. But He still requires our cooperation in working with Him.

If we refuse to go and tell other people about Jesus, that removes the moisture from our hearts, and will ultimately result in a soul that is hard, dry, and cracked. If we allow distractions, worldliness, or other priorities to take our time and attention off God's priorities, those distractions will become weeds and thorns that will suck the spiritual vitality from our lives and make us spiritually sterile. It is the one who stays intimately connected to God, the good, fertile, clear soil, who will see the eternal life growing in their own hearts multiplied many times over in the lives of those with whom they share the gospel.

Pray with me:

Father, I want to be fruitful for you, sharing and reproducing the eternal life that You have planted in me. Help me always to keep You and Your mission for me in first place in my own life. Help me to be conscientious about sharing Your good news with everyone, so that you can reap a continual harvest as Your kingdom continues to grow. Amen.

WHEN WE LISTEN

MARK 4:9-12

Read with me:

Then he said, "Let anyone who has ears to hear listen."

*When he was alone, those around him with the Twelve, asked him about the parables. He answered them, "The secret of the kingdom of God has been given to you, but to those outside, everything comes in parables so that **they may indeed look and yet not perceive; they may indeed listen, and yet not understand; otherwise, they might turn back and be forgiven.**" [Isaiah 6:9-10]*

Listen with me:

As Jesus preached the parable of the sower, as it was with every parable that He told, He knew that representatives of each of the four kinds of soil were right there in the crowd. Not just the good soil that would receive His word and begin to grow into the kingdom, but also those whose hearts were so hardened that His words bounced right off; those whose hearts were shallow, whose lives were emotionally driven, and who would fall away at the first trial; and those whose lives were so crowded that, even though they would receive His word, they would not produce fruit for the kingdom. His call, *"Let anyone who has ears to hear, listen,"* reflected that many people in the crowd would not be able to hear what He was saying. He was doing more than referring to the truth that spiritual truths are spiritually discerned (1 Corinthians 2:14). He was pointing to the fact that His coming was for two purposes, depending on the hearts of each person, and how they received Him.

Every time Jesus appeared in public, every time He spoke, people ended up divided into two, and only two, groups. One group was composed of those who received Him and His words, and so were being saved. The other group was made up of those who rejected Him and His words, and so were being condemned.

When Jesus spoke in parables, those with open hearts ("ears to hear") received His word: their eyes lit up, and the concepts took root in their minds and hearts. But those who had closed their hearts to Jesus showed no insight or understanding, writing off His teachings as ridiculous stories that made no sense. They weren't condemned because they didn't' get the story; instead, their hardened hearts that would not receive Jesus were displayed by their lack of understanding.

The truth of this is shown by Jesus' quote from Isaiah 6:9-10. Those were words that God spoke to Isaiah when He first commissioned him as a prophet and sent him to speak God's words to the people. Through this warning, God told him that his words would be rejected by many of those to whom he was being sent. God's greatest desire for His people was that all would hear, listen, repent, and be saved. He knew that the captivities in Assyria and Babylon were looming just over the horizon, and He longed for His people to repent and turn back to Him before He had to bring that strong judgment on them.

But God also knew His people: that many of them had already hardened their hearts against His word, had already closed their eyes so that they could no longer find His path, and had already plugged their ears against His voice. This had made them liable to His judgment. But even knowing all of that, God sent His messenger, because He also knew that there was a remnant, a portion of the people whose hearts were seeking Him, who would have eyes that would see and ears that would hear.

Some reject the idea that Jesus' first visit had anything to do with judgment or condemnation, and quote John 3:17 in support of their position: *For God did not send his Son into the world to condemn the world, but to save the world through him.* And that is true. But it was not Jesus who was condemning the hard hearted in the crowds; it was they who condemned themselves by their refusal to receive Him, as the very next verse clearly states: *Anyone who believes in him is not condemned, but anyone who does not believe is already condemned, because he has not believed in the name of the one and only Son of God.* (John 3:18)

WHEN WE LISTEN

Pray with me:

Father, there are many today as well who do not receive Jesus, who do not believe in His name, and who are therefore living the lives of the condemned. But there are also more than we think whose hearts are searching for the truth, and who are waiting for us to sow the seed of the gospel into the prepared soil of their hearts. Help us, all of Your people, to be faithful to Your Great Commission, to be trustworthy witnesses who keep the work of Your kingdom first in our agendas. And, Lord, I also pray for the hard-hearted among us. I have seen You work in those hard hearts to soften and break them up in response to the passionate prayers of Your people. (I'm one of those formerly hard-hearted individuals!) Help me to never give up, to never grow weary, and to be faithful in praying for my family members, my friends, my neighbors and coworkers, even for those who seem to have completely hard hearts, so that, with Your help, I can help them to be reconciled to You. Amen.

MARK 4:21-23

Read with me:

He also said to them, "Is a lamp brought in to be put under a basket or under a bed? Isn't it to be put on a lampstand? For there is nothing hidden that will not be revealed, and nothing concealed that will not be brought to light. If anyone has ears to hear, let him listen."

Listen with me:

The key to understanding this somewhat obscure saying is to realize that Mark tended to group Jesus' teachings by topic rather than chronologically. This saying re-emphasizes the teaching about the good soil in the preceding parable. The good soil multiplied the seed that was sown into it thirty, sixty, or even a hundred times.

Jesus' next point is that disciples cannot reproduce themselves by staying quiet, keeping the eternal life in them a secret. A secret disciple is as incongruous as a lamp that is lit and then hidden under a bowl, or under a bed. Everyone knows that for a lamp to do its job, it must stay out in the open, visible, pushing its light out into the surrounding darkness and dispelling it.

It is the same way with the "secret" of eternal life: it is meant to be shared. Jesus was presenting this "secret" openly to everyone in the crowds that surrounded Him. He knew that only those with "ears to hear," whose hearts were prepared, would receive His words, but He spoke them openly anyway, because His words not only planted seeds, it tested the soil of the heart, showing clearly who was really hungering to know God.

This was the pattern that Jesus put forward: share the gospel always, and don't worry about the response of the people. Some will turn away, others may even be hostile, but if you keep the gospel to yourself, the seed will never get planted in the good soil, either, and your own plants will remain sterile and unproductive.

WHEN WE LISTEN

Paul emphasized the same thing to Timothy in his charge: *Preach the word; be ready in season and out of season.* (2 Timothy 4:2a) And it is the same charge that all of God's people have been given today. We must never be secret Christians. We must never hide our testimony or the good news under a bowl or under a bed because we fear the reaction of some people to our message. How will the good soil people ever hear and respond to our message if we don't speak it, clearly, loudly, and often?

Pray with me:

Father, You are absolutely right. Forgive me for keeping such good news to myself far too often. Open my lips as well as my life to those around me who need to hear, so that all of the good soil in my area can be planted.

MARK 4:24-25

Read with me:

And he said to them, "Pay attention to what you hear. By the measure you use, it will be measured to you--and more will be added to you. For whoever has, more will be given to him, and whoever does not have, even what he has will be taken away from him."

Listen with me:

This saying of Jesus continues to tie in to the parable of the sower. There were many in the crowds that surrounded Jesus who just let His words bounce off their hardened, packed-down hearts. They would not ponder or consider carefully what they had heard. If His words did not make immediate sense to them, they rejected them out of hand. That was the reason that Jesus' words so often divided the people.

A good example of this is when Jesus told the crowd: *"I am the good shepherd. I know my own and my own know me, just as the Father knows me, and I know the Father. I lay down my life for the sheep. But I have other sheep that are not from this sheep pen; I must bring them also, and they will listen to my voice. Then there will be one flock, one shepherd. This is why the Father loves me, because I lay down my life so that I may take it up again. No one takes it from me, but I lay it down on my own. I have the right to lay it down, and I have the right to take it up again. I have received this command from my Father."* (John 10:14-18)

At this, the crowd responded in two diametrically opposite ways. Those who were hard-hearted and refused to carefully consider Jesus' words responded negatively: *"He has a demon and he's crazy. Why do you listen to him?"* (John 10:20) But those who pondered Jesus' words, those for whom the light was starting to show, responded differently: *"These aren't the words of someone who is demon-possessed. Can a demon open the eyes of the blind?"* (John 10:21)

This is the way it is today, not only with Jesus' words, but with all Scripture. To the hard-hearted, the words of the Bible seem senseless, even contradictory, and they won't seek God and His wisdom to help them understand them. Instead, they use themselves as the measure of truth and wisdom, and so reject God's word out of hand. These not only miss out on the treasure that lies beneath the surface of what they read and hear, they also lose the truth that they may have already possessed, because they are cutting the foundation out from under it by not seeking God in His word.

But those who read or hear God's words with soft, pliable, open hearts, who consider carefully what is before them, pondering and meditating on things that may be hard to understand at first, who consider God to be the measure of all truth and wisdom, will receive a great treasure. All of His mysteries will be laid open before them. They will receive the wisdom and knowledge that they are seeking, and even more besides; more than they ever imagined!

Pray with me:

Father, help me to read and listen to Your words with a soft, pliable, open heart. Help me to know that You are the only source of true wisdom, and so seek Your face so that I can truly hear Your voice and know Your will. Amen.

MARK 4:26-29

Read with me:

"The kingdom of God is like this," he said. "A man scatters seed on the ground. He sleeps and rises night and day; the seed sprouts and grows, although he doesn'tt know how. The soil produces a crop by itself--first the blade, then the head, and then the full grain on the head. As soon as the crop is ready, he sends for the sickle, because the harvest has come."

Listen with me:

Many people work at growing their congregation through the same means that one uses to grow a business or an organization. They use advertising techniques, new and improved programs, phone marketing, and "customer" follow-up. You can indeed grow a congregation that way, but growing the kingdom of God takes different techniques.

First of all, the seed, God's word, must be intentionally sown into the lives of the people (the soil). It must then be provided good conditions to grow. For a farmer, the soil must be keep moist, and appropriate fertilizers must be applied. For the seed of the gospel, the water and fertilizer are prayer and the love of God working through the lives of His people, liberally applied to the lives and hearts of those being targeted.

But the mystery is that, even though the farmer provides the best possible circumstances and surroundings, he is powerless to actually make the seed actually germinate and grow. That potential is in the seed itself. Each seed, having been planted, watered, and warmed by the sun, will automatically germinate, put out roots, and reach upward toward the source of life-giving energy until it breaks the ground. And then it will continue to grow, developing the leaf, stalk, and stem. Finally it will produce the head, which ripens into the wheat, the desired end. At that point, the farmer brings in the harvest.

In the same way, when we are working to grow the harvest for the kingdom of God, there are certain steps that we need to take. We need to be conscientious about planting the right seed for the crop that we want to harvest. Our goal must always be souls for God's kingdom, souls that will ultimately grow into strong, Christlike, reproducing disciples of Jesus. We need to make sure that we don't sow the seed of programs, or light shows, or carnivals, which are the seeds of consumerism, and will only grow a crop of consumers. The seed that we have been given is the good seed of the gospel, the truth of Jesus Himself.

We also need to make sure that we don't use the genetically modified seed of Jesus according to this person or that person, or Jesus plus this program or that activity. All we need is the pure, unadulterated seed of Jesus Himself, as clearly presented in the gospels. And, finally, we need to keep the soil watered through prayer and love.

But even if we do everything right, we always need to remember that the growth into a harvestable soul is not something that we can program or speed up. God has put into the good gospel seed all that is needed to produce salvation. As He said through Isaiah, His word *"will not return to me empty, but it will accomplish what I please and will prosper in what I send it to do."* (Isaiah 55:11)

Some might think that this exonerates them from the need to tell people about Jesus, or help them to find Him. "After all," they think, "I can't save anyone; only God can." But every farmer knows that seed that is never sown into receptive soil will never produce a crop. Just because the farmer can't cause a seed to germinate and grow, only God can, he is not exonerated from doing his part of the process, which is to prepare the soil and get the seed in the ground. Each of God's people must constantly be telling others the good news of the gospel. And sown seed that is not watered will never grow, so God's people must bathe the souls of those we have told in constant prayer and loving interaction. And if the farmer doesn't keep a sharp eye on the crop, he won't see that it is ripe, the harvest will never happen, and all of the previous work will be lost. So God's people must stay engaged with those we are "farming," always looking for the softness of heart that shows that the harvest is near. And then we must put in the sickle. Right at that moment, we need to pray with that person to bring the harvest into God's kingdom.

Only God can make the seed of the gospel grow. But without steadfast commitment on our part to do the work of sowing, tending, and, ultimately, harvesting, He will have nothing to work with.

Pray with me:

Father, it is so easy to excuse ourselves, or to exempt ourselves from the real work of the kingdom. But, Lord, that's what we are here for! That's the job You left for us to do! For us to hope and pray that You will just drop someone on our path who wants to be led to You is like a farmer who wants to just happen upon a field of wheat, already grown and ripe, that he did no work on. It would be nice if it happened, but he will never feed his family or make a living praying that kind of prayer and hoping it will happen. Lord, the work is too important to hope that others will do the hard work of telling others so that I can just happen to show up to do the harvest, or maybe just to cheer when someone else does the reaping. Help me, Lord, to be diligent in sowing, tending, and harvesting, the real work of the kingdom that You have given to me. Amen.

WHEN WE LISTEN

MARK 4:30-32

Read with me:

And he said, "With what can we compare the kingdom of God, or what parable can we use to describe it? It's like a mustard seed that, when sown upon the soil, is the smallest of all the seeds on the ground. And when sown, it comes up and grows taller than all the garden plants, and produces large branches, so that the birds of the sky can nest in its shade."

Listen with me:

This parable actually speaks about the kingdom of God on two levels. At the time of Jesus' ascension, He had about 120 committed followers, some of whom only became committed after His resurrection. After more than three years of teaching and doing miracles, many would consider that a very small and insignificant number. But it was a mustard-seed beginning. On the day of Pentecost, the minute that seed broke through the ground, it sprang quickly into a majestic tree when 3000 were added to the kingdom in a single day. That clearly demonstrates the powerful growth that is inherent in the seed of the kingdom.

But this parable also applies on an individual level. When the gospel seed is planted in the receptive soil of a person's heart and grows to the harvest, it completely changes that person's life from the inside out, making them into a genuinely new creation (2 Corinthians 5:17). That alone is spectacular. But that is also only a small beginning, much like those 120 believers gathered in the upper room. Changing a single life is never all that God has planned for that seed! Remember the seed planted in the good soil that produced thirty, sixty, or even a hundred times what was originally planted (Mark 4:8, 20).

MARK 4

When the seed of the gospel takes root in a believer's heart and is empowered by the Holy Spirit, the number of people that can be transformed by that new life is virtually unlimited. The small seed that has begun to grow begins to naturally stretch out and produce branches and twigs that grow and divide, continuing to impact and transform the lives of those around them.

It is impressive to see people like Billy Graham and believe that we could never lead so many people to the Lord. But it is the same small beginning that is planted in every believer's life. The difference in the fruitfulness of that seed is simply how committed to God's kingdom agenda each person is. Those who give themselves completely to be used by God, who become clear channels through whom the Holy Spirit can work unhindered, will produce the huge kingdom growth that His seed within them is designed to produce. Those who hold part of themselves back from God's transforming power, who won't leave behind their old habits and patterns of thought, or who won't get intentionally involved in bringing more people to Jesus, will find the growth in themselves stymied. They won't produce the astonishing kingdom growth of which they are capable in Jesus, and they will ultimately see even the small beginning that He has made in them shrivel up and die.

Pray with me:

Father, how easy it is for us to look at ourselves and say, "I could never tell people about Jesus. I could never be used by God to grow His kingdom in spectacular ways." It sounds humble and self-effacing, but in reality it shows a deep lack of faith in what Your power and Holy Spirit can accomplish, even in someone like me. Lord, help me today to grow Your kingdom - to produce even a small branch or two that will grow and multiply, until Your kingdom fills the earth. Amen.

WHEN WE LISTEN

MARK 4:33-34

Read with me:

He was speaking the word to them with many parables like these, as they were able to understand. He did not speak to them without a parable. Privately, however, he explained everything to his own disciples.

Listen with me:

To many of those who heard Jesus' parables, they were a closed book, foolish tales with no point. These were the ones who had already rejected Jesus, who by doing so had also rejected the Father who had sent Him, and whose minds and hearts were thus darkened, incapable of seeing the light.

Many others, however, hungered for the truth, and found it in Jesus. To these, the stories Jesus told were like rays of light that showed them God's love, and revealed the glories of His here-and-now kingdom in vivid colors. Jesus continued to teach these, as much as they could understand. They were the good soil people, who were even willing to wrestle a bit with the difficult concepts until the light turned on.

But it was important that Jesus' core group of disciples, those whom He had selected to lead the Church after His ascension, had far more than a basic understanding of those kingdom principles. After all, they would be responsible for teaching the next generations not only what He said, but what He meant. So Jesus spent lots of time with them, talking these things over, showing them the deeper meanings behind the parables.

In a sense, Jesus was like a spiritual father to them, and taught them as God commanded fathers to do: *"Teach them to your children, talking about them when you sit in your house and when you walk along the road, when you lie down and when you get up."* (Deuteronomy 11:19) Without this clear teaching, passed on conscientiously from one generation to the next, much would get lost.

It's exactly the same today. Even if the next generation of people are believers, if they aren't consistently taught the "truth behind the stories" that Jesus told, the truths of the kingdom that are essential to effective Christian living, their foundation will be less stable and strong than the preceding generation of believers. And the generation that follows them will be even less stable and strong than they are, because they will have even less to pass on. Sunday School and sermons, an hour or two each week, can never take the place of parents, siblings, friends, and mentors who, like Jesus, pass on the truths of the kingdom as they live their lives together with those whom they are teaching.

Pray with me:

Father, in this as in everything, Your ways are always the best. Forgive us, Lord, for leaving it to the Sunday School teachers and preachers to tell our kids, our friends, our loved ones the truths of Your kingdom. We can be so much more effective in helping these loved ones of ours to understand, because we live with them and can talk over these truths daily. And we also love them and care about their future in ways that no Sunday School teacher of pastor can. Help us, whether it is our own children or grandchildren, or those we mentor and disciple, to faithfully and consistently pass on all that we know of You, and to keep on learning, so that we will have even more to teach. Amen.

WHEN WE LISTEN

MARK 4:35-38

Read with me:

On that day, when evening had come, he told them, "Let's cross over to the other side of the sea." So they left the crowd and took him along since he was in the boat. And other boats were with him. A great windstorm arose, and the waves were breaking over the boat, so that the boat was already being swamped. He was in the stern, sleeping on a cushion. So they woke him up and said to him, "Teacher, don't you care that we're going to die?" (NIV)

Listen with me:

Jesus never did anything that God the Father did not specifically tell Him to do. He never went anywhere that God the Father did not specifically tell Him to go. He never even said anything that God the Father did not specifically tell Him to say. It was not that He was a robot or lacked a mind or will of His own. Instead, He was completely surrendered to the will of His Father (John 5:19). Therefore all of God's power was able to flow through Jesus' humanity constantly. It would never have occurred to Jesus to decide on a course of action and then ask God to bless it. He would never have come up with an idea, and then tried to tell the Father what He needed to do to make it happen.

So when Jesus said, "Let's go over to the other side," it was because God had told Him that that was what He wanted Him to do. And because it was God's idea, and because Jesus was confident about when and where God had planned for His journey to end (on a cross in Jerusalem), He had absolutely no fear for His life (or the lives of His disciples) when the storm clouds arose. He just lay down in the back of the boat and took a nap.

But His disciples had not yet figured all of this out. When the storm roared out over the sea, to the point that even those with years of experience feared for their lives, they couldn't understand how anyone could just sleep, as if nothing important was going on. Didn't He know that people often died on the Sea in storms like this? Wasn't He aware that their boats were filing up with water faster than they could bail them out? Didn't He care that they were all going to drown?

But they had not yet learned how Jesus operated. (Remember that this was early on in their relationship with Him.) They had not yet understood that Jesus always walked in God's ways, fully in accordance with His will, so that nothing outside of God's will could touch Him. They didn't realize that as long as they stuck with Jesus, going where God sent Him, doing what God told Him to do, that they were kept safe by the same power that kept Him safe. If it wasn't Jesus' time to die, it wasn't their time either.

Pray with me:

Father, how easy it is to still miss those points. How easy it is to not live our lives like Jesus did. All too often, I'm afraid, we set our agenda, and then ask Your blessing. We come up with a plan, and then inform You how You need to work in order to bring it about. Help me instead, Lord, to yield myself, my agenda, and my whole life completely into Your hands. Then, no matter what storms arise, I can rest secure, knowing that I am right in the center of Your will. Amen.

WHEN WE LISTEN

MARK 4:38-41

Read with me:

He was in the stern, sleeping on a cushion. So they woke him up and said to him, "Teacher, don't you care that we're going to die?"

He got up, rebuked the wind and said to the sea, "Silence! Be still!" The wind ceased, and there was a great calm. Then he said to them, "Why are you afraid? Do you still have no faith?"

And they were terrified and asked one another, "Who then is this? Even the wind and the sea obey him!"

Listen with me:

When the storm first arose on the Sea of Galilee, the disciples, especially those who had made their living for years in fishing boats on that Sea, just tried to push through it. Very soon all of them were rowing, or bailing, doing what they could to keep the boat afloat. But it soon became obvious that they were losing the fight.

When they woke Jesus, it was not because they expected Him to do a miracle - they just thought that He should help in the desperate struggle to keep the boat from going down. They had seen Jesus heal all kinds of sickness. They had seen Him cast out demons. They had even heard as He had proclaimed that the sins of a paralytic were forgiven. But this was a Galilee storm, a kind of fierce wind and rain storm that several of them were familiar with, and afraid of. It never occurred to them that Jesus could actually do something about the storm itself.

But when they had woken Him, Jesus stood, faced Himself directly into the wind and rain, and shouted, "Silence! Be still!" And instantly, so suddenly, in fact, that the disciples nearly stumbled on the now level deck, the storm just stopped. The wind became calm, and the sea grew flat and serene.

100

The disciples were stunned at this sudden reversal. Whatever they were expecting from Jesus, this wasn't it! They weren't even sure how to react. Jesus turned to them and calmly said, "Why are you afraid? Do you still have no faith?" Then He went back to His place, lay back down, and seemed to fall asleep at once.

The disciples were completely freaked out. It was amazing to see Jesus heal someone, or send an unclean spirit running for cover. But to see Him shout a command to the wind and waves and have them obey, that was bizarre! They wondered aloud, "Who is this guy?" The possible answers terrified them even more than the storm had. The words of Psalm 107:23-32, especially verses 28-29 probably flashed through their minds: *Then they cried out to the Lord in their trouble, and he brought them out of their distress. He stilled the storm to a whisper, and the waves of the sea were hushed.* They knew that Jesus was an amazing man, a great prophet, maybe even the Messiah Himself. But now they seriously wondered if He was even more than that!

Pray with me:

Father, I think it is human nature to trust You most easily for those things that we can handle on our own, or at least those things that we can see how they can be handled. When I face an insurmountable task, a life-threatening situation in which I am powerless and overwhelmed, it is all too easy for me to turn to You, not in faith and trust, but in anger and accusation that You don't care, or that You aren't doing Your part in my plan to get me out the situation. How much better it would be if, instead of railing, "Don't You care?!" I simply plead *my case to you and watch expectantly* (Psalm 5:3). Amen.

WHEN WE LISTEN

MARK 5:1-10

Read with me:

They came to the other side of the sea, to the region of the Gerasenes. As soon as he got out of the boat, a man with an unclean spirit came out of the tombs and met him. He lived in the tombs, and no one was able to restrain him anymore—not even with a chain—because he often had been bound with shackles and chains, but had torn the chains apart and smashed the shackles. No one was strong enough to subdue him. Night and day among the tombs and on the mountains, he was always crying out and cutting himself with stones.

When he saw Jesus from a distance, he ran and knelt down before him. And he cried out with a loud voice, "What do You have to do with me, Jesus, Son of the Most High God? I beg You before God, don't torment me!" For he had told him, "Come out of the man, you unclean spirit!"

"What is your name?" he asked him.

"My name is Legion," he answered him, "because we are many."

And he begged Him earnestly not to send them out of the region.

Listen with me:

The disciples had seen several people who were possessed by demons as they had traveled with Jesus. Often, until something triggered an "attack," they looked and acted like normal people. Some looked ill, but they usually looked and acted like a normal ill person. But this man was something entirely different. He looked more like an animal than a human being. He had been living among the tombs for quite a while, miserable and driven from all human companionship. He had cuts all over his body in various stages of healing and infection. And he was filthy.

This man, who was filled with an unimaginable number of demons (a legion was a Roman army unit composed of 3,000 to

6,000 men), was practically torn in two when Jesus walked ashore. The mass of demons just wanted to flee as fast as they could from His presence, but the human part of the man was drawn so powerfully to Jesus that he ran as fast as he could right up to Him, and fell at His feet.

The disciples weren't sure what to do. Some of them wanted to run back to the boat when they saw this wild thing racing toward them shrieking. But Jesus just stood and waited while the man approached. They were positively stunned when this creature cried out at the top of his lungs, *"What do you have to do with me, Jesus, Son of the Most High God?"* How did this man know anything about Jesus? And "Son of the Most High God"? They hadn't heard Jesus called that before!

But Jesus was firmly focused on the business at hand. He ordered the demons within the man to come out of him. That was when the man shouted, *"I beg you before God, don't torment me!"* And when Jesus asked the demon his name, he screamed out, *"My name is Legion, because we are many."*

In those days, like today, a single demon was enough to freak out anybody. And here was a man apparently inhabited by thousands of them! But Jesus wasn't in the least intimidated. The demons had hit the nail on the head: Jesus was no ordinary man; He wasn't going to run away from them. He really was the Son of the Most High God. And, when it came down to it, the demons weren't even willing to put up a fight. Even though the numerical odds seemed strongly in their favor, the real power was all on Jesus' side. They knew Who He was, and they knew that He could easily send them all reeling into the abyss (Luke 8:31) to be imprisoned forever. Instead of one man running from thousands of demons, thousands of demons were reduced to pitiful groveling at the feet of this one man, begging for their very existence.

No one who belongs to God, no one in whom His Holy Spirit dwells, should ever be afraid of a demon - even thousands of them. When we receive Jesus as our Lord and Savior, the same presence that was in Jesus comes to reside in us. The Bible tells us over and over again that the apostles exercised the same power over the demons that they encountered every time they met one

(For example, Acts 16:16-18). There was no fear, no struggle, no ceremonies. A simple command, and the demon instantly fled from them. That is what God's presence in each of us can do!

Pray with me:

Father, it is amazing to realize that when we receive Jesus as our Lord and Savior, it is more than just believing in a creed, or subscribing to a religion. When we turn to You in faith for salvation, Your Holy Spirit actually takes up residence in our hearts, purifying us, empowering us, and transforming us into Your people. It was not Peter's size or Paul's personality that sent the demons scurrying, but Your presence in their lives; the same power that You bring to us when we turn to You. Thank You, Lord. Amen.

MARK 5:11-17

Read with me:

A large herd of pigs was there, feeding on the hillside. The demons begged him, "Send us to the pigs, so that we may enter them." So he gave them permission, and the unclean spirits came out and entered the pigs. The herd of about two thousand rushed down the steep bank into the sea and drowned there.

The men who tended them ran off and reported it in the town and the countryside, and people went to see what had happened. They came to Jesus and saw the man who had been demon-possessed, sitting there, dressed and in his right mind; and they were afraid.

Those who had seen it described to them what had happened to the demon-possessed man and told about the pigs. Then they began to beg him to leave their region.

Listen with me:

Even though when this story is told, the herd of pigs usually seems to get the most attention, there are two key points that are being made by including this event in the gospels that should not get lost in the spectacle of two thousand crazed pigs rushing headlong off a cliff.

The first point is that the multitude of demons was absolutely powerless in the presence of Jesus. Human beings believe that demons are super powerful, a perception fueled by Hollywood. And they do have power that they can use against people who don't belong to God. God protects His people from demons, as a quick overview of the gospels and Acts will show. But any power that they have is insignificant when compared to the power of God, the power that flowed through Jesus.

WHEN WE LISTEN

When Jesus commanded the legion of demons to come out of the man, they had no choice but to obey. There was no epic struggle, no long battle. Jesus simply commanded, and the spirits, all of them, had to obey and leave. The one concession afforded to them by Jesus was that they be allowed to enter the pigs. Jesus already saw what the end of that would be, but the demons were short sighted, and had no idea of the tragedy that their decision would bring. Their only thought was self-preservation, not being banished to the Abyss forever. So Jesus commanded, and into the pigs they went. Their presence in the pigs caused a panic that led to the rapid destruction of their hosts. So much for the demons!

But the second point that needs to be noted is the reaction of the townspeople. These were gentiles who lived on the southeast edge of the Sea of Galilee. When the panicked pig-herders told them about the arrival of strangers, the interaction between them and the demon possessed man, and the bizarre suicide of the whole herd of pigs, they came out to investigate. They found the demoniac, well-known to them, and feared too, now clothed, in his right mind, and sitting at the feet of Jesus, listening as He taught. And it completely freaked them out! The man had been a terror. They had seen him break the chains that they had tried to shackle him with (Mark 5:4). They had heard him screaming and moaning day and night among the tombs. But as long as he stayed away from their houses, they could deal with all of that; it was a known quantity.

But now here was a man who was apparently much more powerful than the demons that had so overpowered the (formerly) demon-possessed man. This was someone who could order demons around, and whom they obeyed. It wasn't the destruction of the pigs that had them so scared - it was being in the presence of someone who was that powerful! They had no idea what to do in the presence of such power. But rather than sit at Jesus' feet to learn from Him, as the former demoniac was doing, they chose to beg Jesus to just go away. He was too powerful, too scary for their taste.

MARK 5

Father, it is easy for us to fear what we do not understand. And there is a lot that we don't understand, especially in the invisible spiritual dimension. Some find comfort for their uncertainty in just denying the reality of what they can't physically touch or see, much like the townspeople wanted to do with Jesus. If they sent Jesus away, banished Him from their lives, they could hide themselves from the reality of the spiritual power that was so obviously working through Him. Others focus on their fear, or even their worship of the spiritual powers that they sense around them, even worshiping demons in the guise of "powers" or "nature gods". But they don't realize that, in doing so, they are worshiping something that is only marginally more powerful than they are themselves, and powerful in a very negative and destructive way. Their myopic focus on the power of evil blinds them to Your infinitely greater power. Help me, Lord, to only fear You, to only worship You, the all-powerful, all-mighty God, whose power and might know no limits. Then I will never have to fear anything that goes bump in the night. Amen.

MARK 5:18-20

Read with me:

As he was getting into the boat, the man who had been demon-possessed begged him earnestly that he might remain with him. Jesus did not let him but told him, "Go home to your own people, and report to them how much the Lord has done for you and how he has had mercy on you." So he went out and began to proclaim in the Decapolis how much Jesus had done for him, and they were all amazed.

Listen with me:

The demoniac is a good illustration of how a mustard-seed beginning (Mark 4:30-32) can produce abundant fruit. No one would have many expectations of this man who had fallen so far, who had lost so many years through being enslaved by a legion of demons. It would have been very understandable if, after being delivered, the people's only expectation for him would be that he would live a quiet and normal life among them.

The man himself had no great aspirations at this point, either. All he knew was that Jesus had freed him, so he wanted to go with Jesus wherever He was going; to serve Him and learn from Him; to devote the rest of his life to Him. But Jesus did have plans and aspirations for this man: *"Go home to your own people, and report to them how much the Lord has done for you and how he has had mercy on you."* Jesus had harvested the crop of this man's life, bringing him into the kingdom of God, and now He was giving those seeds back to the man to be planted, reinvested, so that more people, even among the gentiles, would be able to turn to Jesus.

But the man did even more than Jesus commanded. He told his family; but he was so passionate about what Jesus had done for him that he went all over the whole Decapolis (the "Ten Cities" region east of Galilee), telling his story of captivity and freedom to anyone who would listen. As he shared his own story, he was planting the next crop of seeds, some of which found a place in good-soil hearts, and started growing toward eternal life.

Three things are significant. First, it was the man's gratitude for freeing him that motivated the man's devotion to Jesus, and that drove him to share his story, not just with his family, but with those throughout the whole area. Second, Jesus told the man to tell people how much "the Lord" had done for him. The man's testimony was "how much JESUS had done for him." Even at this stage of his spiritual life, even as a gentile, this man had already placed himself under the lordship of Jesus, obeying Him to the fullest extent. And finally, this man needed no seminary classes, or even evangelism classes to be effective in sharing his faith with many others. The core of his "gospel presentation" was simply "how much Jesus had done for him." It wasn't theologically deep, perhaps, but it was passionately personal every time he told it.

In a nutshell, that is the core of evangelism for every single Christian: obeying Jesus' command to go and tell our story, a passionate, personal, first-hand experience of how Jesus set us free. Powerful theology may sway a few, but a personal experience of life transformation is always compelling, as this man's story illustrates: *"and they were all amazed."*

Pray with me:

Father, we really do make it more complicated that it needs to be. How many of us have taken evangelism classes and workshops galore, but are still hesitant to tell others about Jesus because we "don't know enough"! But it has always been the story of how much the Lord has done for me that must form the core of my testimony. And I know all that I need to know about that! Like the man born blind, the powerful, passionate testimony of "One thing I do know: I was blind, and now I can see!" (John 9:25) is all that I need to make a powerful impact on the lives of those around me who are spiritually blind, but who long to see, too. Thank You for Your work in my life. Amen.

WHEN WE LISTEN

MARK 5:21-24

Read with me:

When Jesus had crossed over again by boat to the other side, a large crowd gathered around him while he was by the sea. One of the synagogue leaders, named Jairus, came, and when he saw Jesus, he fell at his feet and begged him earnestly, "My little daughter is dying. Come and lay your hands on her so that she can get well and live." So Jesus went with him, and a large crowd was following and pressing against him.

Listen with me:

Jairus was a good man. He was conscientious, devout, observant, and God-fearing. As the leader of the synagogue at Capernaum, he was trusted with guarding and overseeing the use of the holy things. And he took that job very seriously.

Like many of the seriously devout people in Capernaum, Jairus wasn't exactly sure what to do with Jesus. How in the world did you categorize someone like Him? He was a God-gifted teacher, that was obvious. But He also healed the sick and diseased, and cast out demons. Some even said that He could raise the dead! He was an amazing man. But was He a marvel-working prophet like Elijah? Was He THE prophet, the precursor of the Messiah? Or could He even be the Messiah Himself?

Those questions had kept Jairus' mind humming during many sleepless nights. Jairus had seen Jesus heal all kinds of diseases and cast out demons with a simple word or a touch. It had happened several times right in the synagogue! It was amazing, awe-inspiring!

On this day, Jairus still hadn't decided how to categorize Jesus, but that no longer mattered. For several days his twelve-year-old daughter's health had been failing. She had continued to grow weaker with every hour that the fever had gripped her, and nothing had helped. This morning she was barely breathing, completely unresponsive. Jairus had quit praying for wisdom for the doctors. He had given up praying that whatever new medicine he had been given would do the trick. The only thing he could pray for now was a miracle.

Then he heard that Jesus had just arrived back in town. Jesus! He could help! This was the answer to his prayers for a miracle!

He ran as fast as his legs could carry him down to the waterfront. The huge crowd showed him in an instant where Jesus was. As he got closer, he could hear that Jesus was in the middle of teaching, but he had to interrupt. His daughter was dying, had maybe died since he left the house. He shoved and elbowed his way through the crowd until he finally reached Jesus.

He fell at Jesus feet, not in worship, but to plead with Him on his daughter's behalf. Gasping from the run, he cried out, *"My little daughter is dying. Come and lay your hands on her so that she can get well and live."*

Jesus looked deeply into his pleading eyes for a single beat, and then, with a nod of His head, He helped Jairus to his feet and started moving through the crowd with him. At that moment it no longer mattered to Jairus how Jesus should be categorized or classified. It no longer mattered how Jesus' miracles fit into his theology. All that mattered was that He really was able to heal broken and sick bodies. He really was able, and willing, to heal His daughter It wasn't in a label that Jairus was now placing his faith, but in what he knew that Jesus could do.

Pray with me:

Father, in times of great crisis many things become crystal clear. All of our arguing about Jesus, exactly what His nature was, exactly what mechanism He used to work salvation, the exact timing and nature of His return, really accomplish nothing to save and heal the lost and broken in our world. It is when we become absolutely consumed with the cold fact that someone we love is lost, doomed, without hope, that all of our "theologizing" falls by the wayside, and we are left with the most important thing: Jesus is the only one who can help. Jesus is the only one who can save. I have seen Jesus on many occasions turn a completely lost soul into a saint; turn a destroyed life around so that it becomes productive, rich, joyful. Father, when push comes to shove, when it is the very souls of my family, friends, neighbors, coworkers that are at stake, help me to not get caught up in my analysis of theological principles. Help me instead, like Jairus, to throw all of that aside, and merely fall at the feet of Jesus, plead with Him to act, to go with me as I go to them, to put His hand on the dying ones that I love, so that they might be saved. Amen.

MARK 5:24-29

Read with me:

So Jesus went with him, and a large crowd was following and pressing against Him.

Now a woman suffering from bleeding for twelve years had endured much under many doctors. She had spent everything she had and was not helped at all. On the contrary, she became worse. Having heard about Jesus, she came up behind him in the crowd and touched his clothing. For she said, "If I just touch his clothes, I'll be made well!" Instantly her flow of blood ceased, and she sensed in her body that she was healed of her affliction.

Listen with me:

As Jesus left to go with Jairus, the crowd followed. Here was an opportunity to see a great miracle, and nobody wanted to miss it.

But in that crowd was a woman whose agenda was different: she had come to see Jesus in hopes of being healed. But as she stood there in the crowd, saw Him heal others, and listened to Him teach, she felt ashamed. The issue of blood which had plagued her for twelve long years had made her ceremonially unclean for that whole time. And not only that, it made everything and everyone she touched unclean, too. (Leviticus 15:25-27) How could she step forward and ask for healing, when her confession of what was wrong would instantly tell everyone who had even casually bumped her in the crowd that they were now unclean? That would be too shameful to even consider!

But as Jesus and Jairus moved through the milling crowd and passed near the woman, she had a bold idea: all she had to do was to touch the edge of Jesus' cloak! She knew that God's power flowed through Jesus. She believed that this power could heal her if only she could make that momentary contact. So she pushed through the mass of people as they moved forward, gaining on Jesus inch by inch. Finally she was close enough. She reached out a tentative hand, and just brushed the edge of His cloak.

It was something like touching another person after shuffling your feet on carpet. There was a noticeable jolt as power jumped from Jesus into the woman's body. She stopped right there in the middle of that jostling crowd as she felt the power course through her whole body. And, in that moment, she knew without a doubt that it had worked; she had been healed!

This woman clearly demonstrated what real faith looks like. Faith is not the ability to work up a strong belief in someone or something. Genuine faith is simply believing that God can do for us all that He has promised, all that He has done for others, and then ACTING on that belief.

If the woman had simply believed, even believed strongly, that Jesus could heal her, and then walked away when Jesus left with Jairus, she would have remained broken and unclean. But her faith in Jesus' ability to heal her, just like He had healed the others in the crowd, moved her to action. She pushed through the crowd, her focus squarely on Jesus, the object of her faith. And then she reached out and dared to touch Him, even if it was only the edge of His cloak. It was that pursuit, that effort, that touch, that transformed simple belief into life-changing faith.

Pray with me:

Father, the action part is so essential. I can believe that You can save the souls of my family members. I can even pray for them. But if I am unwilling to pursue them, to speak very clearly and specifically to them about You, my belief will always stop one step short of true faith. I can believe that You are able to heal someone, but when You direct me to deliver Your healing touch to them personally, or to speak the words, "Jesus Christ heals you" (Acts 9:33-34), if my doubt or timidity holds me back from bold and complete obedience, my belief will not work into true faith. Thank You for the example of this woman. Thank You for this challenge to obey, to boldly move from mere belief into the dynamic obedience of miracle-enabling faith. Amen.

WHEN WE LISTEN

MARK 5:30-34

Read with me:

At once Jesus realized in himself that power had gone out from him. He turned around in the crowd and said, "Who touched my clothes?"

His disciples said to him, "You see the crowd pressing against you, and yet you say, 'Who touched me?'"

But he was looking around to see who had done this. The woman, with fear and trembling, knowing what had happened to her, came and fell down before him, and told him the whole truth. "Daughter," he said to her, "your faith has saved you. Go in peace and be healed from your affliction."

Listen with me:

When the woman with the issue of blood touched the edge of Jesus cloak and was healed, she figured that she could just get in and out without being noticed - a kind of "stealth healing." But when she touched Jesus' cloak in faith, it released power through Him, a release that He could sense (Luke 8:46).

As the disciples pointed out, Jesus was moving through a jostling crowd, with numerous people bumping against Him constantly. But the woman's touch was different; there was nothing causal or accidental about it. It was a touch of faith that released healing power through Jesus. And it wasn't that Jesus felt weaker when she touched Him. He was never a cistern of power that had to constantly be refilled. The Holy Spirit and God's power flowed through Him continually (John 7:38). He just sensed that someone had benefitted from God's healing power by touching Him, and He wanted them to come forward.

Jesus kept looking for the person who had touched Him and released His healing power, not to chew her out, but so that she would be able to give glory to God and to Jesus by testifying about her healing. Of course, she thought that she was in trouble for two reasons: for sneaking up on Jesus and appropriating a healing, and for possibly making Jesus unclean when she touched Him when she herself was unclean from the issue of blood. When she finally stepped forward and threw herself at Jesus' feet, she expected anger and recriminations. Instead, He affirmed her faith and her healing, and sent her on her way in peace.

Pray with me:

Father, it may sound egotistical to some that You require that those who have received a miracle from You testify about it publicly. But we have to remember that You have a much larger agenda than just healing people or providing miracles. You want the whole world to come into a redemptive relationship with You, and that is much more likely to happen when we tell others about all that You have done for us. Lord, open my lips to speak boldly about what You have done in my life, so that everybody can see clearly Your hand at work, and come to know You. Amen.

WHEN WE LISTEN

MARK 5:35-40A

Read with me:

While he was still speaking, people came from the synagogue leader's house and said, "Your daughter is dead. Why bother the teacher anymore?"

When Jesus overheard what was said, He told the synagogue leader, "Don't be afraid. Only believe." He did not let anyone accompany him except Peter, James, and John, James's brother. They came to the leader's house, and he saw a commotion—people weeping and wailing loudly. He went in and said to them, "Why are you making a commotion and weeping? The child is not dead but asleep." They laughed at him, but he put them all outside.

Listen with me:

Twice Jesus heard the judgment of men on this girl: "She is dead." And twice He rejected it. It's not that the girl was still alive; she was obviously physically dead. It is that, unlike the way that other people saw things, Jesus knew that this was not the end of her story. God still had another chapter to write.

Jairus wasn't sure what to think when the men from his household came to him with the news that his daughter, his only daughter (Luke 8:42) had died. He had feared that would happen. She had been failing so quickly when he heard that Jesus had returned. A big part of him wanted to just throw himself into the grief of it all and start wailing and weeping himself. But Jesus looked him right in the eye and said, *"Don't be afraid. Only believe."* It was belief that had sent him to Jesus in the first place - belief that had pushed him through the crowd to Jesus' feet. But could his belief keep him moving forward in the face of this worst-possible news?

Rather than have hundreds of people in tow, Jesus narrowed the group to five: Himself, Jairus, Peter, James, and John. The rest were commanded not to come along. Then they sped through the narrow streets to Jairus' house. They could hear the wailing of the family members and friends even before they turned the last corner. Here was clear testimony that the messengers had not been mistaken. The girl really was dead.

Jesus pushed through the mourners into the house and made the statement that should have changed everything: *"Why are you making a commotion and weeping? The child is not dead but asleep."* The girl really was dead at that moment but, in God's will, this was not an irrevocable state, just temporary "sleep" from which she would soon awake. But Jairus was the only one who was believing Jesus at this point. Everyone else just laughed at the obvious ridiculousness of the statement.

But the unvarying rule is that in every circumstance God has the last word. Even when the situation seems completely hopeless, He can change it all with a single word, with a touch. Even death itself cannot stand firm before God, the very source of life; how much less any smaller tragedy or circumstance!

Pray with me:

Father, thank You that, even when we think some circumstance is completely insurmountable, some enemy is completely unbeatable, some tragedy completely unsurvivable, there is You. You can overcome every circumstance, vanquish every enemy, and walk with us through every tragedy. Even though it is not Your will to reverse every death (many died in Jesus day and were not resurrected), Your promise is that even death itself will be ultimately destroyed. And we can count on that. In the meantime, Lord, help me to hear Your voice in every negative circumstance saying to my heart, "Don't be afraid. Only believe." Amen.

WHEN WE LISTEN

MARK 5:40B-43

Read with me:

He took the child's father, mother, and those who were with Him, and entered the place where the child was. Then he took the child by the hand and said to her, "Talitha koum!" (which is translated, "Little girl, I say to you, get up!"). Immediately the girl got up and began to walk. (She was twelve years old.) At this they were utterly astounded. Then he gave them strict orders that no one should know about this and told them to give her something to eat.

Listen with me:

All of the people who had gathered to support Jairus' family by mourning and grieving over the loss of their only daughter had laughed at Jesus when He had told them that the girl wasn't dead, but only asleep. They didn't pick up on Jesus' real meaning: that the state of death for this girl was only temporary. Jesus was both willing and able to "wake her up."

But Jesus was unwilling to work before a crowd of scoffers. He never did things merely to amaze people, or to build His reputation. He simply obeyed everything that His Father told Him to do (John 5:19). So He first cleared everyone out of the house except the three disciples who were with Him, and the girl's father and mother.

When they went in to where the girl was, it was clear that she really was dead - not a flicker of life anywhere to be seen. But Jesus was completely unfazed. He knew His Father's will in this situation, and He also knew that whatever the Father willed, the Son could do. So His methodology was simple. There were no prayers, no ceremonies, no pleading, no reasoning with God, and no tears to show the sincerity of His request. He simply took the girl by the hand and told her to get up. Immediately life returned to the girl, and she stood up and walked around.

The parents and the disciples were awestruck. They weren't sure what to think! But Jesus helped them to regain their focus by giving them two clear commands: they were to tell no one what had happened there, and they were to feed the girl. The first command was to avoid undue publicity, and to avoid setting up untoward expectations. It is not normally God's will to bring every person who dies back from the dead - resurrections are very rare occurrences, and always happen for specific reasons - and Jesus didn't want a parade of people carrying corpses to Him to be resurrected. The second command was just as practical. The girl hadn't eaten in a couple of days and needed to regain her strength.

A key lesson for God's people in this event is that, when God commands us to speak a word of healing to someone, or even to be part of a resurrection, there is no need for a big ceremony, or rituals, or pleading prayers, begging God to do what he has already commanded. All that is necessary is complete obedience to make the miracle real. (For more examples of this in the lives of real believers, see Acts 3:1-8; 9:32-34, 36-41; 28:7-8. Note in the last two that AFTER Peter and Paul prayed and received God's instruction for the situation, they simply spoke the words that resulted in the miracle.)

Pray with me:

Father, it is very easy to see and understand that when we completely obey Your commands, miracles happen. That, of course, means that we have to listen long enough to hear Your voice, and that we must willingly submit our agendas to Your will. I believe that if I will actually do those things when I find myself faced with needs, I will find that You want to do many more miracles than I imagine, and of a kind that is much more marvelous than what I could come up with on my own. Amen.

MARK 6:1-6A

Read with me:

He left there and came to his hometown, and his disciples followed him. When the Sabbath came, he began to teach in the synagogue, and many who heard him were astonished. "Where did this man get these things?" they said. "What is this wisdom that has been given to him, and how are these miracles performed by his hands? Isn't this the carpenter, the son of Mary, and the brother of James, Joses, Judas, and Simon? And aren't his sisters here with us?" So they were offended by him.

Jesus said to them, "A prophet is not without honor except in his hometown, among his relatives, and in his household." He was not able to do a miracle there, except that he laid his hands on a few sick people and healed them. And he was amazed at their unbelief.

Listen with me:

Jesus had traveled widely, and people from all over the country were clamoring to hear Him and to receive His healing touch. But when He went back to Nazareth, His hometown, the people there responded differently.

Some spurious gospels have been written that try to convince people that Jesus was a miracle worker, even in His childhood. But the response of the people of Nazareth to Him on this occasion show that to be false. Their basic argument was that they had known Jesus since He was a kid. They also knew His parents, and His brothers and sisters. He had never done miracles before; He was just a carpenter. He hadn't been a great scholar with all kinds of insights into Scripture; He had always been just a normal person, as far as they could tell. But now here He was teaching in the synagogue with amazing wisdom and insight. He was able to do the mighty miracles that they had been hearing about: healing sicknesses, casting out demons, even raising the dead!

Instead of welcoming Jesus as God's messenger, all they could see was Jesus as they had always known Him, as he was growing up: the carpenter, the faithful son, that nice young man who really seemed to care about people. Their worldview did not allow them to embrace the concept that, while Jesus was living in their midst, He had always been the Messiah, the Son of God. He had simply been biding His time until God called Him into action. He had been a carpenter, and to them a carpenter He would always be.

And their unwillingness to believe in the difference between the Jesus that they had known and the Jesus that was now standing before them actually prevented Jesus from doing the great miracles for them that He longed to do for them. He would not "perform" just to persuade them. So He healed a few people, and then moved on to the surrounding areas, where the people would be willing to receive what He had to offer.

In a very real sense, the difference that the people could see in Jesus demonstrated the "new creation" life that God brings about in each of us when we come to Him for salvation. God takes normal, everyday people, and, through the power of the Holy Spirit, remakes them into powerful, wise, faithful workers in His kingdom. He takes wicked and sinful people, and remakes them into godly, holy, righteous people, who will be powerful witnesses to His grace and power.

But often, just like the people in Jesus' hometown, those who knew these people before their relationship with God transformed them often have a hard time accepting them for who God has made them, instead of for who they once were. And sometimes even the people themselves find it difficult to believe what God can make of them, and so they limit God's ability to completely transform them into the men and women of the kingdom that He wants to make of them.

WHEN WE LISTEN

Pray with me:

Father, I know that many who knew me before I was transformed by You have a hard time believing that I really have been remade into the person that is so much better, so much more than it ever looked like I had the potential to be. But by Your grace and power, I am what I am, and all the glory goes to You. Help me to never limit You by trusting in the view of others, or even of myself, of what I can be. Instead, Lord, keep molding and shaping me, all the way until I reflect the very image of Jesus to the world. Amen.

MARK 6:6B-13

Read with me:

He was going around the villages teaching. He summoned the Twelve and begin to send them out in pairs and gave them authority over unclean spirits. He instructed them to take nothing for the road except a staff—no bread, no traveling bag, no money in their belts, but to wear sandals and not put on an extra shirt. He said to them, "Whenever you enter a house, stay there until you leave that place. If any place does not welcome you or listen to you, when you leave there, shake the dust off your feet as a testimony against them." So they went out and preached that people should repent. They drove out many demons, anointed many sick people with oil and healed them.

Listen with me:

When Jesus sent out the 12, it was to multiply His ability to get His message out to the people quickly. Their main message was to be, "The kingdom of heaven has come near," (Matthew 10:7) the same message preached by John the Baptist (Matthew 3:2), and Jesus Himself (Matthew 4:17). As a concrete sign that this message was true, Jesus gave them authority over unclean spirits, as well as the ability to heal all kinds of diseases.

When Jesus taught His disciples, He told them that if they would seek first God's kingdom and His righteousness, that God Himself would provide everything that they truly needed (Matthew 6:31-33). So Jesus instructed them to take only the bare necessities, and to trust God for all the rest.

After Jesus left the earth, these disciples, and those who would follow in their footsteps, would have to trust in God many times for their everyday needs. And these twelve, right from the very beginning, would be able to testify to all the rest that God was really able to meet every need that they had when they relied completely on Him. In fact, on the night that Jesus was betrayed, He asked them, "When I sent you out without money-bag, traveling bag or sandals, did you lack anything?" And their response was immediate: "Not a thing." (Luke 22:35)

It is also important to note that the disciples were not traveling about on their own to bring the message of the kingdom to the people. They were doing it at the specific instruction of Jesus, the Messiah Himself, and as His representatives. The miracles and healings that they did were signs that they were legitimate representatives of God and the Messiah. Therefore, if they were rejected by people, those people were not merely rejecting them; they were rejecting Jesus and, by extension, God too! (Luke 10:16) And so, any time they were rejected, the disciples were instructed to shake the dust of that town off their feet as a testimony that their judgment against God made them liable to God's judgment against them!

Pray with me:

Father, we are still Your representatives, Your agents, Your ministers of reconciliation (2 Corinthians 5:18-20). And our message is even the same as that of those first disciples: "Repent, for the kingdom of heaven has come near!" Help me, Lord, every day to faithfully bring Your message to those all around me. Help me every day to rely on You to legitimize my message, even with miracles, healings, and the authority You have given me to stand against and defeat unclean spirits. And as I do the work of Your kingdom, help me to trust in You to supply every legitimate need. Amen.

MARK 6:14-16

Read with me:

King Herod heard about it, because Jesus's name had become well known. Some said, "John the Baptist has been raised from the dead, and that's why miraculous powers are at work in him." But others said, "He's Elijah." Still others said, "He's a prophet, like one of the prophets from long ago."

When Herod heard of it, he said, "John, the one I beheaded, has been raised!"

Listen with me:

Nobody denied the miracles that Jesus was doing. Everyone who hung around Him for any length of time could easily see the amazing things that He was doing, and that there was no trickery or deceit involved. These were powerful miracles; not just one or two that were passed along by word of mouth, but dozens, hundreds, done in broad daylight, with hundreds of witnesses.

Naturally the people tried to figure out a reasonable explanation for how Jesus could do all of these miracles. Many believed that Jesus was John the Baptist raised from the dead. Even though John never did any miracles (John 10:41), they figured that if he had been miraculously raised from the dead, miraculous powers flowing through him would be part of the package. (This was Herod's reasoning, too, although he was driven to his conclusion more by guilt and dread than by logic!)

Others believed that Jesus was Elijah reincarnated. Elijah had done many amazing miracles, and was also prophesied to appear before the Messiah (Malachi 4:5-6). This assumption was logical, but entirely off the mark. In fact it was John the Baptist who had come in the spirit and power of Elijah, and who prepared the way for Jesus, the Messiah (Matthew 17:10-13). Still others believed that

Jesus was a new prophet like those who had done mighty miracles in Old Testament times.

But the simple truth was that all of those people were mere precursors to who Jesus really was: God in the flesh, the Messiah whom God had foretold for centuries. Jesus was more than John, who had come merely to prepare His way. He was more than Elijah, who, even though he proved himself mighty against the priests of Baal and Asherah, was still a mere man, subject to flaws and discouragement. And He was more than any prophet who had ever appeared. All of these spoke on God's behalf, but Jesus was God in the flesh. He was the Messiah Himself, who had come to set all humanity free from the tyranny of sin and death.

Pray with me:

Father, we still have many people with differing opinions about who Jesus was, similar to the opinions that were circulating in His day. To many Jesus was simply a good man, who serves as an example to us of how to live a good life. To others, he was a social reformer, who tried to get people to treat each other more kindly and fairly. To others, He was a great teacher with profound insights into spiritual matters. And to still others, He was a misunderstood religious reformer, who tried to get Judaism back on track. But just like in Jesus' day, all of those fall far short of the truth. Jesus was and is God in the flesh, very God and very man (John 1:1-3, 10:30-33, 14:8-9; Colossians 1:15-20; Hebrews 1:2-3; 1 John 4:2-3). That testimony must be at the center of what we believe, or our beliefs are not in agreement with what You clearly reveal in Your word. Thank You for the truth of Your word that changes everything. Amen.

MARK 6:17-20

Read with me:

For Herod himself had given orders to arrest John and to chain him in prison on account of Herodias, his brother Philip's wife, because he had married her. John had been telling Herod, "It is not lawful for you to have your brother's wife!" So Herodias held a grudge against him and wanted to kill him. But she could not, because Herod feared John and protected him, knowing he was a righteous and holy man. When Herod heard him he would be very perplexed, and yet he liked to listen to him.

Listen with me:

Herod had arrested John under pressure from the woman in his life, Herodias. She had been the wife of Herod's brother, Philip, whom she left for Herod. The law of Moses clearly states that one who marries his brother's wife (while the brother is still living) dishonors his brother, and the couple will be childless (Leviticus 20:21). But Herodias was ambitious, and was afraid that John would persuade Herod to send her away. So she pressured Herod to imprison John, and tried to have him executed.

But Herod knew that John was a holy and righteous man. Even though John's words puzzled Herod and often made Him fearful of God's judgment, he was so fascinated by John that he went down to the prison frequently to listen to him. This freaked out Herodias even more. She could see that John's influence on Herod was growing stronger every day, and grew more determined to do something about it before it was too late.

As for John, he understood from the outset that the role of prophet was almost always an unpopular one, especially when dealing with ungodly monarchs. The Scriptures are full of the histories of God's prophets who were imprisoned, and even executed, merely for speaking God's truth to their rulers. So when John was arrested, he took it in stride. He never stopped telling Herod about God and His kingdom, and the righteousness that He requires of His people.

John also knew that his primary task of preparing the way for the Messiah, and identifying Him when He came, had already been accomplished. He knew that he would soon be exiting the stage as Jesus' renown grew. Even though John had no death wish, he knew that he was likely to be leaving the world very soon, and so his focus was not on staying alive, but on staying faithful and true to God and to his calling, so that when his life was over, he could stand unashamed in the presence of his Lord.

Pray with me:

Father, we all need to be focused on that kind of faithfulness. Our message, even though it is a message of hope and grace, is still not popular with many today, even with many in leadership roles, because Your word is "living and effective and sharper than any double-edged sword, penetrating as far as the separation of soul and spirit, joints and marrow. It is able to judge the thoughts and intentions of the heart. (Hebrews 4:12) And that makes people uncomfortable, even to the point of making them want to silence us. Lord, help me to stay faithful, and to keep on preaching the word "in season and out of season;" to "rebuke, correct, and encourage with great patience and teaching" (2 Timothy 4:2), just like John. Help me to be faithful to Your commission, regardless of personal consequences, all the way to the end. Amen.

MARK 6:21-29

Read with me:

An opportune time came on his birthday, when Herod gave a banquet for his nobles, military commanders, and the leading men of Galilee. When Herodias's own daughter came in and danced, she pleased Herod and his guests. The king said to the girl, "Ask me whatever you want, and I'll give it to you." He promised her with an oath: "Whatever you ask me I will give you, up to half my kingdom."

> *She went out and said to her mother, "What should I ask for?"*
>
> *"John the Baptist's head!" she said.*
>
> *At once she hurried to the king and said, "I want you to give me John the Baptist's head on a platter immediately." Although the king was deeply distressed, because of his oaths and the guests he did not want to refuse her. The king immediately sent for an executioner and commanded him to bring John's head. So he went and beheaded him in prison, brought his head on a platter, and gave it to the girl. Then the girl gave it to her mother. When John's disciples heard about it, they came and removed his corpse and placed it in a tomb.*

Listen with me:

Herod was a man of extravagant tastes and extravagant promises. When someone did something he liked or appreciated, he was quick to show his appreciation. But his haste to make promises held within it the possibility for disaster if the person making the request was selfish or unscrupulous.

Herodias, like her mother, was both. Herod was not her father; to her he was just the man her mother happened to be married to. She had no family loyalty to Herod, and no concern for the welfare of him or his kingdom. So when Herod impulsively promised her whatever she wanted for her dance, and when her mother urged her to ask for the head of John the Baptist (the perfect opportunity to get rid of that thorn in her side), there was nothing in her that shied away from the idea.

Herod, of course, was horrified, and immediately regretted his promise. He had been manipulated by Herodias into arresting John in the first place, and now this! But Herod was more mindful of his reputation before his guests than of the wrongness of the request. If he had had said no, or begged the girl to reconsider, he would have appeared weak before his high officials, military commanders, and the leading men of Galilee who had witnessed the promise, and now wanted to see what he would do. To show weakness before men like those could easily put a king's life at risk, showing a chink in his armor that could embolden people enough to stage a coup. So Herod put his respect for John behind him, and boldly sent the executioner for his head.

It was a moment of triumph for Herodias, but a moment of defeat and humiliation for the king. From that time on he lived in dread of judgment for his dishonorable act on a man that he knew to be supremely honorable. That was why, when he heard about Jesus and the miracles He was doing, his first thought was that it was John returned from the dead (Mark 6:16), and why he kept trying to see Jesus (Luke 9:9), to see if it was true.

Pray with me:

Father, pride and fear of men can place us in a position where we are easily manipulated into doing stupid, or even shameful, things. Lord, help me to never operate from pride, boasting about who I am and what I can do. I have nothing, am nothing, and can do nothing apart from You. And help me to never "fear those who kill the body but are not able to kill the soul," (Matthew 10:28a) so that I end up promising and doing things that bring disgrace to me and shame to Your name. Instead, help me to fear You alone, and to always keep You and Your priorities topmost in my life. Amen.

MARK 6:30-34

Read with me:

The apostles gathered around Jesus and reported to him all that they had done and taught. He said to them, "Come away by yourselves to a remote place and rest for a while." For many people were coming and going, and they did not even have time to eat.

So they went away in the boat by themselves to a remote place, but many saw them leaving and recognized them, and they ran on foot from all the towns and arrived ahead of them.

When he went ashore he saw a large crowd and had compassion on them, because they were like sheep without a shepherd. Then he began to teach them many things.

Listen with me:

When the disciples came back from the mission they had been sent on by Jesus (Mark 6:7-13), they were excited by all that they had accomplished. And they were also exhausted. Intense times of ministry will quickly do that to us. But they couldn't rest when they got back with Jesus due to the needy crowds that continually surrounded Him. They couldn't find time to eat, let alone time to give their excited reports about all they had done and taught!

Jesus knew that they had been all-out for the kingdom for some time, and that they really needed rest and time to regroup. That was why He invited them to the wilderness area outside of Bethsaida (Luke 9:10) to rest and relax. If they just kept on giving of themselves, they would quickly find themselves burned out and out of action for a much longer time.

Of course, the best laid plans can still go awry, and in this case the needy people were the deal breaker. Jesus and the disciples arrived at Bethsaida only to be greeted by the same crowds they had left back in Capernaum.

133

WHEN WE LISTEN

It would have been perfectly natural, and even reasonable, for Jesus to have told the crowds, "Go away. We're on vacation. We'll be back in a few days, and we'll minister to you then." But Jesus never did the natural thing; He always did the supernatural thing. In this case, the supernatural thing was to allow His compassion for these shepherdless sheep to override His need for a break. And so He leaned on His Father for an extra dose of energy, and began to teach the crowds.

It is vital to note that Jesus never did anything in His own wisdom or His own strength (John 5:19). He always listened to His Father's heartbeat, His Father's desires, and then acted accordingly, trusting the Father to provide all the strength and power that He needed to do what He had told Him to accomplish. Jesus took frequent time away from the demands of His ministry, but occasionally, when His down-times were interrupted, He found all of the strength, energy, and power that He needed in the Father. So, even in the midst of meeting overwhelming needs, He avoided burnout.

Pray with me:

Father, it is really easy to get caught up in the seemingly endless needs around us, to keep on doing and doing, and never take adequate time away to rest, relax, and recharge. We can even use this event in Jesus' life as justification for our own lack of time off. But we are also given plenty of instances where Jesus went away from the crowds to spend quantity time with You. It seems to be rare that His time off was interrupted as it was here. So He was able in this instance to respond with compassion. Help me, Lord, to mind my time better; not just manage it or control it better, but to actually plan out frequent on-purpose times away from all of the activity and neediness around me, time away with You, to rest and relax so that You can recharge me, making me more resilient, and better able to respond supernaturally to the needs around me. Amen.

MARK 6:35-37

Read with me:

When it grew late, his disciples approached him and said, "This place is deserted, and it is already late! Send them away, so that they can go into the surrounding countryside and villages to buy themselves something to eat."

"You give them something to eat," he responded.

They said to him, "Should we go and buy two hundred denarii worth of bread and give them something to eat?"

Listen with me:

The disciples really were a considerate and caring group of men. So when Jesus teaching the crowd of more than five thousand people continued on and on, as the sun got lower and lower in the sky, they became concerned that they would suddenly be faced with thousands of hungry people and no way to feed them.

Finally they approached Jesus to remind Him of how late it was getting: *"Send them away, so that they can go into the surrounding countryside and villages to buy themselves something to eat."* It was all perfectly reasonable.

But Jesus' answer floored them: *"You give them something to eat."* Silence fell as they all processed what He had just said. Could they possibly have heard Him right? US give all of these people something to eat? We don't have food for ourselves. How are we supposed to feed more than five thousand people?!

When they expressed these thoughts to Jesus, He quickly realized that this was turning into a teachable moment. These disciples had a view of God and of themselves that was several degrees too small. Plus, they were really bad at connecting the dots! They had just returned from a mission trip, spreading the good news that God's kingdom was becoming a reality right before the eyes of the people. They had been empowered to do miracles, heal people, and cast out demons. And they had been sent out without food, extra clothes, money, or even a purse to carry money in (Mark 6:6-13), putting themselves completely in the care of God. And they had experienced God's provision in every way. Not one of them came back to report to Jesus how they had gone cold, or hungry, or thirsty, or without a place to stay. Not one of them came back with a story of how God had been unable to provide for their basic needs, or had been unable to work through them a mighty miracle that had needed doing.

But here they were, barely twenty-four hours back with Jesus, and they seemed to have completely forgotten all of that. They no longer believed that God could work powerfully through them, so they turned to Jesus. They saw the magnitude of the need all around them, and didn't believe that even HE could meet it with the miraculous power that coursed through Him.

But Jesus knew that God, His Father, could meet this impossible need without breaking a sweat. After all, what was creating food to feed more than five thousand people compared to creating a whole universe from nothing, or even with feeding two million Israelites in the desert of Sinai as He did in the days of Moses! All that was necessary was faith, which Jesus had, and which His disciples lacked right then. All that was necessary was moving forward and acting in concert with what the Father had determined to do. *"You give them something to eat"* was the invitation to be vitally involved in what God was doing right then; to continue learning how to be an effective instrument of God's power in this situation. But the apostles just didn't get it.

Pray with me:

Father, it is so easy to see ourselves as powerless in the face of many of the situations we find ourselves faced with each day. We pray frantic prayers, asking You to do something. But we refuse to consider the possibility that You would answer, "YOU do something.

YOU fix the situation. YOU speak the needed words of healing or freedom." Of course, like the disciples, we could do none of those things in our own strength and power. But, also like them, we can do anything You command us to do, because it would then be Your limitless power flowing through us to accomplish it. Help me, Lord, any time You tell me to do something, to say something, to fix something, to never doubt, to never question, but to simply step forward in absolute faith that whatever You command me to do, You can do through me. Amen.

WHEN WE LISTEN

MARK 6:38-44

Read with me:

He asked them, "How many loaves do you have? Go and see."

When they found out they said, "Five, and two fish." Then he instructed them to have all the people sit down in groups on the green grass. So they sat down in groups of hundreds and fifties. He took the five loaves and the two fish, and looking up to heaven, he blessed and broke the loaves. He kept giving them to his disciples to set before the people. He also divided the two fish among them all. Everyone ate and was satisfied. Then they picked up twelve baskets full of pieces of bread and fish. Now those who had eaten the loaves were five thousand men.

Listen with me:

As much as Jesus would have liked to have seen His disciples instantly spring into action when He told them "You give (these five thousand plus people) something to eat," it was clear that that wasn't going to happen. So Jesus began to work to both fix the problem and to show the disciples how it was done.

First of all , they needed to realize that they weren't completely without resources. After a little research, they found that they had available to them five barley loaves, and two small fish. Of course, that wouldn't do much to feed more than five thousand people! ("What are they for so many?" John 6:9) But that was the wrong question. The right question was, "What can God do with these resources?"

The next step was to impose order on the current chaos (a specialty of God's ever since the creation of the universe!). Jesus had the people sit down in groups of hundreds and fifties. Thus directed and organized, the people grew quiet and attentive, anxious to see what Jesus would do next.

Next Jesus did something that was completely normal, and, at the same time, completely counter intuitive: He prayed. Jesus always prayed before He ate, giving thanks to His Father for providing what He was about to eat. What was counterintuitive was that He didn't vary His normal prayer, even under these extraordinary circumstances. There was no laying out before God the massive challenge - He already knew. There was no pleading for direction - Jesus was always plugged into the Father, and the Father had already told Him what He was going to do before the situation ever manifested itself. There was no pleading for a solution - God was already at work to meet the need. Instead, Jesus merely lifted up the small beginnings that the Father had provided, and thanked Him for what He was going to do with them.

Then Jesus began to break the bread and fish into pieces, which He handed to His disciples, sending them off to the seated groups of people to distribute. As they broke and distributed what had been given to them, there continued to be bread and fish to break and distribute. Like the widow's jar of oil (2 Kings 4:1-7), the food didn't run out until the last person had received what they needed. And even more than they needed. God did not produce only enough for each person to have a mouthful. The people all ate until they were satisfied, and the disciples picked up twelve baskets full of leftovers; more than enough to feed all twelve of them another meal.

The lesson that Jesus was teaching was that when the people of God's kingdom are expressly called to do something, whether it is to share the gospel, or move a mountain, or even to feed more than five thousand people, they can trust God to abundantly provide everything they need.

Pray with me:

Father, this is an amazing lesson for us. But how slow we are to believe and act on it! How easy it is for us to hear Your command, or sense Your will, and then excuse ourselves because we don't feel that we have the skills or resources. But, Lord, Your arm is no shorter today, Your power no less, than it was in the days when You called forth the universe with a word, than when You divided the Red Sea with Your breath, than when You fed five thousand men with five loaves and two small fish. Help me to trust You more, and then to turn that trust into action. Amen.

MARK 6:45-52

Read with me:

Immediately he made his disciples get into the boat and go ahead of him to the other side, to Bethsaida, while he dismissed the crowd. After he said good-bye to them, he went away to the mountain to pray. Well into the night, the boat was in the middle of the sea, and he was alone on the land. He saw them straining at the oars, because the wind was against them. Very early in the morning he came toward them walking on the sea and wanted to pass by them. When they saw him walking on the sea, they thought it was a ghost and cried out, because they all saw him and were terrified. Immediately he spoke with them and said, "Have courage! It is I. Don't be afraid." Then he got into the boat with them, and the wind ceased. They were completely astounded, because they had not understood about the loaves. Instead, their hearts were hardened.

Listen with me:

The disciples were not having a good time. They were trying to obey Jesus' instruction and get to the other shore of the Sea of Galilee, but the wind was against them. They couldn't use the sails in that situation, so they all had to row. Even then, the waves were pushing against them.

After several hours of hard rowing, they had only covered a little more than 3 miles (John 6:19). They were tired and discouraged, and figured that, even having to walk around the lake, Jesus would probably beat them to their destination.

One of them looked toward the stern of the boat, and caught his breath. What was that sticking up out of the water? He poked another of the disciples (it was too windy to talk and be heard) and pointed toward the mysterious object. More of them had noticed the thing, whatever it was, protruding out of the sea, with what almost looked like fabric flapping around it. And it seemed to be getting closer.

Finally it was close enough for them to see it clearly. It looked like a person walking on top of the water right toward them. "A ghost!" someone cried out, and then they were all saying it.

Then, over the sound of the wind and the waves, they heard a familiar voice call out, "Have courage! It is I! Don't be afraid!" It was Jesus walking toward them on the surface of the stormy water; they could see that now. They stopped rowing, and in just a moment He was climbing into the boat with them, smiling at the fear that they had shown. And, as soon as He was in the boat, the wind died down, the sea grew calm, and they were able to quickly get to the other side.

The disciples, far from being comforted by Jesus' presence, were once again mystified, stunned at the things Jesus could do. Calming the storm a few weeks before was amazing; raising the dead was stunning; even feeding a multitude with five loaves of bread and two fish was incredible. But what were they to make of a man who could walk across the surface of a stormy lake like they walked on dry ground? Their minds were completely blown. They had no idea what to do with this. They still had no idea who Jesus really was. Yet.

Pray with me:

Father, we often point fingers of ridicule at the disciples for being so slow to understand. But we are not that much better. We are stunned when we see a real miracle. We still try to work out our own solutions to the major problems we face each day, only turning to You when we can't see a way forward (and even then with more desperation than faith). Even with the Bible and all of the information that we have about You, I think we only have a small glimpse of all that You are, and of all that You are capable of doing. Help me, Lord, to lean on You more fully and more completely , so that I can experience more of You. And then help me to share what I learn with the people around me, so that they can learn more about You, too!

MARK 6:53-56

Read with me:

When they had crossed over, they came to shore at Gennesaret and anchored there.

As they got out of the boat, people immediately recognized him. They hurried throughout that region and began to carry the sick on mats to wherever they heard he was. Wherever he went, into villages, towns, or the country, they laid the sick in the marketplaces and begged him that they might touch just the end of his robe. And everyone who touched it was healed.

Listen with me:

Despite appearances, and despite people's expectations, Jesus did NOT come primarily to heal people or to do miracles. Those things, while quite common in His ministry, were actually the side-effect of His presence, not His purpose. Jesus came to inaugurate the kingdom of God on earth as a here-and-now reality; to reform and re-form God's people into what we were always intended to be: the embodiment of God's presence in the world.

But the people of that day, even the Jewish people, were far from understanding that. Even Jesus' own followers had a worldview that was tainted by false expectations of who the Messiah would be and what He was to accomplish. Many of them still carried the expectation of a largely political Messiah, who would free Israel from its Roman overlords, and raise their nation again to the glory, magnificence, and power that they had in the days of Solomon. To people with those expectations, the miracles were just a bonus - a wonderful blessing that they clamored to take advantage of. But they, like the disciples, missed their deeper significance.

WHEN WE LISTEN

The fact is, where God is, miracles happen, and they happen all the time. Jesus' miracles were proof that He was, in fact, God in the flesh. Where He was, God was, and people were healed, sins were forgiven, and demons fled. When Jesus gave His disciples authority to do miracles and cast out demons (Mark 6:7, 12-13), those miracles were proof that God was present with them, and that they were actively living in God's kingdom and acting in His power to do all kinds of things that were beyond human ability.

Many people have said that miracles are "by definition" rare, meaning, I suppose, that if they were common, they would no longer be "miracles". But the miraculous cannot be defined merely by frequency (or lack of frequency). God provided manna to the Israelites in the wilderness every day for 40 years. Each morning for over 14,000 days it was a new miracle. The fact that it happened every day, and that the people began to take it for granted (and to even look down on it - Numbers 21:4-5) does not diminish the "miraculousness" of it one bit. The fact that Jesus healed dozens, sometimes hundreds of people at a time, and that he did it often (the very opposite of "rare") doesn't make those events "normal" and not miraculous. A miracle is not defined by its frequency, but by its agency. A miracle is something that is done by God's power outside of the normal processes of the physical world, whether they happen once a century, or many times a day.

Sadly today miracles ARE rare. But Jesus came to demonstrate that that was not to be the case among God's people. Miracles happen when God is present in the midst of His people; when we allow Him to work unimpeded in and through us. Even the book of Acts only details a few of the frequent miracles that God did in the midst of His people. The rest are covered with only general statements that still give you the sense that they were frequent. (Acts 2:43; 4:33; 5:12-16; 6:8; 8:6-7, 13; 14:3; 19:11-12.) Because God was present in the midst of His people, miracles happened all the time. It would have been impossible for them not to!

Jesus was the very embodiment of God's kingdom - the model of what kingdom people are supposed to be. He was one through whom all of God's power flowed to bring healing, freedom, and restoration to the people and the world around Him. He embodied the promise of what God can make of all of His people - a promise realized to a high degree in the people of the early Church.

Pray with me:

Father, thank You for this insight. O, Lord, how I long to see this promise of Your kingdom embodied in Your people. How I long to see us become a miracle-living, miracle-producing people. Help me, Lord, to follow You so closely, to open myself to You so completely, and to live for You so thoroughly, that Your miracle power can flow through me into the world, healing, freeing, and restoring the people and the world around me. Amen.

WHEN WE LISTEN

MARK 7:1-5

Read with me:

The Pharisees and some of the scribes who had come from Jerusalem gathered around him. They observed that some of his disciples were eating bread with unclean—that is, unwashed—hands. (For the Pharisees and all the Jews do not eat unless they give their hands a ceremonial washing, keeping the tradition of the elders. When they come from the marketplace, they do not eat unless they have washed. And there are many other customs they have received and keep, like the washing of cups, pitchers, kettles, and dining couches.) So the Pharisees and the scribes asked him, "Why don't your disciples live according to the tradition of the elders, instead of eating bread with ceremonially unclean hands?"

Listen with me:

If we search God's law in the Old Testament, we will not find anything pertaining to washing of hands before eating. This rule came purely from the traditions of men (as the Pharisees and teachers of the law correctly identified it: "the tradition of the elders".) Behind the ritual lay the idea that contact with the things of the world, especially contact with gentiles, or with anything that they had touched, would leave a residual spiritual uncleanness on a person's hands. If a person with that uncleanness on their hands then picked up and ate something without washing their hands first, that uncleanness would be taken into their body, making them spiritually unclean.

It is a good thing to wash our hands before we eat, but that won't keep us from being spiritually contaminated. As Jesus pointed out a little later on in this interaction (v15), spiritual contamination does not come from physical germs, but from allowing corrupting elements to impact our souls. Even those Pharisees who were most conscientious about washing any possible contaminants from their hands before they ate were unconcerned about allowing hate for Jesus to penetrate their hearts. Those who would not dare shake hands with a gentile, or go into a gentile house for fear of contamination that would exclude them from the temple, or from eating a Passover meal (John 18:28), had no problem seeking out false witnesses against Jesus and plotting the murder of a man they knew to be innocent.

Traditions are a fine thing, especially traditions that help people to draw closer to God and to rely more fully on His strength to live holy lives. But when the traditions start to cloud the truth, when they make people believe that they are holy while they are disobeying God's actually commands, or when the traditions become more important than what God actually commanded in His law, they become harmful, even deadly, and must be abandoned.

Pray with me:

Father, I know that we have a tendency to become very comfortable in our traditions, to the point that we don't notice when they become more important to us that You and Your commandments. And when they do hit that point, they become idols, and can actually be a snare to us. Help me, Lord, to always see myself with clear eyes, so that I never lose track of what must always be the main thing: You. Amen.

WHEN WE LISTEN

MARK 7:6-8

Read with me:

He answered them, "Isaiah prophesied correctly about you hypo-crites, as it is written: This people honors me with their lips, but their heart is far from me. They worship me in vain, teaching as doctrines human commands. [Isaiah 29:13] *Abandoning the command of God, you hold on to human tradition."*

Listen with me:

The Pharisees and scribes had moved away from the clear teachings of the Bible and, step by imperceptible step, had been following a faith that was largely based on man's thinking about God, instead of being based on what God had revealed about Himself. And they had been judging others, including Jesus, based on their man-centered faith, and had frequently found them wanting.

The process began innocently enough, with godly men adding interpretations and clarifications to the words recorded in the Scriptures. Some of the events in the Bible were confusing to them, or difficult to understand, so they wrote commentaries about them to try to explain them. Some of the commandments and laws left questions as to how they should be applied, so they wrote applications for those commands. Over time these commentaries filled volumes. Many people, desiring to know and serve God better, intensely studied those writings, crafted by men deemed to be more godly and more wise than ordinary men.

The problem began to manifest itself when those writings became more studied, more well-known, and even more cited than the Scriptures themselves. And the interpretations and commentaries began to be read back into the Scriptures when they were studied, biasing the readers to see things in a certain way, whether or not that way was accurate, not allowing the Scriptures to speak clearly for themselves.

The same phenomena are easily seen in our own times. Many people, even in the Church, read the latest devotional book, the latest "historical fiction" about people in the Bible, the latest commentary, and do so much more frequently, much more regularly, and with much more focus than they do the Scriptures themselves. They look up to the authors of those other books because of their godly reputation and the obvious research that they have done. And they feel that those commentators help them to understand the Scriptures better than they could do if they tried to do it themselves. It is then very easy to begin reading those commentaries, those interpretations, and even those fictions, back into the Scriptures themselves, experiencing biases that can lead them to see things in the Bible in a certain way, that may or may not be accurate.

God wrote the Scriptures in such a way that, if His people will only read them along with Him, asking for and receiving His guidance (Psalm 119:18), and letting His words speak for themselves, they can be understood by the vast majority of people. And whereas the commentaries, devotionals, and companion books can sometimes help people to understand historical contexts and applications more fully, even the best of them can never substitute for careful, Spirit-guided reading of the Scriptures themselves.

Pray with me:

Father, we often do read books about the Bible much more than the Bible itself. We do this under the guise of them being easier to understand, kind of pre-processed. But when we do that instead of reading and digesting the Scriptures themselves, and listening to your voice first-hand, we run the real risk of keeping ourselves mere spiritual infants. Instead, we need to spend lots of quality time in Your word, being guided and directed by You, and being purposefully grown up into people who can rightly handle the word of truth (2 Timothy 2:15). Help me, Lord, to crave the meat of Your word, undiluted, unprocessed, undigested, so that its clear meaning will shine forth in my heart and out of my life, challenging me, informing me, and ultimately changing my life in ways that secondary sources never can. Amen.

MARK 7:9-13

Read with me:

He also said to them, "You have a fine way of invalidating God's command in order to set up your tradition! For Moses said: **Honor your father and your mother** *[Exodus 20:12; Deuteronomy 5:16]; and* **Whoever speaks evil of father or mother must be put to death** *[Exodus 21:17; Leviticus 20:9]. But you say, 'If anyone tells his father or mother: Whatever benefit you might have received from me is corban'" (that is, an offering devoted to God), "you no longer let him do anything for his father or mother. You nullify the word of God by your tradition that you have handed down. And you do many other similar things."*

Listen with me:

Traditions in and of themselves are not bad things. They can serve to keep us connected with those who have gone before us, and they can even enrich our understanding of the faith. But any time a tradition or a "supplemental teaching" contradicts the clear words of Scripture, it becomes a positive evil that can corrupt the faith of God's people, and can even drive a wedge between us and God.

Jesus gave the example of a person who devotes money or other property to God. That sounds very pious and self-sacrificing. However, in some cases it made it impossible for them to uphold one of God's actual commandments: *Honor your father and your mother, so that you may have a long life in the land the Lord your God is giving you.* (Exodus 20:12) One important part of obeying this commandment is ensuring that our parents are adequately taken care of, especially when they are too old or infirm to provide for their own needs. Some in Jesus' day would say, "I'd really like to help, but all of the money that I could use to help you I can't use, because I've dedicated it to God as part of a vow."

151

WHEN WE LISTEN

Again, that sounds very pious, but it ends with that person actively disobeying a direct commandment in order to keep a commitment to God that He did not ask for. The principle behind Jesus' condemnation of this kind of "tradition" is that which was given to King Saul by the prophet, Samuel, when Saul failed to completely destroy the Amalekites as God directed, but saved their king alive to parade in front of his subjects, and also saved the best of their animals, ostensibly to be sacrificed to God as a thank offering. The principle is this: *"Does the Lord take pleasure in burnt offerings and sacrifices as much as in obeying the Lord? Look: to obey is better than sacrifice, to pay attention is better than the fat of rams."* (1 Samuel 15:22)

The irony is that these men, these Pharisees and teachers of the law, who so prided themselves on obeying every fine point of the law, were trying to gain additional blessings from God by those extra sacrifices, those additional acts of devotion. But the thing that would have brought them the maximum blessing was simple obedience to God's clear command. By placing their traditions ahead of what God had commanded, they actually robbed themselves of the very blessings they were trying to earn, and instead were actually bringing down judgment on themselves.

Pray with me:

Father, we still have a tendency to seek Your blessing through extra sacrifices or acts of devotion, while at the same time disobeying Your clear commandments. It is easy to see that simple obedience opens the door to every blessing that You long to give us. I don't have to "sweeten the pot" with extra promises or acts of devotion. Simple obedience to Your clear commands really is better than many sacrifices! Amen.

MARK 7:14-23

Read with me:

Summoning the crowd again, he told them, "Listen to me, all of you, and understand: Nothing that goes into a person from outside can defile him but the things that come out of a person are what defile him."

When he went into the house away from the crowd, the disciples asked him about the parable. He said to them, "Are you also as lacking in understanding? Don't you realize that nothing going into a person from the outside can defile him? For it doesn't go into his heart but into the stomach and is eliminated" (thus he declared all foods clean). And he said, "What comes out of a person is what defiles him. For from within, out of people's hearts, come evil thoughts, sexual immoralities, thefts, murders, adulteries, greed, evil actions, deceit, self-indulgence, envy, slander, pride, and foolishness. All these evil things come from within and defile a person."

Listen with me:

Remember that this whole conversation began when the Pharisees and teachers of the law criticized Jesus for allowing His disciples to eat with unwashed hands, disregarding the traditions of the elders. Jesus' response so far has addressed the pitfalls of man-made religion pushing aside God's commands, and how human traditions can do that as well.

But now Jesus gets to the very heart of the issue, and He does it very publicly, calling the people close to listen: It is not what a person puts into his or her body that makes them unclean; it is what comes out of them that corrupts. All of the food that a person eats, whether meat or vegetables, starches or fats, passes though the body without leaving a single mark on the soul. And this is true whether those foods are eaten with washed or unwashed hands.

WHEN WE LISTEN

Instead, it is the things that come from inside a person, corruption of the heart, that leads to corrupt thoughts (and, ultimately, to corrupt actions). And that is what make a person unclean. That inner corruption corrupts a person even before a single sinful action is committed. That was the problem that the Pharisees had, the problem that led Jesus to paint them as whitewashed tombs - pretty on the outside, but full of corruption within. And those same men, worried so much about corruption working its way into their hearts from the outside, totally missed the corruption that was stinking and festering inside of them.

Their inner corruption can be seen more and more as time went on. Their unwillingness to believe in Jesus, despite His ability to do miracles that they couldn't dream of doing. Their plotting to kill Him, even if it meant trumping up false charges and trying to find false witnesses against Him (Matthew 26:59-60, a direct violation of the 9th Commandment in Exodus 20:16). And even being willing to lie about Jesus' resurrection, and bribing others to lie about it, too (Matthew 28:11-15).

The whole time, these men believed themselves to be wonderfully holy and pure, because they steadfastly kept themselves away from external corrupting influences. What they missed was their own internal corruption, that was actually acting as a corrupting influence on the people all around them!

Pray with me:

Father, it is so easy to see ourselves with bias, to believe that we are righteous, and are doing things (sometimes even wrong things) for all the right reasons. Help me to see myself as YOU see me; to never turn a blind eye to my faults. Instead, any time You point out shortfalls, bad attitudes, or sinful thoughts and ideas, help me to immediately repent, and turn to You, so that You can purify me and make holy every single place in my heart. Amen.

MARK 7:24-30

Read with me:

He got up and departed from there to the region of Tyre. He entered a house and did not want anyone to know it, but he could not escape notice. Instead, immediately after hearing about him, a woman whose little daughter had an unclean spirit came and fell at his feet. The woman was a Gentile, a Syrophoenician by birth, and she was asking him to cast the demon out of her daughter. He said to her, "Let the children to be fed first, because it isn't right to take the children's bread and throw it to the dogs."

But she replied to him, "Lord, even the dogs under the table eat the children's crumbs."

Then he told her, "Because of this reply, you may go. The demon has left your daughter." When she went back to her home, she found her child lying on the bed, and the demon was gone.

Listen with me:

Many people are troubled by this episode in Jesus' ministry - by His seeming callousness toward this needy woman, and by the slap at her inferred by His use of the term "dog." But, as always, the larger picture must always be kept at the forefront.

Jesus had gone up to the area of Tyre in Phoenicia to have some down-time, to get some space between Himself and the controversies and confrontations that now were a regular occurrence in His ministry in Palestine. He should have been able to quietly enter town and just lie low for a few days in this foreign city where He wasn't very well known, but the word got out.

It was a normal occurrence for people to come to Jesus seeking a miracle for themselves or for someone they loved. But those that came were normally Jewish people - people who knew the Scriptures, who had been prepared for the coming of the Messiah, and who would listen to and understand His teachings. But the woman coming to Him now was none of those things. She wasn't even a "God-fearer," a gentile who worshiped the true God. She was just a gentile woman who wanted a miracle from this man who had a reputation as a wonder-worker.

Jesus was reluctant to do this miracle, not because his heart was hard (it never was, toward anybody), but because of the likely results: a miracle given and received without a heart being brought closer to the kingdom of God, the word spreading, and Him then being swamped by dozens or even hundreds of gentiles who didn't want God, but only wanted a miracle.

Jesus' point in His first statement was that He had been sent to those who had been prepared for the gospel - the Jewish people. (Even the Samaritans had been prepared to some extent for the coming of the Messiah by the Jewish Scriptures that they possessed and studied. See John 4:25-26) The time for the gentiles to receive the gospel would come (Acts 1:8), but it was not yet - all of the Jewish people had not yet been told. Jesus wouldn't waste His time performing miracles for those who would not be able to appreciate their deeper meaning and believe in Him.

Jesus' use of the term "dogs" signified that this woman, and most of the people in Tyre, were currently outside of God's kingdom until the time when the gospel would be purposefully extended to them. But it also gave the woman an opportunity to use the same figure of speech herself, and to reframe it to her advantage. Rather than accepting the term to show herself as a wild dog, outside of the kingdom, she changed the picture to one of herself as a pet dog, lying under the table, and willingly receiving even the crumbs that fell from those to whom the bread of the gospel rightfully belonged at the time.

This answer showed Jesus the state of the woman's heart. It was one that was open to receiving Jesus, not just as a miracle worker, but as he truly was: the Deliverer who had come from the true God. So Jesus pronounced her daughter delivered, and from that moment, she was.

MARK 7

Pray with me:

Father, things are not always as they seem on the surface, and I have found that we can discover hearts that You have been preparing for Your good news in unexpected places. Help me, like Jesus, to stay true to Your calling, but at the same time, to be open to any of these wonderful surprises that You place along my way. Amen.

WHEN WE LISTEN

MARK 7:31-37

Read with me:

Again, leaving the region of Tyre, he went by way of Sidon to the Sea of Galilee, through the region of the Decapolis. They brought to him a deaf man who had difficulty speaking and begged Jesus to lay his hand on him. So he took him away from the crowd in private. After putting his fingers in the man's ears and spitting, he touched his tongue. Looking up to heaven, he sighed deeply and said to him, "Ephphatha!" (that is, "Be opened!"). Immediately his ears were opened, his tongue was loosened, and he began to speak clearly. He ordered them to tell no one, but the more he ordered them, the more they proclaimed it.

They were extremely astonished and said, "He has done everything well. He even makes the deaf hear, and the mute speak."

Listen with me:

Everywhere Jesus went at this stage of His ministry, there were opportunities to show forth the power of God that was at work in and through Him. He had gained a reputation as a healer with no limitations. Whether it was an illness, or a condition that had been present from birth; whether it was something caused by a germ or by a demon; it didn't matter. He could instantly provide the needed healing and wholeness.

As soon as they heard that Jesus had come into their area, the family and friends of this man brought him to Jesus to be healed. He couldn't hear, and he couldn't speak clearly.

Some people wonder why Jesus went through all of these actions to perform this healing. It seems a little bit theatrical. Couldn't He have simply spoken a word and healed the man on the spot? The simple and surprising answer is, not in this case. If that method would have been effective, He would have used it. Jesus never did anything that wasn't necessary. He never engaged in theatrics in order to "build people's faith." He never did things in a way that was designed to impress people. Quite the opposite, in fact. He always did things exactly the way that they had to be done - no more, no less.

Sometimes Jesus did heal with a word. Sometimes He healed with a touch. And sometimes He used mud smeared on blind eyes. In this case, He used fingers placed in deaf ears and on a bound tongue. His was never a "one size fits all" approach to healing. He used the appropriate, God-directed method in every case. People are complex creatures, and the things that afflict them stem from many different causes. It makes sense that Jesus would use a different method to cast out a demon than He would to heal a fever. The truth is, He used whatever was the appropriate method for healing whatever disease or infirmity He was presented with in a person.

In this case, the problem were closed ears and a bound tongue. Jesus touched each of these. The spitting symbolized the expelling of what had bound the man's tongue. He then gave the command, "Ephphatha!" ("Be opened."), and the man's ears were instantly opened so he could hear. His tongue was instantly freed up, so that he could speak clearly.

Jesus' command not to spread the word about this healing was another attempt to keep the main thing in the forefront. Jesus had not come primarily to heal people. He had come to inaugurate the kingdom of God. The healings were merely a sign that this new economy of the Kingdom was a reality. But, of course, the people were awed by the power that Jesus possessed, by His overwhelming mastery even over such things as deafness and muteness, things that medical science of their day offered no hope for. They really couldn't resist telling everyone about what they had seen and heard.

WHEN WE LISTEN

Pray with me:

Father, forgive us for trying to use a "one size fits all" method in our lives and ministry, to use something this time, a particular way of praying, or of recruiting, or of organizing, or even of healing, because it has been effective in the past. That is relying on ourselves, and on our own wisdom, our own ability to influence the situation. If Jesus Himself needed specific guidance from You as to how to deal with each situation He faced, how much more do I need to turn to You every single time, and never let myself get caught up in a particular procedure, or a particular methodology. Amen.

MARK 8:1-10

Read with me:

In those days there was again a large crowd, and they had nothing to eat. He called the disciples and said to them, "I have compassion on the crowd, because they've already stayed with me three days and have nothing to eat. If I send them home hungry, they will collapse on the way, and some of them have come a long distance."

His disciples answered him, "Where can anyone get enough bread here in this desolate place to feed these people?"

"How many loaves do you have?" he asked them.

"Seven," they said. He commanded the crowd to sit down on the ground. Taking the seven loaves, he gave thanks, broke them, and gave them to his disciples to set before the people. So they served them to the crowd. They also had a few small fish, and after he had blessed them, he said these were to be served as well. They ate and were satisfied. Then they collected seven large baskets of leftover pieces. About four thousand were there. He dismissed them. And he immediately got into the boat with his disciples and went to the district of Dalmanutha.

Listen with me:

As Yogi Berra famously said, "It's déjà vu all over again!"

It was nearly the same situation as happened a few months before, when Jesus challenged His disciples to feed five thousand men, plus women and children in a remote location (Mark 6:30-44). When the disciples were told, "You give them something to eat" (6:37), they had no idea what to do next. At that time, Jesus patiently demonstrated for them how the Father could multiply five loaves and two small fish to feed the whole crowd.

Now here they were again, in pretty much the same situation: thousands of hungry people, no place to get food, and meager resources - seven loaves and a few small fish. (They should have been encouraged: they had fewer people and comparatively more resources than the first time!) But it was like the previous event had never happened - no flash of understanding, no reaction to the similarity. When Jesus presented them with the opportunity to experience God's amazing power, all they could see were the impossibilities of the situation: the hugeness of the crowd, and the smallness of their resources.

Again Jesus patiently went through the same procedure as before. He had the people sit down on the ground. This quieted everyone, and shifted their attention to what Jesus was doing. He gave thanks to His Father for the bread and fish that was available. He broke the bread and fish, and gave them to the disciples to give to the people. And the same thing happened again: God multiplied the available resources so greatly that everyone ate and was satisfied. And the disciples were able to gather up seven large baskets of leftovers.

These lessons, patiently repeated by Jesus, were important for the disciples to grasp. It would be easy for them to figure that the power to do all of these miracles resided peculiarly in Jesus - that when He wasn't present, no miracles were possible. But Jesus knew that His time on earth would not last forever; He would be leaving one day in the not-too-distant future, leaving the work of the kingdom in the hands of these men. They needed to learn that the power to do these miracles did not reside in Jesus like water in a jar. Instead, it flowed through Jesus from the Father. And the disciples needed to learn that when they were connected to the Father in vital relationship, the same miracle-working power would be able to flow through them, just as it had when Jesus sent them on their mission journey (Mark 6:7-13).

Pray with me:

Father, it is easy to be critical of those disciples for not getting it, but the truth is that we are just as slow to learn this same lesson. We have no real understanding of the power that can flow through us when we stay in vital relationship with You. Understanding that when Your Holy Spirit lives in us, He communicates to us and through us the presence of the whole Godhead, and that we then have access to the power we need to do whatever You ask us to do. Forgive me, Lord, for being slow to learn, slow to believe, and slow to take up the challenge of doing the work of Your kingdom, and allowing Your power to flow unimpeded through my life. Amen.

WHEN WE LISTEN

MARK 8:11-13

Read with me:

The Pharisees came and began to argue with him, demanding of him a sign from heaven to test him. Sighing deeply in his spirit, he said, "Why does this generation demand a sign? Truly I tell you, no sign will be given to this generation." Then he left them, got back into the boat, and went to the other side.

Listen with me:

The Pharisees prided themselves on being loved by God and on being close to God, all because of their righteousness. Yet the best of them could do no miracles. Despite their great learning and their great piety, they were missing something that this simple preacher of God's kingdom had in abundance: power.

By the time they came to Jesus demanding a miracle to prove His authority to teach the things He was teaching, Jesus had done literally thousands of miracles, including casting out demons, healing the sick, feeding multitudes (twice!), and even raising the dead. And some of these same Pharisees had already seen many of them.

What those Pharisees were demanding was that Jesus would show them a miracle of their choosing - that He perform what they demanded as proof of His Messiahship. If He would do that, then they would take that into consideration as they debated just who and what He was.

But Jesus was not a street magician who performed tricks for the amusement of an audience. Nor was he a professional work-er of miracles, a manipulator of people or of nature, who could do what He wanted whenever He wanted. Jesus was God in the flesh; not merely the Messiah, but the Lord Himself. He was not to be ordered about, but listened to and obeyed. And Jesus worked only as the Father directed (John 5:19), never at the whims of people.

The Pharisees were actually being disingenuous here, as they were in most of their dealings with Jesus. If they really needed to see a miracle to believe in Him, any of the thousands that He had already done would have sufficed. Or they could just follow Jesus for a while, and they would be sure to see some miracles that were impressive enough to warrant their respect.

But, as Jesus Himself pointed out, if these men would not believe what their own Scriptures said about Jesus, even so great a miracle as someone rising from the dead wouldn't convince them (Luke 16:31). And this was proven to be absolutely true: after Jesus did rise from the dead, most of the Pharisees still refused to believe in Him, and even concocted a lie to keep others from believing (Matthew 28:11-15). So, at this point, Jesus refused to play into their hands by catering to their desires for more "proof," and simply walked away.

Pray with me:

Father, even today many still clamor for "proof" that You are real, or that Jesus really was God in the flesh. Your testimony, and the testimony of eyewitnesses contained in Your Scriptures don't seem to be enough for them. Nor is the current testimony of those whose lives have been transformed by Your power and love. They demand a sign of their own choosing, or they refuse to believe. But You are still not in the business of catering to the whims of stubborn, unbelieving hearts. You have set the evidence of who You are, and of what Jesus has done all around us, if only we are willing to see. Amen.

WHEN WE LISTEN

MARK 8:14-21

Read with me:

The disciples had forgotten to take bread and had only one loaf with them in the boat. Then he gave them strict orders: "Watch out! Beware of the leaven of the Pharisees and the leaven of Herod." They were discussing among themselves that they did not have any bread. Aware of this, he said to them, "Why are you discussing the fact you have no bread? Don't you understand or comprehend? Do you have hardened hearts? **Do you have eyes and not see; do you have ears and not hear?** *[Jeremiah 5:21; Ezekiel 12:2] And do you not remember? When I broke the five loaves for the five thousand, how many baskets full of leftovers did you collect?"*

"Twelve," they told him.

"When I broke the seven loaves for the four thousand, how many large baskets full of pieces did you collect?"

"Seven," they said.

And he said to them, "Don't you understand yet?"

Listen with me:

It was a very short statement, only 14 words in the CSB; a statement born of frustration: *"Watch out! Beware of the leaven of the Pharisees and the leaven of Herod."* The frustration came from the fact that Herod was the temporal ruler of God's people, but he was completely self-absorbed and corrupt, even to the point of putting John the Baptist to death (Mark 6:21-28) to keep from looking weak politically. If he led God's people anywhere, it would only be to ruin. The Pharisees, those whose hearts were supposed to be completely devoted to God, were looked on by many as the spiritual leaders of God's people. But they, too, were self-absorbed and corrupt, even to the point of rejecting God's Messiah now that He had finally come. If they led God's people anywhere, it would be to rejecting both Jesus and His message of salvation.

When Jesus made the simple 14-word statement, His warning should have been easy to understand. Just as yeast spreads quickly throughout a mass of dough, quickly affecting the whole batch, so self-absorption and spiritual corruption will quickly contaminate individuals, and even whole societies if it is ever allowed to get started.

But this simple statement quickly revealed two huge problems in the disciples. First, they were still spiritually unawake. Jesus was speaking on a spiritual level, but they were only hearing Him on the physical level. They thought He was talking about physical bread, inspired by the fact that they had only brought one loaf with them - not nearly enough for them all when it came time for them to eat.

It was this spiritual dullness that prompted Jesus to ask if they had hardened hearts; if their spiritual eyes were blind, and their spiritual ears deaf; the same accusation that He had made of people outside the kingdom (Mark 4:12). After all this time of living and ministering with Him, and even after being empowered themselves to heal and cast out demons (Mark 6:7-13), Jesus expected more.

The second problem was that the disciples were worried that since they only had one loaf of bread between them, that they would have to go hungry when dinner time came. This troubled Jesus as much as the other problem; maybe even more. It had only been a few weeks since Jesus had fed five thousand men, plus women and children, with only five loaves of bread. It had been an even shorter time since He had fed more than four thousand with seven loaves. But the disciples still didn't understand the meaning of those events. They hadn't put two and two together to realize that when they were on God's mission, God Himself would provide all that they would need, including food. Jesus wasn't worried in the least about the lack of bread. But He was greatly troubled that His closest followers were.

WHEN WE LISTEN

Pray with me:

Father, how easy it is to allow ourselves to be distracted by physical needs and what we seem to lack, and in the process completely miss what You are really trying to show and tell us. Lord, soften my heart so that Your words always find a place in me where they can instantly gain a toehold. Open my eyes so that I can see all that You want to show me, not just on the physical level, but on the spiritual level, too. And open my ears so that when Your words come, I hear and understand each of them clearly. Amen.

MARK 8:22-26

Read with me:

They came to Bethsaida. They brought a blind man to him, and begged him to touch him. He took the blind man by the hand and brought him out of the village. Spitting on his eyes and laying his hands on him, he asked him, "Do you see anything?"

He looked up and said, "I see people—they look like trees walking."

Again Jesus placed his hands on the man's eyes. The man looked intently and his sight was restored and he saw everything clearly. Then he sent him home, saying, "Don't even go into the village."

Listen with me:

This event stands out strongly among all of Jesus' miracles, because it seems to have not been entirely effective at first. In no other case in the gospels did someone require a second touch for the healing to be complete.

This miracle happened during a brief stopover in Bethsaida ("House of fishing"), the hometown of Peter, Andrew, and Philip (John 1:44) on the north shore of the Sea of Galilee. We are told very little about the blind man, except that He did not live in Bethsaida proper (verse 26). But it's important to note that what looks at first like a failure on Jesus' part was actually right in line with God's plan.

We know that Jesus understood that His first touch would not restore the man's sight completely simply because of His question: "Do you see anything?" In every other recorded miracle, Jesus merely touched the person, or spoke the word, and the complete healing immediately followed. In no other case did he ask the person if the healing had worked.

WHEN WE LISTEN

Some think that the man's faith wasn't strong enough to be healed completely. But the man's faith (or lack of it) was never addressed by Jesus. Others wonder if this case was just very complicated. But it was no more complicated than that of the man who was born blind (John 9:1-7) where the healing was completed with a single touch.

The context of this miracle helps us to understand what was going on. It immediately followed Jesus' chastisement of His disciples over their inability to understand God's working and Jesus' teachings (Mark 8:14-21). On the way over to Bethsaida, Jesus had accused them of having eyes but failing to see, and of having ears but failing to hear. And then this blind man is brought to Jesus for healing. (Coincidence? I think not!)

Jesus took the man out of the village, away from the crowds. There He spit on the man's eyes and laid His hands on him, all of which His disciples had seen before, and either of which should have resulted in an immediate healing. But to the disciples' amazement, while the man could now see, his sight was defective - blurred to the point that the disciples looked to him like trees walking around rather than men. To complete both the healing and the lesson, Jesus placed His hands on the man's eyes, and his sight was instantly perfected. Everything was now crystal clear. Jesus then sent the man home, telling him not to go back into the village.

So what was the point that Jesus was trying to make with all of this? Most of the disciples had been with Jesus for a couple of years by now. They had heard Jesus teach so many times, they had experienced so many miracles (including doing some themselves), that they believed that they were quite spiritually advanced. But in reality, even though their spiritual eyes had been opened, their vision was blurred and indistinct, to the point that they were missing some things that should have been obvious to them, and many things that they did see, they misinterpreted.

Jesus knew that what they really needed to help them to see clearly was a second touch, a touch to their hearts and minds that would take away the fuzziness and make everything crystal clear. That second touch would come, but not until the day of Pentecost,

170

when the Holy Spirit would enter into the very core of their beings, and would transform them from the inside out. He would not merely give them power, He would also clarify their sight and enhance their understanding, so that everything would become clear. Until then, Jesus would have to deal with their shortsightedness and their lack of understanding.

Some might be critical of Jesus for "using" this man to make His point, but they shouldn't be. The man was neither harmed nor inconvenienced in this miracle. Instead, over the course of two or three minutes he went from total blindness to completely clear vision. The fact that it happened in two steps didn't bother him a bit.

Pray with me:

Father, it seems the easiest thing in the world to convince ourselves that we can see clearly, especially in the spiritual realm, when the whole time, even though our eyes have been opened, we are so nearsighted that we are still practically blind. (Revelation 3:17-18) Until we are actually given real clarity of sight and understanding, it is difficult to see just how blind we really are. Open my eyes, Lord, so that I can truly see everything you want to show me, and see it all clearly. Amen.

WHEN WE LISTEN

MARK 8:27-30

Read with me:

Jesus went out with his disciples to the villages of Caesarea Philippi. And on the road he asked his disciples, "Who do people say that I am?"

They answered him, "John the Baptist; others, Elijah; still others, one of the prophets."

"But you," he asked them, "who do you say that I am?"

Peter answered him, "You are the Messiah." And He strictly warned them to tell no one about him.

Listen with me:

Jesus' time was growing short, and it was just about time for Him to start heading to Jerusalem for the last few scenes of His life. By this time He had invested about three years into the lives of His closest followers, and He was disturbed that they had shown so little growth in their understanding of Him and of the kingdom which He had inaugurated, and which He would soon leave in their hands.

Jesus knew that there were diverse opinions as to who He really was, so He started this critical conversation with a "soft ball" question: "Who do people say I am?"

Many people believed that Jesus was John the Baptist raised from the dead. This opinion was most prevalent among those who had not seen John, but had merely heard about him. Jesus' message of repentance and the kingdom of God was similar to John's, and people saw his miraculous restoration to life as a reasonable explanation as to why Jesus Himself was able to do miracles.

Others believed that Jesus was the great prophet Elijah. The Jewish people had been awaiting the Messiah for centuries, but they believed (based on Scriptures like Malachi 4:5-6) that Elijah would reappear first to prepare God's people for His coming. Elijah

172

had done a few impressive miracles, so Jesus' miraculous abilities seemed like reasonable evidence that He was, in fact, Elijah, and that the Messiah must be near.

Still others saw Jesus as a mighty prophet, like those written about in the Old Testament. Prophets were not always foretellers of the future. Rather they were spokespeople for God. And some of them, like Moses, and Elijah, did miracles. It had been more than four hundred years since a mighty prophet had arisen. So many saw Jesus as a spokesman for God, a mighty prophet who would help them to know how God wanted them to live.

Then Jesus asked the critical question: "But you, who do you say I am?" Peter acted as spokesman for the group when he answered: "You are the Messiah."

Jesus' disciples knew that He wasn't John the Baptist. They had been with Jesus while John was still in prison, and several of the them had originally been followers of John. Besides, they had seen that Jesus was far above John in every way. As John himself had said, *"One who is more powerful than I am is coming after me. I am not worthy to stoop down and untie the strap of his sandals."* (Mark 1:7) They knew that He was not Elijah come to earth again. He had done things far greater than Elijah had ever dreamed of doing. And they knew that He was not merely a prophet, even a great prophet. Jesus spoke and acted with all of the authority of God Himself; not like one with delegated authority. It was as if He were God in the flesh.

To the disciples there was only one logical answer to the question: Jesus was the Messiah they had been waiting for. He was the long-promised deliverer who would save the people of God and set all things right. They had seen His power at work, they had listened to His teachings, and there was no doubt at all in their minds that He was the One.

Jesus was relieved. It wasn't all that He hoped for at this point, but it was a step in the right direction. However, He swore them to silence, because most people (the disciples included) had a distorted view of the Messiah in their minds. Most people saw the Messiah as a political deliverer; one who would set up an earthly kingdom and a new dynasty of Davidic kings. But He still had a few weeks to help them to understand.

WHEN WE LISTEN

Pray with me:

Father, people still have varied ideas as to who Jesus is. Some see Him as a good man, a great teacher, perhaps even a prophet. But He clearly declared Himself to be the Messiah, the Savior, the very son of God. Help us all to know Him for who He really is, so that we can clearly show Him to others. Amen.

MARK 8:31-33

Read with me:

Then he began to teach them that it was necessary for the Son of Man to suffer many things and be rejected by the elders, chief priests, and scribes, be killed, and rise after three days. He spoke openly about this. Peter took him aside and began to rebuke Him. But turning around and looking at his disciples, he rebuked Peter and said, "Get behind me, Satan! You are not thinking about God's concerns, but human concerns!"

Listen with me:

The preconceived notions of who and what the Messiah was to be ran deep in the hearts of God's people, even among the inner circle of Jesus' twelve disciples. After Peter's confession that Jesus was indeed the Messiah, He began to share with them all that that actually meant.

Jesus had known for some time where His path would lead. He knew that He would be rejected by the elders, chief priests, and scribes, the very ones who were most eagerly awaiting the arrival of the Messiah. He didn't even have to be omniscient to know that this was true, because many of them had already rejected Him as the Messiah because He didn't fit what they had been taught that He should be and do. But Jesus knew that an even deeper rejection was just over the horizon - one that would result in those leaders condemning Him to death.

Jesus knew that He would be killed by those very leaders whom He had come to save, and that the death He had to die would be inconceivable to anyone else. Not only would it be gruesome, shameful, and excruciating from a physical standpoint, it would also include suffering for all of the sins of mankind. It would even include having the Father withdraw His presence from Him, something that Jesus had never experienced from all eternity past.

But Jesus could clearly see beyond the suffering and shame, and even beyond the separation from his Father that He would have to endure. He understood that all of that would last only a few hours, and would then be followed by a glorious resurrection. He would be restored to the glory that He had with the Father before the world began (John 17:5).

But Peter never even heard the part about the resurrection. He was appalled at Jesus' prediction of rejection and suffering, and when Jesus spoke about being killed, he simply stopped listening and began to move toward Jesus, to pull Him aside, to convince Him that this was not the path that He should follow. After all, there were a sizable number of people who adored Jesus, enough to make up a small army. Surely there were more than enough of them to prevent even the whole Sanhedrin from taking Jesus away and killing Him.

But Jesus immediately recognized the spirit behind those words. In them He heard an echo from His time in the Judean wilderness. Three times Satan had tried to get Him to turn aside for God's plan, to follow the "easier" and "safer" path of self-satisfaction, self-aggrandizement, and self-preservation. Satan had promised that if Jesus would only turn aside to HIS path, all of His goals could be met without any pain or suffering. But all of that was a lie then, and it was a lie now. God's ways are not ways that make sense to the enemy, or even to most human beings.

Tainted by self-interest, most people shy away from the path of self-sacrifice that God lays out before them. But, just as in the wilderness, one sharp rebuke put an end to this temptation, and provided an opportunity for the disciples to really hear what Jesus was trying to tell them.

Pray with me:

Father, we do tend to shy away from the hard paths, the hard choices, even when we know that those paths and choices are the ways that You have laid out before us. How much time have we wasted trying to explain to You that our way is better? How many opportunities have we missed while wavering and second guessing Your clear commands? Forgive em, Lord, and help me to yield myself more fully to Your complete will for my life. Amen.

MARK 8:34-38

Read with me:

Calling the crowd along with his disciples, he said to them, "If anyone wants to follow after me, let him deny himself, take up his cross, and follow me. For whoever wants to save his life will lose it, but whoever loses his life because of me and the gospel will save it. For what does it benefit someone to gain the whole world and yet lose his life? What can anyone give in exchange for his life? For whoever is ashamed of me and of my words in this adulterous and sinful generation, the Son of Man will also be ashamed of him when he comes in the glory of his Father with the holy angels."

Listen with me:

Peter was disturbed that Jesus was talking about His upcoming crucifixion. Jesus was disturbed that Peter was disturbed. But the problem lay in the fact that most people's understanding of the kingdom of God differed markedly from the reality that Jesus had come to inaugurate.

Jesus' twelve disciples especially had a vision that was wide of the mark. They doubtlessly pictured Jesus marching into Jerusalem at the head of a massive throng, throwing out the Roman governor, and then all of them participating in His coronation as king. From then on, it would be marvelous! All twelve of them would become heads in the new government, making up Jesus' privy council, and enjoying all the perks that went along with it.

But Jesus saw a much different picture, and He knew that it would be His picture that would come true. He knew that, even though many in the crowds would cheer Him into Jerusalem, five days later He would die on a cross and be buried in a borrowed tomb. Even though He would rise on the third day, and ascend back into heaven a few weeks later, He would be leaving a massive and difficult job in the hands of these disciples. They would be tasked with taking the gospel to every corner of the globe, with confronting the forces of evil and darkness, and pushing forward the kingdom of love and light.

Jesus knew that as they did this, darkness and evil would be constantly pushing back against them. He knew that their paths would lead them through dark and treacherous valleys, and that suffering and pain would dog their steps. He knew that often they would have to choose between obeying God and their own safety.

Jesus' word was not just for the twelve. He gathered all of the people around them to hear. Anyone who wanted to follow Him, to be counted among the people of the kingdom, had to be willing to deny themselves - to put all of their plans not just on the back burner, but off the stove altogether. Jesus' disciples don't live out their own lives; they are to live out the life of Jesus. They no longer own their hopes and dreams. Instead they take up God's plan, pursue His vision, and take up His goals as their new hopes and their dreams.

Anyone who wants to follow Jesus cannot shrink from the cross. Instead, they must take up their own cross willingly; be willing to die rather than turn away from the task to which Jesus has called them. Anyone who denies the gospel to save their life will ultimately lose their soul. But anyone who lays down their life for the sake of the gospel will save their soul for eternal life.

It was vital for Jesus' followers to understand this. If they were shrinking back now, when Jesus' suffering on the cross was only an idea in their minds, what would they do when the choice had to be made for themselves - surrender or suffering; compromise or condemnation; denial or death? Jesus wanted His words to stick in their minds and hearts for the rest of their lives. He knew that on the day of Pentecost the Holy Spirit would give them the power that they needed to be witnesses. But even then, the decision to obey regardless of the cost would have to originate in their own will.

WHEN WE LISTEN

Pray with me:

Father, the standard is still the same today. There are a thousand ways in which we can deny You each day instead of pushing boldly forward with the gospel; a million little compromises and ways of holding back so that people won't think poorly of us. But we are not our own. We have been bought with a price, and our lives are now to be lived as Your life. Help me to receive Your word deeply into my heart, and to make my decision to follow you now, no matter where the path leads, so that when the time comes, I will respond with boldness - no shame, no compromise, just obedience. Amen.

MARK 9:1

Read with me:

Then he said to them, "Truly I tell you, there are some standing here who will not taste death until they see the kingdom of God come in power."

Listen with me:

Jesus had just shocked His inner circle by predicting His death at the hands of the Jewish leaders, and He had just shocked a whole crowd by insisting that those who wanted to follow Him must be willing to consciously lay down their own lives, to take up their own crosses. In essence, all of Jesus' followers must be willing to follow Him all the way, even if that way lies to death.

The mood was pretty somber as they all processed this news. It was a lot to think about. But then Jesus made this announcement that turned their minds into another channel altogether: *"Truly I tell you, there are some standing here who will not taste death until they see the kingdom of God come in power."*

Many have taught that Jesus was referring to the transfiguration that was to occur six days later, and which comes immediately after this statement in all of the synoptic gospels. But there are a few problems with this view. First, Jesus' statement strongly implies that at least one of His followers would die before the event that He was predicting, and there is no hint of that death anywhere in the gospels. Second, only three people, Peter, James, and John, were witnesses to the transfiguration, whereas Jesus seems to be predicting something much larger. Finally, although Jesus' transformation was stunning to those who witnessed it, it cannot be said that anything appreciable changed that would be able to be described as "the kingdom of God coming," or that any additional power was evident afterwards. The miracles that Jesus did after the transfiguration were of the same quality and quantity as before;

His teachings were of the same kind and on the same subjects. The only reason that the transfiguration comes immediately after Jesus' statement in the gospels is not that it was the fulfillment of that promise, but it was the next significant event to happen.

So what was Jesus pointing to with this statement? On the day of Jesus' ascension, He told the gathered disciples, *"you will receive power when the Holy Spirit comes on you, and you will be my witnesses in Jerusalem, in all Judea and Samaria, and to the end of the earth."* (Acts 1:8) This promised power filled the disciples (120 of them) on the day of Pentecost, and in a matter of hours, God's kingdom exploded onto the scene and grew to over three thousand people (Acts 2).

This fits Jesus' predication much better. Although the kingdom of God, the people who follow God as their Sovereign in the new life of the Spirit, awaits its final consummation at Jesus' return, it definitely began and started its exponential growth on the day of Pentecost. It also came with the power that Jesus promised. From that day on, signs and wonders, miracles, and powerful witness that brought dozens, hundreds, even thousands of people at a time into the kingdom, were all experienced by the Church. But all of Jesus' disciples did not live to experience this coming of the kingdom of God with power. One of them had indeed tasted death before the kingdom became a reality. Judas had hanged himself in remorse over betraying Jesus into the hands of His enemies, just as Jesus Himself had predicted.

Ever since that day, the same Holy Spirit comes into the hearts of those who trust in Jesus for salvation, providing the same power to be a witness everywhere we live, everywhere we work, everywhere we go. Since that day, all of us who have come to the Lord by faith have come into His kingdom. We become His subjects, doing His will. And we wait eagerly for the final consummation of the kingdom when Jesus returns.

MARK 9

Father, thank You for this truth. A single sentence from Jesus, but it points us to a powerful reality that we get to experience in our own lives. Help me, Lord, to live as a member of Your kingdom. Help me to serve You every day with my whole heart. Amen.

MARK 9:2-8

Read with me:

After six days Jesus took Peter, James, and John and led them up a high mountain by themselves to be alone. He was transfigured in front of them, and his clothes became dazzling—extremely white as no launderer on earth could whiten them. Elijah appeared to them with Moses, and they were talking with Jesus. Peter said to Jesus, "Rabbi, it's good for us to be here. Let us set up three shelters: one for you, one for Moses, and one for Elijah"—because he did not know what to say, since they were terrified.

A cloud appeared, overshadowing them, and a voice came from the cloud: "This is my beloved Son; listen to him!

Suddenly, looking around, they no longer saw anyone with them except Jesus.

Listen with me:

Jesus' time was short. It was time for Him to start heading south, and soon it would be the Passover, when His final journey would end in Jerusalem. Jesus often prayed, especially before the major transitions in His ministry, and this was definitely one of those times. He wanted to tag up with the Father to make sure what His next steps would be.

The transfiguration that the three disciples saw was for their benefit, not for the benefit of Jesus. And what they actually experienced was a brief look "behind the curtain," a glimpse of Jesus' glory that was ensconced in His human flesh. (John saw this glory even more clearly on Patmos - see Revelation 1:12-18.) Moses and Elijah were speaking to Jesus specifically about His departure (the Greek word Luke used is "exodus") that He would shortly be undergoing in Jerusalem (Luke 9:30-31).

These two people had great symbolic significance to the disciples. Moses stood for the Old Testament, the Law that Jesus had come to fulfill through His life, death, and resurrection (Matthew 5:17). Elijah stood for the Prophets, and he was also prophesied to come to usher in the Messiah (although this was fulfilled not in this "cameo" appearance, but through the ministry of John the Baptist - Matthew 17:10-13.)

As wonderful as all of this was, and as privileged as these disciples were to be there to experience it, they were mostly just terrified at the time. Peter was so overwhelmed by the glory of these three people that he felt that something should be done to honor them, but he had nothing to do it with. So he came up with the idea of at least building shelters for the three of them.

That was where God the Father stepped in, covering them with a cloud of glory, and speaking directly to them. It was not important for them to DO anything. What was important was for them to see clearly and understand who Jesus was, the Messiah, the beloved Son of God, and to listen to Him. Their time with Him was coming quickly to an end, and events were just over the horizon that would make them doubt what Peter had so strongly expressed just a few days ago. Now was the time to drive the truth deep into their hearts.

Pray with me:

Father, sometimes we get overconfident in what we think we know. Peter, James, and John knew that Jesus was the Messiah, but they really had no idea all that that meant. Even this small glimpse of His real glory terrified them. In the same way, all that we know of You, all that You have revealed of Yourself through Your word, is really just the edge of Your garment. We believe that we want to see Your glory, but even seeing a small bit of You as You truly are would be enough to completely overwhelm us. Help me, Lord, to simply rest in what I do know of You, and of Jesus. Help me to hold Him up always as Your beloved Son, and to really listen to Him, as You instructed those disciples that day. Amen.

MARK 9:9-13

Read with me:

As they were coming down the mountain, he ordered them to tell no one what they had seen until the Son of Man had risen from the dead. They kept this word to themselves, questioning what "rising from the dead" meant.

Then they asked him, "Why do the scribes say that Elijah must come first?"

"Elijah does come first and restores all things," he replied. "Why then is it written that the Son of Man must suffer many things and be treated with contempt? But I tell you that Elijah has come, and they did whatever they pleased to him, just as it is written about him."

Listen with me:

Teachings that people have received in the past, even false or erroneous teachings, are terribly difficult to modify or remove. And new teachings, even if they are absolutely correct and biblical, often have a hard time working into people's hearts, especially if they challenge or contradict non-biblical teachings that are already there. And Jesus' closest followers were no exception to this rule.

There were many teachings about the Messiah that were popularly believed in Jesus' day. But since the Jewish Scriptures about the Messiah were scattered throughout the various Scriptures, and since some of them seemed somewhat ambiguous until Jesus fulfilled them, these teachings were sometimes accurate, sometimes incomplete, and sometimes completely false.

Many people knew that the Messiah would be born in Bethlehem from the line of David (Matthew 2:4-6, 22:41-42), but some believed that He would just magically appear, and that no one would know where He had come from (John 7:27), which led to some rejecting Jesus right off the bat. Most people believed (correctly) that the Messiah would live forever (John 12:34), but few were willing to accept the Scriptures that He had to first be tortured, killed, buried, and rise again (Isaiah 52:13-53:12).

So it was understandable that Jesus' disciples were confused about what Jesus was now telling them. The whole idea that the Messiah would have to die and then rise from the dead before He would live forever had no place to take root in the traditions that they had received. It mystified them.

Jesus swore the three disciples that had witnessed the transfiguration to silence, because the experience alone could lead them to false assumptions, which would then be shared with others right along with the narrative of the experience. After Jesus rose from the dead, this would all make much more sense to them, and they would have a much more solid context from which they could accurately share what had happened. But in the meantime, they were still troubled by all of this talk about "rising from the dead."

They were also troubled by the seeming non-fulfillment of the teaching that the Messiah would be preceded by the return of the prophet Elijah. They had now seen Elijah in the (glorified) flesh, and realized that he had not come yet - at least they hadn't seen him before.

This teaching about Elijah was actually solidly based on Scripture (Malachi 4:5-6), but the fulfillment was a little different than the literal reading would suggest. Jesus knew that John the Baptist (who actually dressed like Elijah and spoke as boldly as he did – compare 2 Kings 1:7-8 & Matthew 3:4) had already fulfilled that role, preparing the way for Jesus. John's father, Zechariah, had been told by Gabriel before John was even conceived, "And he (John) will go before him (the Lord), in the spirit and power of Elijah, to turn the hearts of fathers to their children, and the disobedient to the understanding of the righteous, to make ready for the Lord a prepared people." (Luke 1:17)

All of these new teachings were strange to the disciples, and it was difficult for them to find a place for them in their heads among the potpourri of Messianic teachings that they had already received. But it was critical that they begin to see and understand how the things that God had actually spoken through the prophets were being fulfilled right before their eyes, so that, after Jesus rose from the dead and ascended back into heaven, they would be able to teach others accurately.

Pray with me:

Father, it is a sad truth that bad teachings about the Scriptures can actually close people's eyes to the real truths that are right there before them. That is probably why You point out that "we (who teach) will receive a stricter judgment" (James 3:1). Help us all, Lord, to be open to all that You want to show us from Your word. Help me to root out of my heart any teachings that are not in accordance with the full counsel of Your word, and replace them with the actual truth, so that I can show those same amazing truths to others. Amen.

MARK 9:14-19

Read with me:

When they came to the disciples, they saw a large crowd around them and scribes disputing with them. When the whole crowd saw him, they were amazed and ran to greet him. He asked them, "What are you arguing with them about?"

Someone from the crowd answered him, "Teacher, I brought my son to you. He has a spirit that makes him unable to speak. Whenever it seizes him, it throws him down, and he foams at the mouth, grinds his teeth, and becomes rigid. I asked your disciples to drive it out, but they couldn't."

He replied to them, "You unbelieving generation, how long will I be with you? How long must I put up with you? Bring him to me."

Listen with me:

Jesus, Peter, James and John had just spent time in a heavenly scene, a genuine mountain-top experience. Now, as they came down from the Mount of Transfiguration, they were confronted with a scene, not just of earth, but with the demonic smell of sulfur all over it.

The first thing they noticed was the argument. On one side were Jesus' disciples; on the other were the scribes. And around them stood a crowd of onlookers, watching and listening. This was no polite theological discussion, but appeared to be a heated argument.

When the people in the crowd saw Jesus walking toward them, they instantly lost interest in the argument, and ran to Him. It was, after all, Him that they had come to see. The disciples came too, red in the face from the emotion of the argument.

Jesus had frequent disagreements with the Pharisees and teachers of the law, but on His side it never devolved into an argument. He simply stated where they were wrong, and told them what the truth was. But whatever the issue was that the disciples were "discussing" with these teachers of the law, the emotions surrounding them obviously went very deep on one side or the other to result in the scene Jesus had just witnessed. So He asked, *"What are you arguing with them about?"*

The answer came not from the disciples or the teachers of the law, but from the man at the center of the controversy: a father who had brought his demon-possessed son so that Jesus could heal him. The spirit that had control of the young man had made him completely unable to speak, and from time to time it sent him into convulsions. The disciples had tried to cast out the demon themselves, but had been completely ineffective. And their inability to cast out the demon, their lack of power, was what had started the argument. They were emotionally involved because their own reputations were at stake.

Jesus' outburst was directed at His disciples: *"You unbelieving generation, how long will I be with you? How long must I put up with you?"* After three years with Jesus, after watching Him work, after being empowered themselves to cast out demons, they were completely powerless in the face of this one challenge. As strong as this demon might be, as frightening as the convulsions that it caused were, the disciples, working in God's power, should have been able to cast it out easily. But they hadn't been able to. They had been totally defeated.

Jesus' frustration stemmed from his keen awareness that these were the men in whose hands He would be leaving the future progress of the kingdom of God in just a few short weeks. But instead of their faith and power growing stronger, here they were trying to defend their inability to cast out this demon.

Ultimately the demon was just a demon. The father had brought the young man to Jesus for release from bondage, and his faith would be rewarded. Jesus' simple statement, *"Bring him to me,"* marked the transition point of the whole event.

MARK 9

Father, I sometimes wonder if Jesus gets just as frustrated with us as He got that day with His disciples. We are, after all, the ones who are currently tasked with growing Your kingdom by making disciples of all nations, including those right in our own back yards. We are the ones tasked with allowing Your power to flow through us to heal the bodies and souls of men. And, sadly, we have not done a very good job. We have allowed ourselves to get distracted by our games, our shows, and our recreations, allowing the work of the kingdom to fall far down on our list of priorities, so that when we are called upon to respond to the deep needs around us, we are reduced to praying feeble prayers and hoping for the best. Lord, this is far from the vision that You paint for us in Your word - far from the promises of power that You have given us. And the fault lies in us, in our lack of focus, our lack of devotion, our lack of passion for Your kingdom, and the compromises we make that restrict Your power in our lives. Forgive me, Lord. Help me to recapture, or even to capture for the first time, a real passion for You, and for the kingdom work that You have called me to do in Your power. Amen.

WHEN WE LISTEN

MARK 9:20-24

Read with me:

So they brought the boy to him. When the spirit saw him, it immediately threw the boy into convulsions. He fell to the ground and rolled around, foaming at the mouth. "How long has this been happening to him?" Jesus asked his father.

"From childhood," he said. "And many times it has thrown him into fire or water to destroy him. But if you can do anything, have compassion on us and help us."

Jesus said to him, "'If you can'? Everything is possible for the one who believes."

Immediately the father of the boy cried out, "I do believe; help my unbelief."

Listen with me:

They didn't even get the boy to Jesus before the evil spirit took one look at Him, and threw the boy into a convulsion. He was rolling around on the ground, foaming at the mouth, and making a huge scene. The noise and the disturbing sights made the people who were nearby back away from the scene. It was an impressive display of power, dismaying to the disciples, who had been completely powerless to do anything to remove the demon.

Jesus questioned the father. This was not something that had just started happening; it had been a normal occurrence with this young man since he was a child. The doctors hadn't been able to do anything (it wasn't, after all, a physical ailment, but a demon that was causing the problem), and the father had eventually given up hope, figuring that sooner or later the demon would end up destroying the boy.

Then the man had heard about Jesus, and that He had been

able to cast demons out of people, freeing them body and soul. But when the man had gotten to where he had been directed, Jesus wasn't there. In hope he had approached the disciples with his sad tale, but the disciples ended up being as ineffective as the doctors had been. It was this additional frustration and disappointment that caused the father to blurt out his nearly hopeless plea: *"If you can do anything, have compassion on us and help us."*

Jesus' response sounds indignant, and has been widely misunderstood: *"'If you can'? Everything is possible for the one who believes."* This has been taught as pointing an accusing finger at the man, as if it was his lack of belief that had caused the failure of the disciples. But if there was any accusation at all, it was pointed directly at the disciples who had failed to dislodge the spirit. The man was not looking for a reason why the previous attempt had failed, but he was wondering out loud if Jesus was actually able to do anything to help. "If you can…"

Jesus' answer pointed out that of course He could. He Himself believed, and everything (and the Greek word here means EVERYTHING) is possible for the one who believes. Jesus had no doubt that would get in the way of His evicting this demon. There was no hesitancy, no needing to test how strongly the spirit was lodged in the young man. (Remember, Jesus had already cast out a whole legion of demons and sent them into a herd of pigs with a simple word. Mark 5:1-13) Since Jesus believed, getting rid of this demon was going to be no problem at all. It was the disciples lack of belief that had led to their failure.

The father's follow-up statement, ("I do believe; help me overcome my unbelief!") has led some to establish a doctrine that only those with adequate faith can receive healing. Of course, if someone doubts that God can heal them, or someone that they care about, they won't be able to pray effectively for that healing. But, in this instance, Jesus is not talking about the faith of the victims (after all, the boy, the actual victim here, was currently rolling around on the ground in the midst of a demonic convulsion, completely unable to exercise faith of any kind!). He's not talking about the faith of the family members (who weren't the ones who were going to have to cast out the demon). In this case, He was talking very specifically about the belief, the faith, of the one who was doing the casting out.

Matthew's version of this event includes a fuller response to the disciples' later question (*"Why couldn't we drive it out?"*) than Mark's does, and verifies this conclusion: *"Because of your little faith. For truly I tell you, if you have faith the size of a mustard seed, you will tell this mountain, 'Move from here to there' and it will move. Nothing will be impossible for you."* (Matthew 17:19-21) The disciples' faith was weak. They had doubted that they could remove the demon, so they ended up being powerless. Jesus had no doubt at all that He could cast out the demon, and so the demon would be gone. It was a foregone conclusion. EVERYTHING is possible for him who believes!

That is still the lesson for the disciples of today. God still calls us to action. And when we have full faith in God that He will help us and empower us to do whatever it is that He has called us to do, whether that is speaking a word of healing, casting out a demon, or sharing the gospel with someone who is lost in the darkness of sin, nothing will be impossible for us.

Pray with me:

Father, this father's prayer needs to be OUR prayer far too often: "I do believe; help my unbelief!" There are so many times when we know beyond a doubt that you want us to speak a word of healing, a word of encouragement, or a word of salvation to someone, but we let our doubts stop us cold. If we do manage to struggle on and do what you have prompted us to do, we do it haltingly, with great fear and trembling, and without the mountain-moving faith that our strong relationship with You should engender. And, all too often, we fall flat because we have so little faith. Help me to realize that everything really IS possible for me if I will only believe and have faith, not in my own ability or power, but in Your ability, Your power to accomplish through me whatever you have called me to do. Amen.

MARK 9:25-29

Read with me:

When Jesus saw that a crowd was quickly gathering, he rebuked the unclean spirit, saying to it, "You mute and deaf spirit, I command you: Come out of him and never enter him again!"

Then it came out, shrieking and throwing him into terrible convulsions. The boy became like a corpse, so that many said, "He's dead." But Jesus, taking him by the hand, raised him, and he stood up.

After he had gone into the house, his disciples asked him privately, "Why couldn't we drive it out?"

And he told them, "This kind can come out by nothing but prayer."

Listen with me:

Jesus noticed that a whole crowd of people were running toward where He was speaking to the father of the demon possessed boy, drawn by the noise and violent action of the young man's convulsions. The time for talking was over; the time for action had come.

Jesus' technique in dealing with demons was always simple and effective. In this case, all He had to do was speak a command (*"I command you: Come out of him and never enter him again."*), and the demon left with a shriek, and a final spasm. There was no wrestling with the demonic forces, no incantations, no ritual. Jesus didn't need any of that. The demon already knew that he was doomed as soon as He saw Jesus. He understood that he had no power over the Son of God. And the smoke screen that he tried to throw up by convulsing the young man didn't intimidate Jesus even the smallest bit. One command, and out.

Those who saw the young man lying motionless on the ground after the violent shriek and final convulsion, could be excused for believing that the final attack had left him dead. But Jesus knew better. It was only the violence of the actions immediately before the demon left that made the normal quiet seem like death; the normal shallow breathing of his exhaustion seemed like no breathing at all. But when Jesus pulled him to his feet, the young man stood strong before them in full health.

The disciples were silent as they went into the nearby house. Jesus had made this exorcism seem so simple, but they had been completely unable to pull it off. So they asked, "Why couldn't we drive it out?" After all, they had driven out many demons not long before, when Jesus had sent them out ahead of Him, two by two. What had gone wrong?

Jesus' answer in Mark's gospel is different than in Matthew's, but the two versions are complementary. Matthew (who was one of those who had tried to drive the demon out and failed) remembered most clearly the part of Jesus' answer in which He said, *"Because of your little faith. For truly I tell you, if you have faith the size of a mustard seed, you will tell this mountain, 'Move from here to there' and it will move. Nothing will be impossible for you.* (Matthew 17:20) Mark's version, remembered by Peter, who had been coming down from the Mount of Transfiguration with Jesus while the original failure was happening, is much shorter, and seems to go in an entirely different direction: *"This kind can come out by nothing but prayer."*

So how can it be that these two answers are complimentary? Prayer and faith go together hand-in-hand, each being indispensable to the other. Jesus' response that this kind of demon can only be cast out by prayer (especially when there is no record in any of the gospel versions of this event of Him praying as part of the exorcism), is really talking about what we would call today being "prayed up." The disciples had approached the exorcism by just doing what they had always done to cast out a demon, relying on their own power, their own skill, their own techniques. Jesus never did that. Instead, He was always "prayed up," always intimately connected to the Father, and always relied on God's direction and God's power, not mere human technique.

Faith is closely related to this. When a person spends consistent time in prayer, he or she is able to clearly hear God's voice guiding and directing them in every situation. Whether faced with a demon or an illness, or even a person who has died, a person who is consistently in prayer, and who has stayed "prayed up" throughout the day, can easily hear what God's plan is for the situation, and then act in faith to do what God has directed them to do.

Pray with me:

Father, it is so easy for us to let our focused prayer time with You get pushed to the side by our schedules, our agendas, our general busyness. But when we do that, we can so easily end up unable to hear You as You try to guide and direct us through the events of our day. Help me, Lord, to be more consistent, to spend regular time with You in prayer - quantity time, not just what passes for a small amount of quality time. Then, when you speak, when I hear, I can move forward in faith to move mountains. Amen.

WHEN WE LISTEN

MARK 9:30-32

Read with me:

Then they left that place and made their way through Galilee, but he did not want anyone to know it. For he was teaching his disciples and telling them, "The Son of Man is going to be betrayed into the hands of men. They will kill him, and after he is killed, he will rise three days later." But they did not understand this statement, and they were afraid to ask him.

Listen with me:

Even though Jesus clearly told His disciples (several times) exactly what was going to happen to Him just a short time in the future, they never got it - at least not until after the resurrection.

This problem in their ability to understand came from several sources:

• Even though they knew that the Pharisees, Sadducees, and scribes were out to get Jesus, they could not imagine how they could act against the rising positive public opinion that seemed to be continually growing around Him. He seemed unassailable.

• They couldn't imagine who would "betray" Jesus. The inner circle of twelve had been with Jesus for a couple of years, and all of them seemed deeply committed to Him.

• The idea of Jesus being killed ran completely against their expectations and their theology. They believed that Jesus was the Messiah beyond a shadow of a doubt. But to them, that meant that Jesus would soon take control of the government, and set up a whole new theocracy that would launch Israel to the top of the world scene, and that would

198

last forever. The death of the Messiah did not fit into any picture they had of this future.

- Even if they could have accepted the idea of Jesus' death, they could not understand the concept of Jesus rising from the dead on the third day. There had been resurrections in the deep recesses of biblical history, and Jesus himself had raised a few people from the dead. But if Jesus was dead, who would be there to raise Him up!?

Every time Jesus talked about these things, these same issues perplexed the disciples. They didn't understand them at all. They wondered if maybe it was another parable that they weren't quite getting. But He always seemed so earnest and so deadly serious when He talked about them, that they never dared to ask for an explanation.

After the resurrection, of course, it all became perfectly clear. This was no parable, but a clear foretelling of events exactly as they would happen. They also quickly realized that the problem was not with God's plan, but with their own misunderstandings of what the Scriptures really said. When Jesus opened their eyes and showed them what the prophets had actually written, it changed everything and helped them to see more clearly how every piece of the puzzle contributed to the finished picture of the Father's love and salvation for all mankind.

Pray with me:

Father, it is easy to shake our heads at the disciples, and maybe even sneer at them a bit. But we can easily fall into the same trap. We can allow the theology we have been taught to obscure the truths that are clearly and repeatedly expressed in Your word. We can end up skipping over passages of the Bible that we find disturbing or hard to understand, instead of asking and listening carefully until we get it. Help me, Lord, to rely on You and Your Spirit to guide me into all truth, even truths that will challenge me, and change what I believe. Amen.

WHEN WE LISTEN

MARK 9:33-37

Read with me:

They came to Capernaum. When he was in the house, he asked them, "What were you arguing about on the way?" But they were silent, because on the way they had been arguing with one another about who was the greatest. Sitting down, he called the Twelve and said to them, "If anyone wants to be first, he must be last and servant of all." He took a child, had him stand among them, and taking him in his arms, he said to them, "Whoever welcomes one little child such as this in my name welcomes me. And whoever welcomes me does not welcome me, but him who sent me."

Listen with me:

The disciples were ashamed to admit that they had been arguing about which of them was the greatest among Jesus' disciples. The twelve had good reason to think of themselves as more important than the many others who followed Jesus consistently (Acts 1:21-23), because Jesus had singled them out from the others, and had given them special authority, and had even called them His "apostles." Peter, James, and John had good reason to think that perhaps they were more important than the other nine apostles, because Jesus had called them apart for special duties on several occasions (Mark 5:37, 9:2), making them a kind of "inner circle."

The problem was not that they recognized that they had been called to follow Jesus, or even that they had been set apart for special things. The problem was that they still had their minds set on an earthly kingdom, not the kingdom of heaven. They were still looking forward to Jesus setting Himself up as an earthly king, and saw themselves as the natural choices for the top spots. They had completely missed the things that Jesus had been telling them were awaiting them in Jerusalem.

They were also missing the whole point of what Jesus had been doing and teaching. He had not come to be the king, to have others serve Him and meet His every need. He had lowered Himself to come as a servant, to serve others, and to meet their most profound needs.

Jesus' words sounded illogical to them: If you want to be first in the kingdom, you must make yourself last among men, instead of striving for the top spot. If you want to be the greatest, you must make yourself the servant of all instead of working your way up to a position in which you would be served. To strive to be number one in men's opinions made sense in a worldly kingdom. But Jesus always strove to be number one in God's opinion, and the only way to do that was to live a life of humble obedience, complete submission, and loving service to others.

Jesus then brought a little child into the middle of their group. Children have no power, and they have many needs. If you are trying to climb the so-called ladder of success, a child is of absolutely no help. They have no connections and can pull no strings to help us on our climb. For that reason, the needs of children are frequently overlooked by those who are striving to be the greatest in the system of this world.

But Jesus told the disciples that their greatness would be measured by God in a different way. Whoever welcomes a child (and, by extension, any person who has no connections that can help us, but who has great needs) in Jesus' name welcomes Jesus. And whoever welcomes Jesus in this way welcomes the Father who sent Him.

Jesus didn't come to remake the disciples into government officials. He came to remake them into His own image, representatives of God's kingdom, who, even though they have access to all the power of God, use that power not for themselves or their own benefit, but who use it to serve others, to bring healing and wholeness into the lives of others, and to bring light into their dark lives.

WHEN WE LISTEN

Pray with me:

Father, the lure of this world, of power and position, of gaining the honor and respect of others, can be very strong. Those things seem so much more desirable than to be a servant of others, one who puts all of our own ambitions aside to serve You by serving others. But the ways of this world, the climbing of the hierarchies of business or government, will never put us in a place of being able to bring genuine light and life into the lives of those around us as effectively as simply allowing ourselves to be molded into Your image; humbling ourselves like You, in order to serve others; giving ourselves, like You, to the Father's kingdom and to His agenda. Amen.

MARK 9:38-41

Read with me:

John said to him, "Teacher, we saw someone driving out demons in your name, and we tried to stop him because he wasn't following us."

"Don't stop him," said Jesus, "because there is no one who will perform a miracle in my name who can soon afterward speak evil of me. For whoever is not against us is for us. And whoever gives you a cup of water to drink in my name, because you belong to Christ — truly I tell you, he will never lose his reward."

Listen with me:

This is a continuation of the conversation that began when Jesus chided the disciples about arguing over who was the greatest. John now told Jesus that they had seen a man using His name to drive out a demon, and they had told him to stop doing it, since he was not one of the twelve to whom Jesus had given specific authority to do that.

They probably expected Jesus to commend them for not allowing outsiders to use His name against demons. But they got chastisement instead of commendation. Jesus' point was that if someone believed in Jesus strongly enough to use His name to cast out demons, that person would not be someone who would turn against Jesus. They truly believed in Him, and were most likely to continue in that belief, especially when His name was effective in casting out demons!

This scene is reminiscent of Numbers 11:26-29, when God put His Spirit on seventy of the elders of Israel so that they could share the load with Moses. Two of the men chosen to receive the Spirit, Eldad and Medad, would not come to the tent of meeting. But God poured His Spirit on them anyway, and they began to prophesy. Joshua, Moses' aide, heard about it and said, *"Moses, my lord, stop them!"* Since they seemed to be outside of the chosen group, Joshua believed that they shouldn't be allowed to be filled with God's Spirit, and definitely shouldn't be allowed to prophesy.

But Moses asked him, *"Are you jealous on my account? If only all the Lord's people were prophets and the Lord would place his Spirit on them!"* Moses understood that Spirit-filled believers would not rebel against God, or against His chosen leader - a situation not to be feared, but to be desired.

In a very short time, Jesus' disciples would see the tide of public opinion turn against Him, and a few short days after His triumphal entry into Jerusalem, they would see Him crucified, dead and buried. Then they would realize that their real enemies did not include those who had sincerely believed in Jesus and the power of His name.

Today there are many divisions in the body of Christ - different sects and denominations. And there is a strong tendency for each group to see each other as competitors, or even as adversaries; to struggle against each other, to compete with each other, and to try to tear each other down. But God's people need to realize that those others who believe in Jesus, who speak His name with reverence, and who trust in Him for salvation are not their enemies, but their coworkers.

There actually are strong enemies of Christianity out there, those who are intent on corrupting, or even destroying God's people. But often they can do their work freely, with little or no restraint, because God's people are busy attacking each other, or defending themselves from attacks by other Christians. We really need to take Jesus' words to heart: *"whoever is not against us is for us,"* and start to work together, to pray for each other that healing may take place, so that all of God's people may be one; so that those parts of the body of Christ that have wandered from the truth may be restored; and so that, together, all of God's people may accomplish the work that Jesus left for us to do.

MARK 9

Pray with me:

Father, this really is a problem that we, the Church, have had for a long time - competing against each other, speaking against each other, tearing down one another. This has prevented us from working together to bring the lost to You, and has greatly diminished our effectiveness. Instead of praying for the healing of those parts of Your body that have wandered from the path, we turn our backs on them, and Your body is diminished. Father, help us to become truly one as Your people. Help us to heal the divisions, and to pray for the restoration and healing of those groups that have gotten off track, so that we can be united, and so that we can have a powerful victory over our real enemy. Then we can see Your kingdom grow in our nation, and around the world. Amen.

MARK 9:42-48

Read with me:

"But whoever causes one of these little ones who believe in me to fall away—it would be better for him if a heavy millstone were hung around his neck and he were thrown into the sea.

> *"And if your hand causes you to fall away, cut it off. It is better for you to enter life maimed than to have two hands and go to hell, the unquenchable fire. And if your foot causes you to fall away, cut it off. It is better for you to enter life lame than to have two feet and be thrown into hell. And if your eye causes you to fall away, gouge it out. It is better for you to enter the kingdom of God with one eye than to have two eyes and be thrown into hell, where **their worm does not die, and the fire is not quenched.**" [Isaiah 66:24]*

Listen with me:

Look at how far Jesus went to try to communicate how bad sin is! If anyone leads a little one (not just a child, but any believer who is still learning the basics of the faith) into sin, it would be better for them to have a hundred pound weight tied around their neck and then be dropped into the deepest part of the ocean than to have to stand before God on the day of judgment with that kind of guilt on their soul. If your hand, or your foot, or even you eye causes you to sin, it would be better to cut it off or gouge it out than to end up suffering in hell for all eternity.

Of course Jesus understood very well that it is not a person's hand that causes them to take sinful action. It is not their feet that cause them to walk into sinful situations. It is not their eye that causes them to look against their will at sinful things. He knew and taught that sin originates in the heart of a person (Mark 7:14-23). But here He is pointing out, as clearly as human language can say it, that sin is such a drastic and heinous thing, and its consequences are so horrendous (condemnation at the judgment seat of God and eternal suffering in hell) that it must never be ignored, never be excused, and never be tolerated in our lives. Like cancer in a person's body, the presence of sin in our lives must be dealt with strongly and gotten rid of before it causes our death.

Since the real source of sin in our lives is our hearts (the spiritual dimension of our lives), the solution is a spiritual heart transplant - removing our heart of stone that has been warped and twisted by sin, and replacing it with a heart of flesh, soft and responsive to God's leading. Instead of responding to the urgings of our own spirit, we must receive God's Holy Spirit to guide and direct us into the right paths. (For promises concerning both of these, see Ezekiel 36:26-27.) We must allow our hearts and minds to be completely transformed through the renewal of the Holy Spirit (Romans 12:1-2). We must be made into a new creation in Christ (2 Corinthians 5:17).

All of these seem very radical to many people. It actually feels like a death to who we know ourselves to be. This kind of "replacing" and transformation feels as drastic as - well, as drastic as cutting off a hand or foot, or gouging out an eye! But, as two thousand years of Christian experience have proved, this kind of death to self, this kind of radical transformation, this complete excision of the true source of sin in our lives, is the ONLY effective method of making it possible for us, as God's people, to live genuinely holy lives.

Pray with me:

Father, You are absolutely right! We so want to live holy lives, and we try to do it in our own strength. But we ultimately discover that we just can't pull it off. The disease runs so much deeper than just our surface actions. But we shy away from the drastic surgery that is necessary to remove the true source of our sin. Instead, we try again; we develop rationalizations for our sinfulness; we even convince ourselves that it's not a big deal to You. But then Jesus' words come to us, and show us that sin is a VERY big deal - something that must be dealt with drastically, or it will have drastic consequences. Thank You for not only showing me how serious this situation is, but for also providing all that is necessary for me to receive a completely new heart, for me to be completely transformed into a new creation, for me to be able to live a life completely pleasing to You, in YOUR strength, and by YOUR grace. Amen.

MARK 9:49-50

Read with me:

For everyone will be salted with fire. Salt is good, but if the salt should lose its flavor, how can you season it? Have salt among yourselves, and be at peace with one another."

Listen with me:

Salt in Jesus' day was considered primarily a preservative. It was very valuable because it was the only means of preserving meat. Without salt, meat would be completely inedible in just a day or two.

This saying of Jesus is a cousin to that in the Sermon on the Mount: *"You are the salt of the earth. But if the salt should lose its taste, how can it be made salty? It's no longer good for anything but to be thrown out and trampled under people's feet."* (Matthew 5:13)

When Jesus talked about the disciples having salt in themselves, He was pointing to the truth that Jesus' followers, because of the Holy Spirit's presence in their lives, have the ability to act as a preservative in society, to keep it from rotting and going bad. But if salt loses its saltiness, if it no longer keeps the decay from taking place, it is worthless. Likewise, if Jesus' disciples stop acting as a preservative in their society, they become worthless as well, good for nothing but to be thrown into the street and trampled on by men.

Jesus' urging to the disciples to have salt in themselves, and to be at peace with each other, is an urging for them to keep their focus on the main thing: being a preservative force, keeping society from decaying and rotting by consciously working to expanding the kingdom of God. If they will keep that goal clearly in view, it will prevent them from focusing on worthless things, like who is the greatest one of Jesus' disciples, and who will get the top spots in His administration, and it will unify them instead of dividing them.

Pray with me:

Father, I wonder how many of Your people really understand the power that Your Holy Spirit brings into our lives - the power to be a preservative, to keep our society from sliding into decay. I'm afraid most of us see the decay that seems to be engulfing us these days, and we allow ourselves to fall into a state of despair, pleading with You to do something about it. But we fail to realize that You already have done something about it: You have put us here to act as a preservative, to push the doors of Your kingdom wide open, and urge everyone in, so that our whole society can be changed one life at a time, and preserved from decay. Help us to never lose our saltiness, but to be powerful and effective, working in Your name. Amen.

MARK 10:1-9

Read with me:

He set out from there and went to the region of Judea and across the Jordan. Then crowds converged on him again, and as was his custom he taught them again.

Some Pharisees came to test him, asking "Is it lawful for a man to divorce his wife?"

He replied to them, "What did Moses command you?"

They said, "Moses permitted us to write divorce papers and send her away."

But Jesus told them, "He wrote this command for you because of the hardness of your hearts. But from the beginning of creation God **made them male and female.** *[Genesis 1:27; 5:2]* **For this reason a man will leave his father and mother and the two will become one flesh.** *[Genesis 2:24] So they are no longer two, but one flesh. Therefore what God has joined together, let no one separate."*

Listen with me:

The Pharisees came to Jesus with a hot-button issue to "test Him;" to see where He landed on the theological spectrum. Was he on the side of the more liberal interpreters of the law, who declared on the basis of Deuteronomy 24:1 that if a man finds ANYTHING displeasing in his wife (for example, if she burns his food, or if she is not as attractive as she once was), then he is permitted to divorce her? Or was He on the side of the more conservative interpreters who (on the basis of the same Scripture) declared that only adultery was adequate grounds for divorce?

Like any good theology teacher, Jesus turned their attention to the Scriptures: *"What did Moses command you?"* Theology is

211

much too important, with consequences that are far too significant, to be left to opinion. And these Pharisees, who knew the Scriptures forward and back, were ready with their answer: *"Moses permitted us to write divorce papers and send her away."* (Deuteronomy 24:1 again.)

The problem was, they were looking at the wrong Scripture, because they were thinking about the wrong topic. They were researching for Scriptures on divorce. But Jesus wanted to help them to approach the issue from the other end: What did Moses say about the nature of marriage? Jesus acknowledged that Deuteronomy 24:1-4 talked about the rules for divorce, but divorce rules were put into place only because the hard hearts of the Israelites made adultery and divorce a possibility. It was a concession, not a command.

Jesus pointed clear back to the origin of marriage to give the true answer to the question. In the beginning, God created humanity male and female (Genesis 1:27), creating the woman from the bone and flesh of the man (Genesis 2:21-24). In marriage, the man and the woman become one flesh again. That is what marriage is all about: two people becoming one flesh for a lifetime. Divorce is then tearing this one-flesh creation in two, rather like tearing a person in half. It causes untold pain and damage to both halves. Therefore Jesus' answer to the question is based on the Scripture about marriage, not the Scripture that allowed divorce as a mere concession to those with hard hearts. Jesus' decision, which is ultimately God's decision, was *"Therefore what God has joined together, let no one separate."*

Pray with me:

Father, this is not a very popular viewpoint these days - neither part of it, in fact. The idea that marriage is something that You designed in the beginning, and the fact that Jesus had anything at all to say about the nature of marriage, has come under heavy attack. And the further idea that divorce shouldn't be allowed any time people decide that they don't want to be married any more ("no fault" divorce) is also unpopular. But Your truth has never been subject to popular opinion or majority vote. When we are looking for how You want us to live our lives, man's opinions are of no value at all. Only Your word gives us the truth, and the true values to live by. Help me, Lord, to continue to search Your word, not just for my "theology," but for direction and truth in every area of my life. Amen.

MARK 10:10-12

Read with me:

When they were in the house again, the disciples questioned him about this matter. He said to them, "Whoever divorces his wife and marries another commits adultery against her. Also, if she divorces her husband and marries another, she commits adultery."

Listen with me:

Jesus' words sound harsh to the ears of 21st century Americans - hopelessly out of touch with the times. But again, Jesus' context is not really the topic of divorce, but the topic of marriage.

The people of Jesus' day, much like the people of today, had developed a very cavalier attitude toward marriage. They had devolved to the point where they believed marriage to be a social contract, entered into by two consenting adults (and/or their families), ratified by a ceremony, and celebrated with a party. Therefore, they believed that the contract could be nullified at the consent of either of the two parties, and a new contract entered into.

But Jesus' frame of reference (which is also God's frame of reference), is that marriage is not a contract, but a covenant. It is not something that originated in the mind of man, but is a key part of God's original design for people. It is one more thing that separates man, created in God's image and likeness, from the animals - the ability to enter willingly into a covenant with God.

Even many of those who do believe in marriage as a covenant see it as being a three-way arrangement: a covenant primarily between the man and the woman, with God overseeing it - kind of like a triangle with God at the top. But in reality, marriage is a two-sided covenant. On one side is God, the author and guarantor of the covenant. On the other side is the one-flesh entity of husband

and wife. That is the source of Jesus' saying, *"What God has joined together, let no one separate."* (Mark 10:9) God is the one who ratifies the covenant because, even though many promises are made by the husband and wife to each other, the covenant between the husband-wife entity is made with Him.

Therefore, marriage must be entered into with great seriousness. A man or woman who divorces to marry another, as the people of Jesus' day were prone to do if they found someone more to their liking, did not avoid adultery by merely breaking the previous covenant through divorce. As long as God remains true to His covenant promises (and He always does), divorce does not nullify the covenant. Only adultery by one of the parties nullifies it, breaking the covenant from the human side (Matthew 19:9).

Again, this language sounds harsh and unreasonable to the ears of the people of today, just as it did to the ears of the disciples. (*"If the relationship of a man with his wife is like this, it's better not to marry."* Matthew 19:10) But this viewpoint is not based on narrow-mindedness, lack of compassion, or staunch traditionalism. It is based on a true understanding of what marriage actually is, and the clear, straightforward, non-nuanced command of the One who created marriage in the first place.

It is also vital to understand that divorce, even divorce and remarriage, is not an unforgiveable sin. As in every other case of disobedience, God can provide forgiveness, restoration, and a fresh start to anyone who sincerely turns away from their sinful actions and attitudes (repentance), and turns back to Him for forgiveness.

Pray with me:

Father, it is easy to see that the reason that this view of divorce sounds so "antiquated" and even harsh to many today is that we hold a different view of the nature of marriage than You do. Of course, because You are the one who designed marriage in the first place, Your view of what it is and how it is to be conducted is always the correct one, no matter how "progressive" or "enlightened" we think our viewpoint is. Forgive us, Lord, for treating something as holy as marriage with such disregard. Forgive us for taking a covenant relationship that You created, and recasting it in our own image, doing untold damage to it in the process. Help us, at least Your people, those called by Your name, to recapture Your design for marriage, and to live it out in our own lives. Amen.

MARK 10:13-16

Read with me:

People were bringing little children to him in order that he might touch them, but the disciples rebuked them. When Jesus saw it, he was indignant and said to them, "Let the little children come to me. Don't stop them, because the kingdom of God belongs to such as these. Truly I tell you, whoever does not receive the kingdom of God like a little child will never enter it." After taking them in his arms, he laid his hands on them and blessed them.

Listen with me:

It was understandable that the disciples wanted to be protective of Jesus. He was almost continually surrounded by people wanting something from Him, continually beset by those who had important things to talk to Him about. These were just parents wanting Jesus to touch and bless their children. Surely Jesus had better things to do than to deal with a bunch of kids! So they blocked the way and wouldn't let the parents bring the children to Jesus.

As soon as Jesus realized what was going on, He was indignant. What did they think they were doing!? He told the disciples, "Don't stop the children; let them come to me. Let the parents bring them over here." Jesus wasn't put off at all by these parents or by their children. He wasn't too busy for them at all. "The kingdom of God belongs to such as these."

No one was sure whether Jesus meant the children or the parents by this statement. Actually, it is true for both. The parents demonstrated a couple of key characteristics of people who live in the kingdom of God:

- Faith: They brought their children to Jesus for a touch because they had faith that the touch would have an overwhelmingly positive effect on their lives.

- Evangelistic Impulse: They believed in Jesus (or else they would not have brought their children to be blessed by Him), and they wanted to bring their children into contact with Him, even at an early age.

The children also demonstrated characteristics of the people of God's kingdom:

- Trust: The children came to Jesus and let Him bless them. They were innocent enough to not worry that He would hurt them.

- Poverty: The children would never try to earn or pay for the blessing that Jesus gave them. They had nothing that would even come close to paying back even a small portion of His blessing. So they simply received what Jesus had for them, with no thought of whether or not they deserved it.

- A teachable spirit: Children are like sponges, readily learning everything that anyone is willing to teach them.

It was these last three characteristics that Jesus had in mind when He said, *"Whoever does not receive the kingdom of God like a little child will never enter it."*

- We must trust, believing that when Jesus opens the door to the kingdom for us, that everything He is offering us is for our good, never for our harm. We must also trust that anything He requires us to leave at the door must be left behind for our good.

- We must come in poverty, realizing that there is nothing that we could ever do that would make us good enough for salvation, or that can pay Jesus back for His sacrifice. "Nothing in my hand I bring, simply to the cross I cling." (From *Rock of Ages*)

• We must come with a teachable spirit, willing to lay down all we think we know of God, of His kingdom, and even of how to live our lives. We must be completely open to learning about God and about His ways directly from the Holy Spirit.

Pray with me:

Father, I thank You that You didn't make Your blessings available only to the scholars and theologians. You made it available to the little children, all of us who love You for Yourself, who trust You for all that You promise, and who, out of our own poverty, come to You to receive the blessings of Your kingdom, so that we can learn from You. Amen.

MARK 10:17-18

Read with me:

As he was setting out on a journey, a man ran up, knelt down before him, and asked him, "Good teacher, what must I do to inherit eternal life?"

"Why do you call Me good?" Jesus asked him. "No one is good except God alone."

Listen with me:

This rich young man had achieved much in his short life. He could have just taken it easy and lived on his wealth. But he had a spiritual hunger in his life, an emptiness in the core of who he was, that took the joy out of all of the material riches that he had amassed.

This man had heard about Jesus, the miracle worker and great teacher, who many believed knew the way to eternal life. So when he heard that Jesus was in the area, he rushed off to talk to Him. When he saw Jesus and His followers starting down the road, he threw himself on the ground at Jesus' feet and panted, *"Good teacher, what must I do to inherit eternal life?"* No introduction, no small talk, just blurting out the question before Jesus had a chance to move on.

Jesus' first response has puzzled many over the ages: *"Why do you call me good? No one is good except God alone."* Some take this to mean that Jesus was denying that He was God, and that He was denying that He was good, thus undermining both the doctrine of the Trinity, and the doctrine of Jesus' sinlessness. But this is not what He was doing at all.

This young man did not come to Jesus to acknowledge that He was God. He knew nothing about Jesus or His life other than what he had heard. He came to Jesus purely as a "good" man, and a great teacher of spiritual things. His hope was that this teacher would help him to find the way to a relationship with the true God, without ever realizing that this man Himself WAS the way.

Jesus' response was actually ironic - even a little tongue in cheek. The young man had called Him "good," but no mere human being could rightfully claim that adjective for himself. And any that readily did should probably be eyed with suspicion. Only God is truly good. Any goodness that people may have shrinks to nothingness when compared to the true goodness of God. So was this young man just trying to butter Jesus up? Or was He ready to acknowledge that Jesus was in fact God in the flesh?

Jesus knew that the young man was merely using the polite formula of the day. He did not come to Jesus because he realized who He was. He had come to a teacher, a guru, someone who could help him to find the real relationship with God that he desired. Jesus would tell him all that he wanted to know. But the man's spiritual eyes were so misfocused that, in the process, he would miss the God whom he was seeking standing right in front of him!

Pray with me:

Father, how treacherous it can be to take our own spiritual perceptions as ultimate truth. How treacherous it can be to go to fallible human beings for spiritual direction, believing them to be "good" and able to lead us to you, instead of just coming straight to You. The reality is that You are as accessible to us today as Jesus was to that rich young man. But all too often people still come to Jesus so that He can show them the way, instead of coming to Jesus because he IS the way. They come to Jesus, the "good teacher," to learn about God, instead of coming to Jesus because He IS God. Help us all, Lord, to see clearly. And, in seeing clearly, help us to lead others directly to You. Amen.

MARK 10:19-22

Read with me:

*"You know the commandments: **Do not murder; do not commit adultery; do not steal; do not bear false witness; do not defraud; honor your father and mother.**" [Exodus 20:12-16; Deuteronomy 5:16-20]*
He said to him, "Teacher, I have kept all these from my youth."
Looking at him, Jesus loved him and said to him, "You lack one thing: Go, sell all you have and give to the poor, and you will have treasure in heaven. Then come, follow me." But he was dismayed by this demand, and he went away grieving, because he had many possessions.

Listen with me:

The rich young man's question was, *"What must I do to inherit eternal life?"* (Mark 10:17b) Jesus naturally pointed him to the law. A person who lives a life contrary to God's requirements can never inherit eternal life. As Paul wrote, *Don't you know that the unrighteous will not inherit God's kingdom? Do not be deceived: No sexually immoral people, idolaters, adulterers or males who have sex with males, no thieves, greedy people, drunkards, verbally abusive people, or swindlers will inherit God's kingdom.* (1 Corinthians 6:9-10) It is only when we repent, turn away from those things contrary to God's will, and receive forgiveness and cleansing that we can inherit God's kingdom and, along with it, eternal life.

Jesus began with the things that most people would quickly identify as sin, the second part of the Ten Commandments, knowing that this man, like most "good people" of His day (and ours), would have been scrupulous about obeying. And, as expected, this man verified that he had kept all of those commandments since his youth.

Jesus' heart was filled with love for this young man. Here was a person who really was seeking God's kingdom, who was trying to avoid sin, who was trying to do the right things. But there was one part of this man's life that was misaligned, and was standing in the way of his coming into God's kingdom to experience eternal life: the orientation of his priorities, the core of his heart. He was missing the mark on the first two commandments, the ones that specifically address a person's relationship with God.

- *Do not have other gods besides me.*

- *Do not make an idol for yourself, whether in the shape of anything in the heavens above or on the earth below or in the waters under the earth. Do not bow in worship to them, and do not serve them* (Exodus 20:3-4a)

Even though this young man would never have considered making or buying an actual idol to worship, his possessions had become just that. They had become his god. They had become the thing that took up his time and attention; the thing that all of the best of his time and energies were devoted to. So Jesus pointed his finger right at this key area of his life. *"Go, sell all you have and give to the poor, and you will have treasure in heaven. Then come, follow me."*

This man could not follow Jesus yet, because his heart belonged to something else: his possessions. And no clearer indication of this is needed than the next two sentences: *But he was dismayed by this demand, and he went away grieving, because he had many possessions.* The price for eternal life, turning away from amassing wealth, was greater than he was willing to pay. *"No one can serve two masters, since either he will hate one and love the other, or he will be devoted to one and despise the other. You cannot serve both God and money."* (Matthew 6:24)

WHEN WE LISTEN

Pray with me:

Father, as always, Jesus put His finger right on the core issue. This man ultimately had to choose who and what he would serve; where his focus would be. And it is clear that we today must make the same choice. We have so many things to which we devote our time and energy: our cars, our houses, our television shows and computer games, our jobs, our relationships, our investments, our stuff. Any and all of these can grow to the point where they begin to take first place in our lives and hearts, so that we don't have time to pray adequately, or worship, or read our Bibles. Many times they take resources that rightfully belong to You, so that we cannot tithe or give as you direct us to. At that point they have become our god, that which we love most, focus on the most, and give the best of our time and energy to. At that point they will stand between us and inheriting eternal life. At that point, we must make a choice. Help me to keep my priorities exactly in line with Your word, and to choose correctly. Amen.

MARK 10:23-27

Read with me:

Jesus looked around and said to his disciples, "How hard it is for those who have wealth to enter the kingdom of God!"

The disciples were astonished at his words. Again Jesus said to them, "Children, how hard it is to enter the kingdom of God! It is easier for a camel to go through the eye of a needle than for a rich person to enter the kingdom of God."

They were even more astonished, saying to one another, "Then who can be saved?"

Looking at them, Jesus said, "With man it is impossible, but not with God, because all things are possible with God."

Listen with me:

Jesus' words to His disciples cause as much consternation today as they did when He first spoke them. *"It is easier for a camel to go through the eye of a needle than for a rich person to enter the kingdom of God."* Obviously, to fit a camel through a needle's eye (the word for needle in Matthew and Mark is a regular sewing needle, while that in Luke is a suturing needle, entirely appropriate for a physician) is a physical impossibility.

The concept of it being impossible for a rich person to get into heaven is so distasteful to people that some have tried to explain Jesus' words away. For a while it has been taught that there was a small "after hours" gate next to the main gate in Jerusalem called "the eye of the needle." It was so small that a camel could get through it only after having all of its burdens removed, and only if it crawled in on its knees. It's an interesting picture with some good imagery. But that small gate never actually existed. Others have tried to change the camel into a rope by changing a letter in the text. (Not that getting a thick rope through the eye of a needle is any easier than getting a camel through it!)

But no hedging or "re-imaging" is necessary. Jesus was using hyperbole, as He frequently did to make His point. (For example, the beam of wood sticking out of the judgmental person's eye in Matthew 7:3-5.) The context for His remark is the fact that the rich young man had just opted out of the kingdom of God, deciding that the cost (selling all that he had, giving it to the poor, and then following Jesus) was too high a price to pay. Jesus was simply pointing out that this is the way it is with many (most?) people whose focus has been on amassing worldly riches. Those riches become an idol for them, gaining such a stronghold in that person's heart that they are usually unwilling to give it all up for the much simpler life that is focused on Jesus.

The disciples' disbelief came from two sources. First, it was common theology that rich people were rich because they had been specially blessed by God. The idea that such people were not already in God's kingdom was a shocking thought. Second, the disciples were still looking forward to serving as top members of Jesus' cabinet when He took over as king in Jerusalem. And, yes, that included gaining LOTS of worldly riches, too. This whole statement by Jesus, that riches could be a block to entering the kingdom, and not a sign that one was already in it, tapped their kaleidoscopes sharply, changing their whole view of how worldly riches fit into the picture of God's kingdom.

But Jesus' answer to the disciples' amazed question, *"Then who can be saved?"* showed a small ribbon of light around the seemingly closed door: *"With man it is impossible, but not with God, because all things are possible with God."* The claws of worldly wealth sink deep into the hearts of those who are focused on it. But God can break those claws loose. The lure of riches can blind the eyes of those focused on them to the point where they can see nothing else clearly. God can open those eyes to the glory of His kingdom. But He will do that only if the person wants to live in His kingdom enough to be willing to be set free.

MARK 10

Pray with me:

Father, I agree that the quest for riches can easily ensnare our hearts, and move us further from You and Your kingdom. Help me, Lord, to always put the interests of You and Your kingdom first on my list of priorities. And help me, when You do bless me with material wealth, to think first of how to use if for the good and the growth of Your kingdom. Amen.

WHEN WE LISTEN

MARK 10:28-31

Read with me:

Peter began to tell Him, "Look, we have left everything and followed you."
"Truly I tell you," Jesus said, "there is no one who has left house
or brothers or sisters or mother or father or children or fields for my sake
and for the sake of the gospel, who will not receive a hundred times more,
now at this time—houses, brothers and sisters, mothers and children, and
fields, with persecutions—and eternal life in the age to come. But many
who are first will be last, and the last first."

Listen with me:

It is safe to say that, even though both the disciples and Jesus were talking about the same subject, the disciples were hearing Jesus say something different than what He was actually saying. That frequently happened during the run-up to Jerusalem, because the disciples' worldview had them firmly focused on the things of this world, not on the kingdom of heaven.

Peter had just heard Jesus tell the rich young man that the one thing he lacked to gain eternal life was a wholehearted devotion to God. His heart was torn because of the hold his wealth had on him. In order to break that hold, he needed to sell all that he had, give all of the proceeds to the poor, and THEN he could follow Jesus with singleness of heart. But, of course, his wealth meant too much to him, so he went sadly away. This provided the opportunity for Jesus to point out that it was impossible, without God's help, for the rich to get into God's kingdom, because worldly wealth can so quickly and effectively pull a person's heart away from God and His priorities.

That's when Peter wanted to know where he (and the rest of the disciples) stood. They had given up a lot to follow Jesus - their jobs, their families, their old way of life. So what about them?

Jesus' answer has been embraced by those who preach a prosperity gospel, and explained away by those who don't seem to have received all that it promises. But the principle in this one sentence is true, and the disciples did experience this dynamic working in their own lives.

Jesus promised that those who left all behind to follow Him - home, family, and possessions, such as fields - would receive a hundred times as much in this world. Jesus' disciples never became rich in worldly possessions, but they did get to experience all of this huge blessing.

They had all left their homes for Jesus, but, as each traveled through the world sharing the gospel, each found homes with those who were living in or interested in the kingdom. (For example, Peter's sojourn with Simon the Tanner in Acts 9-10, and Paul, who stayed with people who feared the Lord in every town that he visited.)

The disciples had left family (and some, no doubt, had family leave them because they were not willing to follow Jesus themselves), but in exchange, they found brothers, sisters, mothers, and fathers in abundance among those in God's kingdom; people who grew to be even closer than flesh-and-blood family.

And the disciples had left worldly wealth behind, but in a short time they found people bringing their wealth and money and laying it at the disciples' feet (Acts 5:34-35). The difference was that the disciples realized that none of this property or money belonged to them, but to the kingdom. So they distributed it to all of those in need. John Wesley was much the same. In his later years, great wealth passed through his hands. But he only took a meager salary, eating very plain food, and wearing plain and durable clothing, and passed the rest on to those in need.

Jesus noted also that even through those blessings would come with persecutions and trials, and that the disciples would be counted as the bottom of the barrel, that they would also end in eternal life, where those who claim nothing of their own will receive a kingdom from God's own hand (Matthew 5:3, 10).

WHEN WE LISTEN

Pray with me:

Father, some might feel cheated or short-changed by seeing things in this way, but that is only because our eyes are too much focused on the things of this world, including worldly wealth. Help me to see clearly, Lord, that even if I was to gain multiplied millions of dollars in this world, that this world and all that it contains is passing quickly away, and that only that which I give away, that which passes through my hands in the name of Jesus to those in need, goes with me into the next world. Help me to turn away from pursuing the things of this world, and instead to first seek Your kingdom, and Your righteousness. Then all that I truly need will be given to me. (Matthew 5:33) That is great riches indeed!

MARK 10:32-34

Read with me:

They were on the road, going up to Jerusalem, and Jesus was walking ahead of them. The disciples were astonished, but those who followed him were afraid. Taking the Twelve aside again, he began to tell them the things that would happen to him. "See, we are going up to Jerusalem. The Son of Man will be handed over to the chief priests and the scribes, and they will condemn him to death. Then they will hand him over to the Gentiles, and they will mock him, spit on him, flog him, and kill him, and he will rise after three days."

Listen with me:

As the group headed to Jerusalem, Jesus led the way, and was intent on getting there. This confused and worried the disciples. Jesus had already told them a couple of times that terrible things were waiting for Him there. If that was all true, wouldn't it make way more sense to stay away from Jerusalem instead of marching boldly right into the lion's mouth?

But Jesus had come to the world for precisely this time. All else that had gone on had been waiting and laying the groundwork for the coming of God's kingdom which His suffering, death, and resurrection would make a reality. He had told His followers, *"I have a baptism to undergo, and how it consumes me until it is finished!"* (Luke 12:50) And so He was anxious to go, anxious to get to Jerusalem to play out the last act of His ministry, and anxious to get to the other side of the suffering that was waiting for Him.

Jesus saw with absolute clarity all that He would have to go through. First, He would be betrayed to the religious leaders by one of His closest disciples. They would try Him and condemn Him to death. Then, because the Jews were not allowed to execute anyone

(John 18:31b-32), they would hand Him over to the Gentiles, the Romans, to have Him crucified. Both the religious leaders and the guards would mistreat Jesus, mocking Him, spitting on Him, and flogging Him. Finally they would nail Him to the cross and kill Him.

All of that was terrifying to the disciples, and they couldn't see any possible hope beyond it. Even when Jesus proclaimed the coming victory that would make it all worthwhile, *"And he will rise after three days,"* they couldn't hear Him; their ears were so full of the coming terror, that there was no room to hear of victory on the other side. So Jesus pressed on toward the victory, while all the disciples could see was that they could very well be walking into a great tragedy.

Pray with me:

Father, it is easy for us, who already have the testimony of these witnesses, to sneer at their fear, and to wonder at their deafness. But if we had been them, I don't think we would have been any different at all. Even today, we let fear of trouble, fear of persecution, fear of tragedy stop us cold in our tracks. We, like them, cannot see the victory that lies on the other side of these earthly trials if we will only be steadfast and obedient. We fail to believe Your promise to be with us always, to the very end of the age (Matthew 18:20b) when we find ourselves facing trouble or tragedy. Father, help me to be more steadfast where my own rubber meets the road, so that I can do Your work powerfully and bring glory to Your name. Amen.

MARK 10:35-37

Read with me:

James and John, the sons of Zebedee, approached him and said, "Teacher, we want you to do whatever we ask you."

"What do you want me to do for you?" he asked them.

They answered him, "Allow us to sit at your right and at your left in your glory."

Listen with me:

There could be no more "tone deaf" request than this one. Jesus no sooner tells His followers about His impending betrayal, suffering, and death (with a resurrection soon after), than James and John, two of His inner circle, start jockeying for position in His administration.

James and John had no clue what *"in your glory"* really meant. Their eyes were still on an earthly kingdom. So to them, Jesus' coming glory would be like the glory of Solomon when he had been the king of all Israel a thousand years before. Even though they had just recently seen Jesus' heavenly glory for a few minutes on the Mount of Transfiguration (Mark 9:2-3), they had no idea of what Jesus would have to go through before He actually received the kingdom; before He came out the other side, victorious over death.

James and John were emboldened to make this request because they formed 2/3 of Jesus' inner circle, along with Peter. They believed that there were only two top spots in the kingdom, one at Jesus' right hand, and one at His left, and they wanted to get their bid in before Peter, who was also obviously in line for a high position. This showed clearly that they did not yet have hearts that were set on the priorities of the kingdom of God. They had not yet assimilated Jesus' earlier words: *"If anyone wants to be first, he must be last and servant of all."* (Mark 9:35) They were probably willing to serve others, as long as they could do it from a high position. They may even have been willing to magnanimously make themselves last, as long as they could do it from the top spot.

James and John would eventually understand. But at this juncture, their request merely showed how far even these closest disciples still were from the heart and mind of the kingdom.

Pray with me:

Father, we can look at those two disciples and shake our heads and click our tongues at them. But are we really any better? We are still fond of positions and titles, and of having our accomplishments recognized. We still feel much more able to serve others if we can do it from a position above them; to humbly make ourselves the last when we know in our hearts that we are really among the first. Father, help me to be willing to not just play the role of the servant of all, but to really BE the servant of all. Help me to not act like the very last, but to allow myself to actually be made the very last. Amen.

MARK 10:38-40

Read with me:

Jesus said to them, "You don't know what you're asking. Are you able to drink the cup I drink or to be baptized with the baptism I am baptized with?"

"We are able," they told him.

Jesus said to them, "You will drink the cup I drink, and you will be baptized with the baptism I am baptized with. But to sit at my right or left is not mine to give; instead, it is for those for whom it has been prepared."

Listen with me:

James and John were incredibly naïve at this point. They wanted the top two spots in Jesus' administration, believing that they knew what those top spots were, and believing that they knew what Jesus' administration was all about. They were dead wrong on both counts.

Jesus asked them clearly if they could drink the cup that He would drink, or be baptized with the baptism that He was baptized with. Jesus' implied answer was "absolutely not." But they both gave a hearty, "We can!" They had no idea that the cup Jesus was preparing to drink was a cup full of such agony, such physical suffering and torment of soul, that Jesus Himself asked to be spared from it if there was any other way (Mark 14:35-36). If they had any idea what this cup really was, they would not have been so quick to believe that they were up to it.

They had no idea that the baptism Jesus referred to was not a single event, a ceremony or ritual. He was referring to being completely inundated by the Holy Spirit at all times, to the point that His life was not His own. He was possessed by God the Father, completely submissive to His will, to the point that He no longer had any plans, hopes or dreams apart from God's plans, hopes, and dreams. His baptism meant that he had completely committed Himself to God in a way that these two disciples could not begin to fathom.

Jesus knew that the mere earthiness of these disciples, their cocksureness that they could, in their own strength, do whatever was required of them, was a clear indicator that they were nowhere close to being ready to do that. But He also knew what lay in the not too distant future for both of them. He knew that they would be filled with the Holy Spirit, and at that moment, they would throw their lives completely at the feet of God - they would be totally committed to all that He would call them to be and to do. He knew that they would indeed drink from His cup of suffering for the kingdom, although not to the same measure as Jesus Himself would. They would go through great physical suffering and loss for the sake of the gospel, and would not turn back because of it.

But neither of them were ready to hear all of this yet. That understanding would have to wait until the far side of the cross; until the day of Pentecost, when the Holy Spirit would burn the dross of the world from their hearts, and give them incredible power to be a witness to Jesus' life and ministry, to His death and resurrection, and to the grace and love of God.

Pray with me:

Father, it is easy for us to get cocky, to think that we are strong enough, or smart enough, or even committed enough in our own strength to serve You and your kingdom effectively. But, like James and John, all of our confidence turns to mush when the going gets tough; when things turn powerfully against us. Lord, I need the powerful baptism of Your Holy Spirit if I am going to be effective for You. I need all of the earthy parts of me consumed in Your fire, so that I come forth pure of heart, clear of mind, focused completely on Your agenda, and empowered to be and to do all that You are calling me to. Help me, Lord, to surrender myself to Your hand, to Your Spirit. Melt me, mold me, shape me, fill me, so that I can be all that You need me to be. Amen.

MARK 10:41-45

Read with me:

When the ten disciples heard this, they began to be indignant with James and John. Jesus called them over and said to them, "You know that those who are regarded as rulers of the Gentiles lord it over them, and those in high positions act as tyrants over them. But it is not so among you. On the contrary, whoever wants to become great among you will be your servant, and whoever wants to be first among you will be a slave to all. For even the Son of Man did not come to be served, but to serve, and to give his life as a ransom for many."

Listen with me:

The concept of "downward mobility" that Jesus taught and lived out is very difficult for the people of the world to grasp, let alone implement in their lives. That's because it militates so strongly against everything that the world system tells us about how to be successful.

According to the ways of the world, the race goes to the swift and clever, and the victory to the strong and smart. If you want to be successful, you have to ruthlessly seize every opportunity to get into the higher-up slots when they come into view. To be honest, the other ten disciples were indignant with James and John, not because those two had done something morally wrong, but because they had simply beaten them to the punch. James and John had seen an opening and had taken it while the other ten were still waiting for the perfect opportunity.

But Jesus needed to show them that the whole paradigm that they were thinking in was in complete contrast to the ways of the kingdom. Jesus' kingdom was not a kingdom of the world, to be run by the rules of the world. It was the kingdom of God, which operates on God's priorities and principles, and is based on His character.

WHEN WE LISTEN

Instead of the leaders of God's kingdom lording it over those beneath them in the hierarchy, they live to serve others and help build those others up. Instead of exercising authority over those below them, they intentionally lower themselves to the position of slave, serving the needs of those others. Instead of building a fortune and a comfortable lifestyle for themselves, and looking to make their own lot more pleasant and secure, the leaders in God's kingdom willingly lay down their lives for those beneath them.

The model for this new paradigm was and is Jesus Himself. Jesus never laid aside any earthly treasure for Himself, but relied on God the Father to provide what was needed each day. He did not try to build an empire that would give Him power and authority over others, but lived each day to exalt the name of God by showing forth His glory in His every thought, word, and deed. In fact, Jesus' focus was never for a moment on the things of this world and the things that people tend to rely on for security. His eyes were continually on eternity, and His every thought on how to draw as many people into that eternity as possible.

The reason that this paradigm shift was such a hard sell for His disciples was that they were still at this point creatures of the world. Their priorities, their worldview, and the way that they thought were all worldly, and kept them, at this stage of the game, from living out the ways of the kingdom. But Jesus patiently taught them, over and over again, realizing that in just a few weeks, on the day of Pentecost, the Holy Spirit would transform their minds and change their hearts, and then they would be able to start living out the ways of the kingdom in their lives.

Pray with me:

Father, it is still often difficult for us to think in the ways of the kingdom, to instinctively react in self-sacrificing kingdom ways. But every time we catch ourselves thinking like the world, or strategizing like the world, or jockeying for position like the world, we need to recognize that that is a symptom of a place in our heart that has not been fully transformed and recast into the image of Jesus.

Help me, Lord, to see myself clearly, to evaluate myself honestly, and any time I find a worldly place in my heart or mind, help me to bring that part of myself to You to be transformed and filled to overflowing with Your Spirit. Amen.

WHEN WE LISTEN

MARK 10:46-49

Read with me:

They came to Jericho. And as he was leaving Jericho with his disciples and a large crowd, Bartimaeus (the son of Timaeus), a blind beggar, was sitting by the road. When he heard that it was Jesus of Nazareth, he began to cry out, "Jesus, Son of David, have mercy on me!" Many warned him to keep quiet, but he was crying out all the more, "Have mercy on me, Son of David!"

Jesus stopped and said, "Call him."

So they called the blind man and said to him, "Have courage! Get up; He's calling for you."

Listen with me:

Even though Bartimaeus couldn't see, he could hear perfectly well and, as he sat begging by the road out of Jericho, he heard a large and noisy crowd approaching. When he asked someone what was happening, they told him that it was Jesus.

Bartimaeus had heard about Jesus, the miracles He had done, the demons He had cast out, and the thousands He had healed from every disease and disability. Jesus had healed blind people - even one who had been born blind (John 9)! Bartimaeus saw that this could be his chance, maybe his only chance, to see.

The crowd between Him and Jesus was large and moving along at a good pace. Even a seeing person would have a hard time getting to Jesus; what hope did a blind man have? But he had to get Jesus' attention. What could he do?

He did the most natural thing he could think of: he yelled. And not just a small, timid yell; he gave it all he had, and out came a scream that had the people around him holding their ears, and those far away turning to find the source of this desperate cry: *"Jesus, Son of David, have mercy on me!"*

This caused quite a stir among the people, especially when he used the term "Son of David," a popular term for the long-expected Messiah. Who did this shabby, blind fellow think he was - interrupting the teaching Jesus was doing as He walked along with the crowd; drawing attention to himself; and calling Jesus the Messiah to top it off! They tried to shut him up, to shut him down, but he wouldn't be silenced. This was his one chance, and he wasn't going to let it escape. Louder and louder he cried out, to make himself heard over the competing shouts: *"Have mercy on me, Son of David!"*

Jesus heard him and stopped. Why were people always trying to keep people away from Him? And, just as he had done when His disciples tried to stop parents from bringing their children to Him to be blessed (Mark 10:13-16), He put a stop to their interference, this time with two simple words: *"Call him."*

Pray with me:

Father, sometimes we get so caught up in our conversations with our Christian brothers and sisters, and with our theological discussions, that we walk unheeding right past the people all around us who have great needs, who want to know You, who are searching for You, if only someone would show them the way. Forgive me, Lord, for sometimes seeing the needy people around us as a problem, a nuisance, an interruption of my ministry, instead of seeing them as the very reason You came - to seek and to save what was lost (Luke 19:10). Amen.

MARK 10:49-52

Read with me:

Jesus stopped and said, "Call him."

So they called the blind man and said to him, "Have courage! Get up; he's calling for you." He threw off his coat, jumped up, and came to Jesus.

Then Jesus answered him, "What do you want me to do for you?"

"Rabboni," the blind man said to him, "I want to see!"

Jesus said to him. "Go, your faith has saved you." Immediately he could see and began to follow Jesus on the road.

Listen with me:

Baritmaeus' passionate cries had the desired effect. They stopped everything until he had a chance to bring his request before the Lord. Jesus had called him into His presence, and Bartimaeus threw off his cloak, and strode right up to Him, confident, because he had been invited.

Jesus' question was simple: *"What do you want me to do for you?"* There was no need to wonder about Bartimaeus' faith - he had demonstrated that abundantly by calling out, and by coming into Jesus' presence when invited. All that remained was for Bartimaeus to speak his request, and the miracle would follow.

There was no hemming and hawing. There was no long list of wants that Bartimaeus brought with him to Jesus. He didn't ask for money or resources. He didn't ask for good health or long life. He had only one shot with Jesus, and He had to make it count. So he brought only a single request, the very desire of his heart: "I want to see."

Jesus didn't touch him; He spoke no specific words of healing; there was no show of power, no lights flashing, no hairs being raised on the back of necks. He simply told Bartimaeus to go - that his faith had saved him. And immediately he could see! He could see everything! It was amazing! Wait until his family and friends found out!

He turned to thank Jesus, but saw that the whole crowd was moving on out of the city, and toward Jerusalem. Bartimaeus didn't even pause a moment to think about what to do. He knew what he HAD to do. He followed Jesus out of the city.

Pray with me:

Father, how often when I come to You do I come with a long list of requests? And not just my own, but numerous requests from others as well. How often do I rattle those requests off to You like reading a laundry list, bringing them before you with neither passion nor power? Lord, help me always to remember what a huge privilege it is to be invited into Your presence to bring my requests. What an amazing thing it is to hear You ask, "What do you want me to do for you?" Help me, Lord, at that moment, to focus all of my heart and mind on You, and to make that one request that is at the very center of my heart; the one request that will make all of the other things fall into place. I know that it will take me some time and some careful consideration to understand what that one thing is, but I believe with all my heart that it will be well worth it. Amen.

WHEN WE LISTEN

MARK 11:1-7

Read with me:

When they approached Jerusalem, at Bethphage and Bethany near the Mount of Olives, he sent two of his disciples and told them, "Go into the village ahead of you. As soon as you enter it, you will find a colt tied there, on which no one has ever sat. Untie it and bring it. If anyone says to you, 'Why are you doing this?' say, 'The Lord needs it and will send it back here right away.'"

So they went and found a colt outside in the street, tied by a door. They untied it, and some of those standing there said to them, "What are you doing, untying the colt?" They answered them just as Jesus had said; so they let them go.

They brought the donkey to Jesus and threw their clothes on it, and he sat on it.

Listen with me:

A seemingly meaningless event to Jesus' disciples, and to most of those standing by. Jesus had walked into Jerusalem many times before; why did He need to ride this time? And if He wanted to ride, why pick an unbroken colt instead of a mature donkey that had experience as a mount?

But for all of this, there was only one reason: Zechariah 9:9: *Rejoice greatly, Daughter Zion! Shout in triumph, Daughter Jerusalem! Look, your King is coming to you; he is righteous and victorious, humble and riding on a donkey, on a colt, the foal of a donkey.*

Up to this time, Jesus had been reluctant to identify Himself as the Messiah, because the term had accumulated a myriad of political overtones that only caused confusion about who He really was, and what He had come to do. But the time for all of that was now past. The Passover would be here in five days, and it was time for Jerusalem's true King to make His ultimate appearance, in complete fulfillment of the prophecy written about Him 450 years before.

Everything was ready. Jesus knew exactly where the donkey would be tied, and He knew the words needed to get those watching over the colt to release it into His care. The disciples experienced everything that Jesus said that they would, and it all worked perfectly. When they got the colt back to Jesus and spread their cloaks over it, Jesus got on and started over the hill to Jerusalem.

The disciples that went ahead of Him and those who followed behind had no idea what kind of reception they would get. They knew that a lot of very important people in Jerusalem would like nothing better than to see Jesus dead and buried. But Jesus knew exactly how the people would respond to Him, and went forward to greet the cheering crowds with His eyes wide open, knowing that in five short days, those cries of acclamation would be replaced by shouts calling for Him to be crucified.

Pray with me:

Father, in this episode we can see so clearly Jesus' complete trust in You. He knew by heart every prophecy that You had ever made about Him. One by one they had been fulfilled - some purposefully, by Him, but many that were beyond His physical control were orchestrated by You, so that everything would find its fulfillment in Him. That way there would be no doubt in anyone's mind, not in ours, and not even in the minds of those who were even then plotting His execution, Who He really was. Help me, Lord, to have that same trust in You, that same reliance, and that same willingness to march into whatever situation You lay out for me. Amen.

MARK 11:8-11

Read with me:

Many people spread their clothes on the road, and others spread leafy branches cut from the fields. Then those who went ahead and those who followed shouted:

> *Hosanna!*
> *Blessed is he who comes in the name of the Lord!*
> *Blessed is the coming kingdom of our father David!*
> *Hosanna in the highest heaven!*

He went into Jerusalem and into the temple. After looking around at everything, since it was already late, he went out to Bethany with the Twelve.

Listen with me:

As the crowd of disciples moved along with Jesus, those who went ahead of Him laid their cloaks on the road in front of His donkey, an ancient sign of commitment to a king (2 Kings 9:12-13). And they began singing songs that pointed to the coming kingdom that they all felt was right on the cusp:

- *Hosanna!* - This actually means "Save us!" and is a call of subjects for a king to intercede on their behalf.

- *Blessed is He who comes in the name of the Lord!* - This is from Psalm 118:26. The original context of this verse was doubtless in the minds of the disciples. It follows two pertinent sections of the Psalm, the first of which talks about entering the gate of the temple through which only the righteous may enter (verses 19-21); and the second of which talks about the rejected stone becoming the capstone (verses 22-23), a section which Jesus applied specifically to Himself shortly afterwards (Matthew 21:42). This verse also comes immediately before a section that talks about joining a festal procession with tree branches in hand, a procession that goes right up to the horns of the altar (verse 27) where the sacrifices are made. All of this context made this single verse more appropriate for the occasion than any of the disciples ever dreamed.

- *Blessed is the coming kingdom of our father David!* - This shows that the disciples still believed that Jesus was coming to fulfill the popular Messianic ideas of the time: to become the earthly king of Israel, to reestablish the Davidic dynasty, to remove the Roman overlords, and to restore the glory of Israel, making her once again a free and sovereign nation. This view had only one spiritual dimension to it - that all of this would demonstrate that God was once more looking with favor on His people.

All of these shouts, which grew and spread among the people all along the way into the city, were received by Jesus (Luke 19:38-40) even though they fell far short of the reality behind His triumphal entry. The people would soon understand what was really happening - but that would only be on the other side of the horrific and miraculous events that were fast approaching. Until then, this would have to do. This step had been accomplished. Not only had one more significant prophecy been fulfilled to the letter, but Jesus had put everyone on notice that He was making His move. The end game had begun. Tomorrow He would take another step.

Pray with me:

Father, it is clear that Jesus was so focused on His mission, the mission that You had sent Him to accomplish, that all of this adulation, all of this popular opinion didn't even turn His head. He had the power and, at least for the moment, the popular support to actually take over the throne if Israel right then. But He had already turned down an earthly kingship once (Matthew 4:8-10), because a worldly kingdom was not Your plan. He had come to establish YOUR kingdom on earth, not through honor and acclaim, but through His suffering, death, and resurrection. And He wasn't going to let anything sidetrack Him. Thank You, Lord! Amen.

MARK 11:12-14

Read with me:

The next day when they went out from Bethany, he was hungry. Seeing in the distance a fig tree with leaves, he went to find out if there was anything on it. When he came to it, he found nothing but leaves, for it was not the season for figs. He said to it, "May no one ever eat fruit from you again!" And his disciples heard it.

Listen with me:

Many point to this event as showing Jesus being peevish and even unreasonable. After all, it was too early in the year for figs, being the very end of March, or the very beginning of April. The leaves would be out on the fig trees, but no fruit yet. So why would Jesus curse a tree that was perfectly normal, just because He looked for fruit and was disappointed?

Jesus never did anything without a clear reason, and He was never peevish or unreasonable. Instead, He was painting a picture for His disciples, much like the prophets of old. (Ezekiel 12:1-14; Jeremiah 19:1-15) Jesus was hungry, just like the world was hungry for the truth of the Lord. Jesus went to a fig tree for food, just as the people of the world looked to the Jewish people to hear God's word. (After all, they claimed to be "God's chosen people," didn't they?)

But Jesus found only leaves - all show and no substance. And that is what the world found when they looked for God's truth among the leaders of the Jewish religion - all show and no substance. They did a lot of showy things, like making their sacrifices by the hundreds and thousands every day, and performing all of their rituals and celebrations. But when the people looked beneath the leaves, the "show," they found no real fruit; no people with a powerful relationship with God Almighty.

In cursing the fig tree for its fruitlessness, Jesus was speaking for God the Father. Just as the tree was cursed to never bear fruit again, so God had pronounced judgment on the religious leaders of Israel: that they would be fruitless. God was even preparing at that moment to remove the "show," their temple, their sacrifices, and all of their grand celebrations in Jerusalem. (That removal would happen in AD 70, when the Romans would destroy Jerusalem and the Temple.) God was planning on doing this because the leaders of the Jewish people were, at that moment, plotting against Jesus, to take His life. And a plot against Jesus is always a plot against God the Father.

That is not to say that all of the Jewish people had rejected God and His Messiah, or that everyone among them was under that same curse (just as every fig tree in the area was not cursed by Jesus). The curse was for those who had rejected God by rejecting Jesus. It fell on those whose religion was only an outward show, and who were so confident in their own righteousness that they rejected the One God had sent to save them from their sins.

Pray with me:

Father, this makes sense. It is easy to see that much of the leadership rejected Jesus, falsely accusing Him before Pilate, and even ended up throwing You under the bus in the process ("We have no king but Caesar!" John 19:15)! They bribed the guards to lie about Jesus' resurrection (Matthew 28:11-15), and the whole time celebrated the Passover and Feast of Unleavened Bread with what they believed were clean hands. They really were whitewashed tombs, and trees with showy leaves but no fruit! Father, help me to never fall into that same trap. Help me to keep my heart open and soft before You, so that You can help me to bear abundant fruit, day and night, every day of the year (Revelation 22:2; Psalm 1:3). Amen.

MARK 11:15-19

Read with me:

They came to Jerusalem, and he went into the temple and began to throw out those buying and selling. He overturned the tables of the money changers and the chairs of those selling doves, and would not permit anyone to carry goods through the temple. He was teaching them: "Is it not written, My house will be called a house of prayer for all nations? But you have made it a den of thieves!"

The chief priests and the scribes heard it and started looking for a way to kill him. For they were afraid of him, because the whole crowd was astonished by his teaching.

Whenever evening came, they would go out of the city.

Listen with me:

When Jesus entered Jerusalem that morning, He already knew what had to be done, because He had looked everything over the previous day (Mark 11:11). So there was no time wasted - He headed straight to the temple.

The temple was a magnificent structure, about 500 years old, and the subject of a nearly 50-year-long refurbishing and beautification project by the Herod dynasty. The average person could never go into the temple itself to see the holy place where the golden oil lamps burned, and where the golden tables were stacked with the bread of God's presence every week. Even fewer, only the high priests, were allowed to go into the Most Holy Place where God's presence and glory were supposed to reside. Regular people could not even go into the courtyard where the sacrifices were made. Instead, they were restricted to a series of outer courts, where they could see the outside of the building and worship the true God.

WHEN WE LISTEN

The Court of Israel was the closest of the courts, and was for the Jewish men. They would bring their sacrifices to this point, and hand them off to a priest or Levite. Then they could watch as those people took their animal into the courtyard and actually made the sacrifice.

The Court of the Women was farther away. From there the women could not actually see the sacrifices being made, but they could see much of the temple façade, and worship from there.

The Court of the Gentiles was huge, and was even further away from the temple itself. It was separated from the rest of the temple complex by a wall on which were signs engraved in three languages, warning Gentiles not to approach any closer under penalty of death. This far outer court was the only place where a Gentile seeker after the true God could come to worship and learn more. In a sense, it was the one place where an evangelistic connection could be made.

But Jesus found that the Court of the Gentiles had been turned into a marketplace. This was where the sellers of livestock and of doves had set up their stands. It was where the money changers had their tables, exchanging Roman coins, contaminated by figures of gods and of Caesar, for "clean" Jewish shekels, which were then able to be taken into the temple for contributions.

Booths and tables filled this whole area, along with the stench of livestock and the loud voices of the sellers and traders, to the point where nobody could worship or seek God effectively. This one place where people from outside could come and worship, this one place that could literally serve as 'a house of prayer for all nations,' had been transformed into a market, filled with livestock pens, and noise, and haggling traders - 'a den of thieves."

And so Jesus cleaned house, driving out the animals and those who sold them, and overturning the tables of the money changers. He also stopped those who were carrying merchandise through the court, sending them back the way they had come.

Of course, this did nothing to win over the chief priests and teachers of the law. The temple was THEIR area of responsibility, their purview and, in their opinion, Jesus had no right to barge in and change things around like that. They looked at things from their own viewpoint: what was most orderly, most convenient, and most profitable. But Jesus saw things from God's viewpoint: what was needed to bring the most people into His kingdom.

Pray with me:

Father, sometimes I admit that we, Your people, still look at things in our churches from the standpoint of what is most orderly, most convenient for us, most to our liking, and yes, even what is most profitable. But, Lord, those are not Your priorities. You still want to reach out through us to those who are far away, and bring them close to You. You are still primarily focused on seeking and saving what was lost. Help us to look at ourselves, our churches, and our procedures with YOUR priorities in mind. And help us to clean out our own churches, so that we can once again be houses of prayer for all nations, drawing them in, showing them Your love, and leading them all the way into Your kingdom through the one way of Jesus. Amen.

WHEN WE LISTEN

MARK 11:20-26

Read with me:

Early in the morning, as they were passing by, they saw the fig tree withered from the roots up. Then Peter remembered and said to him, "Rabbi, look! The fig tree that you cursed has withered."

Jesus replied to them, "Have faith in God. Truly I tell you, if anyone says to this mountain, 'Be lifted up and thrown into the sea,' and does not doubt in his heart, but believes that what he says will happen, it will be done for him. Therefore I tell you, everything you pray and ask for — believe that you have received it and it will be yours. And whenever you stand praying, if you have anything against anyone, forgive him, so that your Father in heaven will also forgive you your wrongdoing.

Listen with me:

Even though the disciples had no idea of the real meaning of Jesus cursing the fig tree, they could clearly see the results. In less than twenty-four hours, the tree had completely withered - dried up from the roots.

People frequently delivered curses on everything in those days, from obnoxious neighbors, to misbehaving children, to stubborn donkeys. But those curses were figurative in the minds of most people. They never really expected the curse to DO anything! But Jesus had cursed this tree, and now, the next morning, the tree was absolutely dead.

Jesus pointed out that the secret was not in magic, or some mysterious power, but simply faith in God. Many people try to define faith as a belief that originates in themselves. They take Jesus' words, *"everything you pray and ask for — believe that you have received it and it will be yours,"* as meaning that if they can make themselves believe strongly enough that they have something, that God will be forced to give it to them. But that interpretation completely ignores Jesus' first words: *"Have faith in God."*

The truth is that Jesus never did anything on His own (John 5:19). He was constantly listening to God's voice, and continually obeying everything that the Father told Him to do. If Jesus healed someone, it was because God told Him to do it. When He spoke to the people, it was the very words of God that He spoke. And when Jesus cursed the fig tree, it was the Father's idea to do it.

The faith part for Jesus came into play when He obeyed what the Father told Him to do. If the Father told Him to heal a man born blind by spitting on the ground, making mud out of the spit and dirt, and then putting that mud on the blind man's eyes (John 9:6-7), He could have thought, "That's a really weird way of doing things. I've never done it that way before. What if I do this and it doesn't work?" And nothing would have happened, because He didn't have faith enough to just do what the Father had told Him to do, exactly the way He was told to do it.

But Jesus NEVER responded that way. Whatever the Father told Him to do, no matter how improbable it seemed, no matter how strange the methodology that He chose, He always obeyed to the letter. His faith was perfect, because He never second guessed, never wondered if God could actually do what He promised. He obeyed completely, believing that what God had told Him to do was a done deal. And miracles happened!

Of course there are a couple of things that will stop the process cold, because they put a separation between a person and God: unforgiven sin in us, and unforgiveness of people's sins against us. And these two are closely interrelated. Jesus cautioned His disciples to never let a sin against us go unforgiven, because it will prevent our own sins from being forgiven (Matthew 6:14-15, 5:23-24). That will cut us off from hearing God's voice clearly, which means that we won't be able to hear what He wants us to do; which means in turn that we won't be able to exercise dynamic faith in His ability to do what He has told us He wants to do. Which ultimately means no miracle.

WHEN WE LISTEN

Pray with me:

Father, it is good to be reminded that the real secret to miracles is that they originate in Your own heart. And our faith even originates in You too! When you give us command, even a command to do something miraculous, we can rest assured that You are right there enabling it, if we will only respond in faith, and obey. Amen.

MARK 11:27-33

Read with me:

They came again to Jerusalem. As he was walking in the temple complex, the chief priests, the scribes, and the elders came and asked him, "By what authority are you doing these things? Who gave you this authority to do these things?"

Jesus said to them, "I will ask you one question; then answer me, and I will tell you by what authority I do these things. Was John's baptism from heaven or of human origin? Answer me."

They discussed it among themselves: "If we say, 'From heaven,' he will say, 'Then why didn't you believe him?' But if we say, 'Of human origin'"—they were afraid of the crowd, because everyone thought that John was truly a prophet. So they answered Jesus, "We don't know."

And Jesus said to them, "Neither will I tell you by what authority I do these things."

Listen with me:

Jesus was not in the least surprised when He was accosted by the chief priests, the scribes, and the elders, demanding where He got off believing that He had any authority to do the things He had been doing. This was more than just a challenge to His clearing out the temple. That action had merely been the final straw.

They were still seething about the triumphal entry, with the crowd declaring as their Messiah someone that they were completely unwilling to endorse, and Jesus not doing anything to stop them. After all, they were the ones who were experts in the Holy Scriptures, especially those having to do with the Messiah. The regular people were ignorant and easily swayed by charisma and appeals to their emotions.

The cleansing of the temple, of course, was particularly galling to them. They had approved both the activities that were taking place in the Court of the Gentiles and their location. And it was those approved activities that Jesus had so violently denounced as outright affronts to God and His agenda. And that basically amounted to a denouncement of they themselves.

And then there was the fact that Jesus was teaching the crowds that gathered around Him by the hundreds, even in the temple complex. Jesus had no credentials, no diploma from one of their approved rabbinical schools, but the people flocked to Him rather than to them, even calling Him Rabbi. And you could add to that the fact that His teachings about what NOT to do were far too often aimed directly at them!

With all of those things burning in their minds, they challenged Him to state before everyone around Him the source of His so-called authority to do those things. They had credentials, they had tradition on their side, and they held the offices of religious leadership.

This was not, by the way, just an idle challenge. It contained a very clever trap. Jesus, they knew, could produce no credentials, so He could not claim that as a source of His authority. And if He said that God had given Him this authority, they were ready to pounce. How could He prove that? Anyone could say that. And those whom God himself had assigned to positions of leadership (themselves) definitely did NOT agree that He had any authority from God to challenge them, to change things, to stir up dissention. When Jesus was left speechless in the face of this logic, as they were sure He would be, all of those listening to His teachings would abandon Him at once, pulling His fangs, and leaving Him vulnerable, without popular support.

But, of course, Jesus knew their hearts, and cleverly saw the trap that they were laying out for Him. So He redirected the whole debate. If it was a matter of authority coming from man or from God, He would challenge them on the same issue: *"Was John's baptism from heaven or of human origin?"*

All eyes expectantly turned back on the leaders. They were unwilling to admit that John's baptism was from heaven, especially since so many of John's denunciations of sin were aimed right at them. (Matthew 3:7-12) But the people believed that John was a prophet sent by God, and a martyr to boot! If these leaders told Jesus directly that they believed that John had no heavenly authority, that he was a charlatan, not a prophet, misguided, not a martyr, these people, some of whom had been baptized by John, would rise up and stone them!

They wouldn't give John credibility by proclaiming him a prophet; they wouldn't put themselves at risk of losing credibility (or even losing their lives) by denying it. So, helpless, they ended up seeing the trap so carefully laid out for Jesus snap closed around their own heads. And they were reduced to a feeble, *"We don't know,"* which, of course, released Jesus from the game.

Pray with me:

Father, how much simpler it is to trust You than it is to fight against You; simply trusting in Your word for the truth that it is. All through history, no one who sets themselves against You or Your Messiah ever came out on top. And they still don't today. Even when they succeed in taking out some of Your people, they still lose. You and Your kingdom still reign supreme, and those whom they killed are still alive with You forever. Praise Your glorious name! Amen.

MARK 12:1-12

Read with me:

He began to speak to them in parables: "A man planted a vineyard, put a fence around it, dug out a pit for a winepress, and built a watchtower. Then he leased it to tenant farmers and went away. At harvest time he sent a servant to the farmers to collect some of the fruit of the vineyard from them. But they took him, beat him, and sent him away empty-handed. Again he sent another servant to them, and they hit him on the head and treated him shamefully. Then he sent another, and they killed that one. He also sent many others; some they beat and others they killed. He still had one to send, a beloved son. Finally he sent him to them, saying, 'They will respect my son.' But those tenant farmers said to one another, 'This is the heir. Come, let's kill him, and the inheritance will be ours!' So they seized him, killed him, and threw him out of the vineyard. What then will the owner of the vineyard do? He will come and kill the farmers and give the vineyard to others. Haven't you read this Scripture: **The stone that the builders rejected has become the cornerstone. This came about from the Lord and is wonderful in our eyes?"** *[Psalm 118:22-23]*

They were looking for a way to arrest him but feared the crowd because they knew he had spoken this parable against them. So they left him and went away.

Listen with me:

It is important to remember the context of this parable. Jesus was only a couple days away from His arrest and execution orchestrated by the same priests, scribes, and elders who had just confronted Him, challenging His right to do the things He was doing. (Mark 11:27-33) And this parable was told directly to those same religious leaders as part of His answer to them. (The chapter break here between chapters 11 and 12 was not in the original gospel but, like all of the chapter breaks, was added hundreds of years later to make finding Scripture passages easier.)

This parable uses several symbols:

• The vineyard was a traditional symbol for Israel, but here it stands for the larger concept of God's kingdom. The people of Israel were supposed to be the people of the kingdom, living in God's blessing, and growing His kingdom by bringing more and more people into it. Just as the vineyard owner in the parable had done everything necessary to make the vineyard safe (building a wall & watchtower) and productive (planting the vines and digging the winepress), so God had done everything He needed to do to enable them to be successful and productive as His kingdom. This included giving them a land, empowering them to be victorious over all of their enemies, and even providing wealth beyond imagination.

• The servants sent at the harvest time symbolize the prophets that God sent repeatedly to the Israelites, trying to refocus them back to their original mission - to work the harvest of the world, and grow His kingdom. But God's people quickly lost track of the mission and the vision that all people of the earth would be blessed through them (Genesis 12:3), and instead were living in His kingdom as if it were theirs to possess and control. As God sent His prophets over and over again to warn and redirect them, the people persecuted them, and even killed them.

• Of course, the last messenger that God would send to these people, to try one final time to redirect them was His beloved son, Jesus - the most important, most authoritative messenger of them all. But the leaders of the Jewish people would not tolerate His clear teachings, and even then were plotting how they might kill Him so that they could regain control of God's kingdom. Jesus predicted what was already in their hearts: in just a couple of days, these leaders would kill him and (so they thought) throw Him out of the vineyard.

- The judgment of the vineyard owner on the tenants foretold events that would follow over the following 40 years. These same Jewish leaders would see God's kingdom given to others, both to Jewish believers who came from outside of their approved circle, and even Gentiles, who would start flooding into the kingdom within the next decade. They would see their beloved Jerusalem and temple destroyed by Rome, and many would die in that conflict.

Even though those leaders, God's tenants, rejected and even killed God's beloved Son, Jesus became the capstone of the kingdom through that very death, and through His resurrection and ascension to the right hand of God that followed.

The vital thing has always been the kingdom of God - His rule in the lives of people who love Him wholeheartedly, and who obediently do the work of building His kingdom, saving souls, and expanding His influence throughout the world. And those who stand against God's kingdom, ultimately end up standing against God Himself.

Pray with me:

Father, how often we fall into thinking that the most important thing to You is our worship and praise. But, as You told Your people in Isaiah 1:10-18, worship without obedience, without doing the work of Your kingdom, without producing a harvest for You, is actually detestable to You. Help us, Lord, to keep Your main thing our main thing. Help us to be the people of Your kingdom, and to regularly present You with an abundant harvest. Amen.

MARK 12:13-17

Read with me:

Then they sent some of the Pharisees and the Herodians to Jesus to trap him in his words. When they came, they said to him, "Teacher, we know you are truthful and don't care what anyone thinks, nor do you show partiality but teach the way of God truthfully. Is it lawful to pay taxes to Caesar or not? Should we pay, or shouldn't we?"

But knowing their hypocrisy, he said to them, "Why are you testing me? Bring me a denarius to look at." They brought a coin. "Whose image and inscription is this?" he asked them.

"Caesar's," they replied.

Jesus told them, "Give to Caesar the things that are Caesar's, and to God the things that are God's." And they were utterly amazed at him.

Listen with me:

The next challenge for Jesus came from an unlikely alliance: the Pharisees, who were focused on righteousness through keeping all of the fine points of the law, and the Herodians, who were focused on loyalty to the king, and thus were generally seen as being in cahoots with the Romans. Their only point of commonality was that both groups saw Jesus as a threat.

The Herodians were threatened by Jesus' widespread acclamation as the Messiah, the rightful king of the Jews, a direct challenge to the legitimacy of the Herodian dynasty. They also worried that if a popular uprising against Herod ever got a foothold, it would bring down on everyone's head the considerable wrath of the Roman Empire.

The Pharisees, on the other hand, were threatened by Jesus' credibility with the common people. Jesus made no secret of the fact that He had little use for the rituals, rules, and traditions around which every Pharisee built his life. They saw Him as a heretic, a Sabbath breaker, and a rebel against the traditions of the elders. (And someone likely to bring God's wrath down on all of their heads!).

In what looked like a sincere question on a hot-button issue of the day, they asked Jesus whether or not they, as Jews, should be paying taxes to Rome. But in that question was a trap. If Jesus said that they should pay taxes to Rome, the people would rise up against Him, considering Him a shill for the hated Romans. At best (for Jesus), they would desert Him en masse, leaving Him with no influence. At worst, they would rush Him out of the temple and stone Him.

If, on the other hand, Jesus said that they should not pay the taxes that Rome demanded, He could be denounced to the governor as trying to undercut the Empire, a charge that carried the death penalty. Either way Jesus answered, His goose would be cooked!

But Jesus saw through their duplicity at once. Roman taxes were paid with Roman coins, the currency of the Empire, which had the image of Caesar on their faces. These coins, because of this image, were not allowed to be used to pay the temple tax – they had to be exchanged for Jewish shekels through the money changers in the temple courts. But outside of the temple, these were the coins that everybody, Jew as well as gentile, carried and traded with.

When Jesus requested and was given a denarius, and asked whose image it bore, He was not ignorant of whose face was on the coin; He was simply making His point. Since the coin bore the image of Caesar, it belonged to Caesar, so should be given to him when he demanded it. However, Jesus had an even more significant point that He was making. The thing that bears the image of God, which is us as human beings, belongs to God, and so should be given to Him.

The Herodians had given themselves to the king. The Pharisees had given themselves to their rituals, and rules, and traditions. Both groups, despite their profession of being God's chosen people, had not been faithful in giving to God what belonged to God. So in the end, both groups left without their prey, and stinging from well placed slaps from their intended victim.

Pray with me:

Father, how many of us today can say that we have given ourselves unreservedly to You? How many of us even understand that, because we bear Your image and likeness, we are Yours by right? And even more so since You have redeemed us! But instead we give ourselves to so many other things, so many activities, so many pursuits, so many causes that are not Yours. And in the process, we steal ourselves from You, and end up deserving Your condemnation. Forgive us, Lord, and help us to set things right, by giving ourselves entirely to You from now on. Amen.

MARK 12:18-27

Read with me:

*Sadducees, who say there is no resurrection, came to him and questioned him: "Teacher, Moses wrote for us that **if a man's brother dies**, leaving a wife behind, but **no child, that man should take the wife and raise up offspring for his brother**. [Genesis 38:8; Deuteronomy 25:5] There were seven brothers. The first married a woman, and dying, left no offspring. The second also took her, and he died, leaving no offspring. And the third likewise. None of the seven left offspring. Last of all, the woman died too. In the resurrection, when they rise, whose wife will she be, since the seven had married her?"*

*Jesus spoke to them, "Isn't this the reason why you are mistaken: you don't know the Scriptures or the power of God? For when they rise from the dead, they neither marry nor are given in marriage but are like angels in heaven. And as for the dead being raised—haven't you read in the book of Moses, in the passage about the burning bush, how God said to him: **I am the God of Abraham and the God of Isaac and the God of Jacob?** [Exodus 3:6, 15-16] He is not the God of the dead but of the living. You are badly mistaken."*

Listen with me:

The Sadducees, the line from which the priests and high priests had come ever since the rebuilding of the temple (Ezekiel 44:15-16), only accepted as authoritative the first five books of the Bible, called the law, or the Pentateuch: Genesis, Exodus, Leviticus, Numbers, and Deuteronomy. Since these books did not contain any explicit teaching that there would be a resurrection from the dead, they rejected the concept out of hand.

When they came to Jesus that day, they came with what they believed to be an iron-clad argument against the whole idea of the resurrection from the dead. They approached the idea from a purely logical standpoint: a resurrection would be too confusing, with too many problems that would have to be resolved. In their story, this woman had been legally (and rightfully, Deuteronomy 25:5-6) married to each of seven brothers. So when the resurrection came, it's was going to be a mess! Each of the seven brothers would have a legitimate claim on her as husband. So whose wife will she end up being?

The Sadducees finished with smug looks on their faces. The best legal minds in their schools had wrestled over this question, and no consensus had been able to be reached. Therefore, they considered the problem unsolvable, and any advocate of a resurrection from the dead (like Jesus) sadly ignorant.

But Jesus was neither ignorant nor mistaken when He promised a resurrection from the dead – first His own, and ultimately everyone else. Instead, it was the Sadducees whose understanding was lacking.

Jesus presented His rebuttal to the Sadducees under two headings: they were ignorant of what the Scriptures really said, and they were ignorant of God's power and ability to pull off what might seem impossible or illogical to the human mind.

First, as far as God's power, when He raises the dead (which, with his infinite power, is really not difficult), He will not just reanimate what was dead and decayed. Instead, He will actually recreate us, making us new and imperishable (1 Corinthians 15:42-44a), so that our bodies will last forever, without pain, disease, or aging. And the life that we will live in our resurrected bodies will not just be a continuation of the life we have lived here, with our need for things like possessions and spouses. Instead, we will be consumed with our love for God, and completely occupied with serving Him. There will be no marriage to other people, and marriage relationships that we had here on earth will be subsumed into our mutual focus on God.

As far as the Scriptures are concerned, even the five books that the Sadducees accepted as authoritative contain enticing hints that there is more to our lives than this earthly existence. When God identifies Himself to Moses, and through Him to the Israelites,

WHEN WE LISTEN

He said, *"I am the God of Abraham and the God of Isaac and the God of Jacob."* This statement is in the present tense, even though all of these had been dead for four hundred years or more. Jesus' point was that God's statement indicated that His relationship with these three patriarchs was ongoing and current, not a thing of the past. Abraham, Isaac, and Jacob, though physically dead and buried for centuries, were still alive in God's presence. And since their lives clearly continued beyond their physical deaths, contrary to the Sadducees' view that this life was all that there is, a resurrection from the dead becomes neither impossible nor illogical.

Jesus' final sentence is very important. The Sadducees' mistaken notions about the nature of life and of God's power had caused them to build their spiritual foundation on the wrong stuff. Even though they were the ones entrusted with the holiest things of God, their focus had become completely locked onto the things of this world. They relished material gain and material comforts because, in their worldview, this life was all that existed for human beings. And, because of that, their concept of God had slid into a mode of believing that God's favor was shown only through material prosperity, a notion that Jesus completely rejected (Luke 12:15).

Pray with me:

Father, it is easy for us to sneer at the Sadducees, but at the same time fall into the trap that they were in. How often do we live like this world is all that there is, or at least like it is all that matters now? How often do we paint heaven in our minds as merely the world that we know, except with better weather and a healthier body? How often do we limit our ideas of what is true by the Scriptures that we personally know and believe, instead of constantly allowing the entirety of Your word to stretch us? And how often do we measure Your blessing in our lives or in our churches merely by the material blessings we possess? Help me, Lord, to keep my focus on the things of the Spirit instead of the things of this world. Help me to love You and Your word, so that I am continually learning more of You. Amen.

MARK 12:28-30

Read with me:

One of the scribes approached. When he heard them debating and saw that Jesus answered them well, he asked him, "Which command is the most important of all?"

*Jesus answered, "The most important is **Listen, O Israel! The Lord our God, the Lord is one. Love the Lord your God with all your heart, with all your soul, with all your mind, and with all your strength.** [Deuteronomy 6:4-5; Joshua 22:5]*

Listen with me:

Among the Jewish leaders and teachers that day in the temple, many were intent on destroying Jesus – laying traps for Him that would either destroy His credibility with the people who followed Him, or that would form the basis of official charges that they could bring before the Roman government officials. But some among these leaders were sincere and devout and craved the truth, wherever that truth might lead.

Among those who sincerely sought the truth was this man, a scribe, or teacher of the law, who had made studying and obeying God's commands the very core of his life. The scribes had counted 613 discrete commands in the law, the first five books of the Bible. And there was always a lively debate as to how to divide those commandments up. Which were critical to a life of godliness? Which were just nice to do if you could work them out? Which one was the most important? And over hundreds of years, the scribes and commentators had worked out many different organization systems, none of which truly satisfied those who genuinely desired to please God.

WHEN WE LISTEN

So this man, after listening to Jesus display His depth of scriptural knowledge, decided to ask his own question: Of all of the commandments, all 613 of them, which one is the most important?

To the surprise of many, Jesus didn't go to the Ten Commandments for the most important one. Instead, He went to the book of Deuteronomy, Moses' summation of God's law and of God's history with the Israelites from the time of the Exodus to the day of Moses' death about 40 years later. By the way, Jesus had already shown His deep respect and knowledge of the book of Deuteronomy three years earlier during His temptation in the wilderness. Every answer that Jesus had given to Satan had come from the book of Deuteronomy.

Jesus went straight to Deuteronomy 6:4-5. The first line of these verses were very well known by the Jewish people, forming part of their regular synagogue liturgy: *Listen, O Israel, the Lord our God, the Lord is one.* This basic statement reveals that God is the only true God, the God of not just Israel, but of the whole world. There is no other God besides Him, so He is to be worshiped by all of His people exclusively.

But that line is not to be separated from the very next sentence, which shows the natural outgrowth of the former truth, and forms the core of the commandment: *Love the Lord your God with all your heart, with all your soul, with all your mind, and with all your strength.* Since there is no god besides the one true God, all of His people are to love and serve Him completely.

Some have tried to break down what is included in each of these categories, but that is not necessary – the command is actually much simpler than a close analysis would suggest. God's people are to love and obey Him in every dimension of their lives, and with every part of themselves: mentally, spiritually, emotionally, and even physically.

The reason why this is the most important commandment is simple. If a person is willing to acknowledge that God is the only true God, and if they will commit themselves to love and obey Him in every dimension of their lives, then everything else will naturally fall into its proper place. If, however, a person is unwilling to acknowledge who God is, or if they hold back any dimension of themselves from His lordship, it will open the door to every kind of sin and compromise that will ultimately reach into and contaminate every area of their lives.

Pray with me:

Father, it really is very simple, isn't it? If You are acknowledged as the uncontested God of every part of my life, there is no possibility of my compromising my beliefs with other things, and allowing them to jump into first place in my life (the definition of idolatry). And if I love You and am committed to serving and obeying You with every dimension of my life, there will be nothing that could motivate me to willingly disobey You. This single command, elegant in its simplicity, really is the hinge-pin of a life committed to loving, following, and obeying You. Amen.

WHEN WE LISTEN

MARK 12:31

Read with me:

*"The second is, **Love your neighbor as yourself.** [Leviticus 19:18] There is no other command greater than these."*

Listen with me:

The greatest commandment is that God's people are to love Him with every part of themselves: heart, soul, mind, and strength. The second greatest commandment comes from Leviticus 19:18: we as God's people are to love our neighbors as ourselves.

The reason why these two commandments are the keystones of the entire law (Matthew 22:40) is this:

• If a person loves God completely, with every aspect of who they are, there is no way that they will willfully sin against God, doing what they know is displeasing to Him; no way that they would worship or serve anything apart from Him. Those are the complete opposite of loving God completely. And if they ever find that they have inadvertently trespassed against something that God has commanded, absolute love for God will drive them instantly to repent so that the relationship between them and God can be restored.

• If a person loves their neighbor in the same way and to the same degree as they love themselves, there is no way that they will willfully sin against their neighbor, killing them, committing adultery against them, stealing from them, lying about them, or coveting what they have. Those are the complete opposite of loving their neighbor. And if they ever find out that they have inadvertently wronged their neighbor in any way, love for that person will drive them to instantly repent, and to do what is necessary to make things right so that the relationship can be restored.

By the way, the focus of this second commandment is our neighbor, not ourselves. A teaching makes the rounds from time to time that before we can love our neighbor as ourselves, we have to first learn to love ourselves appropriately. But this command has nothing to do with feelings or emotions. It is about action and attitudes. It really ties in most closely with the golden rule: *"Therefore, whatever you want others to do for you, do also the same for them, for this is the Law and the Prophets."* (Matthew 7:12) Just as we want to be treated with honor and respect, loving our neighbor honors and respects them instead of doing things that will kill body or soul. Just as we want our marriage commitment to be honored by others, love for our neighbor honors their marriage commitment instead of engaging in adultery with their spouse. Just as we want our property rights to be respected by others, love for our neighbor respects their rights to what they own, and doesn't steal from them, or covet what they have. Just as we want our reputation to be respected, love for our neighbor will never lie or gossip about them, tearing down their good name.

And love like this is not just about avoiding evil. It is about doing positive good to our neighbor every chance we get. Just as we would want to receive food when we are hungry, clothing when we are cold, and shelter when we have none, love for our neighbor willingly shares what we have with others in need. Just as we would want to be encouraged in times of struggle, visited when we are lonely, and comforted in times of grief, real love for our neighbor looks for opportunities to do those things for them.

This kind of love is easy to see when it is present – no one has to wonder whether they have received it or not. If we are doing these things consistently, it is easy for us to know it. And if we aren't, we will know that, too. But we, as God's people, need to realize that this kind of love for others is not an option, a nice addition to our faith if we have the time and energy and means. It is a commandment – the second most important commandment in the whole Bible, from Jesus' own lips.

Pray with me:

Father, it is easy for us to think that this kind of self-sacrificial love in action is "optional equipment," or something that we might be able to do some day. But there is no escaping the truth that Jesus identified this as an outright commandment for Your people, second in importance only to loving You with every part of ourselves. Forgive me, Lord, for too often putting something so important to You on my back burner, or for disregarding it altogether. Help me to live in Your love, so that it flows all the way through my life into the lives of everyone around me. Amen.

MARK 12:32-34

Read with me:

Then the scribe said to him, "You are right, teacher. You have correctly said that he is one, and there is no one else except him. And to love him with all your heart, with all your understanding, and with all your strength, and to love your neighbor as yourself, is far more important than all the burnt offerings and sacrifices."

When Jesus saw that he answered wisely, he said to him, "You are not far from the kingdom of God." And no one dared to question him any longer.

Listen with me:

This teacher of the law, unlike many of them at that time, was not out to get Jesus. Instead, he was in pursuit of a solid relationship with God that would lead him to eternal life. In Jesus' answer, he heard the same truth that he himself had arrived at through years of arduous study.

He had found, contrary to the beliefs of the Pharisees, that the answer was not to be found in rituals and sacrifices. He had seen countless numbers who were scrupulous in their sacrifices and ritual observances, and had been for years, but had not the slightest scent of God about them.

He had found, contrary to the beliefs of the Sadducees, that the answer was not to be found in worldly wealth, power, position, and prestige. Many of that party had all of those things, and pointed to them as signs of God's favor, but at the same time they had corrupt and ungodly hearts.

And he had found, contrary to the beliefs of the other teachers of the law, that the answer was not to be found in devotion to the study of books. Many in his own group could recite long passages of Scripture and the opinions of the great rabbis of the past forward and backward, but were no more godly than those who were largely ignorant of the finer points of Scripture.

He had come to realize that the real key lay in complete devotion to God, loving Him with the entirety of his heart, soul, mind, and strength. If he withheld any part of himself from that devotion, he understood that it would quickly become a toehold for the enemy, and would corrupt all of it, leaving him ultimately in the dark.

But that love for God could not be considered real unless it showed itself in wholehearted love for others. This was echoed by James: *What good is it, my brothers and sisters, if someone claims to have faith but does not have works? Can such faith save him? If a brother or sister is without clothes and lacks daily food and one of you says to them, "Go in peace, stay warm, and be well fed," but you don't give them what the body needs, what good is it? In the same way faith, if it doesn't have works, is dead by itself.* (James 2:14-17) It was also John's point in 1 John 2:9-11: *The one who says he is in the light but hates his brother or sister is in the darkness until now. The one who loves his brother or sister remains in the light, and there is no cause for stumbling in him. But the one who hates his brother or sister is in the darkness, walks in the darkness, and doesn't know where he's going, because the darkness has blinded his eyes.* Both commands, whole-hearted love for God and sacrificial love for others, have to be obeyed. If either is absent, it betrays that darkness is still abiding in the soul.

Jesus could clearly see that this man had searched long and hard for the truth, and had found it. He was not far from the kingdom of God. Good theology is not enough to be in the kingdom, but bad theology will blind us to the truths necessary to enter. All that was missing in this man's life was saving faith in Jesus Himself, which would come soon enough.

Pray with me:

Father, thank You for making these truths clear. We, as New Testament Christians, have been commanded by Jesus Himself to love

You with every part of ourselves, and to love our neighbors, caring for them in the same way that we care for our own needs. But in addition to that, we must enter Your kingdom through the one way of Jesus, the Lamb of God (cf. John 14:6). Help me, Lord, to walk in this way of obedience and faith, starting right now. Amen.

MARK 12:35-37

Read with me:

While Jesus was teaching in the temple, he asked, "How can the scribes say that the Messiah is the son of David? David himself says by the Holy Spirit: **The Lord declared to my Lord, 'Sit at My right hand until I put your enemies under your feet.'** *[Psalm 110:1] David himself calls him 'Lord'; how then can he be his son?" And the large crowd was listening to him with delight.*

Listen with me:

The teachers of the law taught very clearly that the Messiah (Greek: Christ) was the son, or descendant, of David. By this, they meant that he would be a great earthly king, descended from the line of King David. Their expectation was that when He came He would take over the rule of Israel, oust the Romans, and restore the nation of Israel to the freedom, military might, prestige, and wealth that it had during the reigns of David and Solomon.

Jesus' argument did not deny that the Messiah was a physical descendant of David. That was actually God's plan based on His promise to David that one of his descendants would sit on his throne forever (2 Samuel 7:16). And Jesus was a descendant of David, both on His earthly father's side (Matthew 1:6-16), and on His mother's side (Luke 3:23-31).

Jesus' point was that by limiting their expectations of the Messiah to an earthly Davidic king who would pick up the loose threads of the kingdom and reestablish Israel as a political, military, and economic power, they were expecting far less than what God had promised. The clues to who the Messiah would be are scattered throughout the history and prophecy of the Old Testament. Isaiah 9:6, for example, says that, among other things, the Messiah would be called Mighty God and Everlasting Father (or, perhaps, Father of Eternity), titles hardly suited to a mere earthly king. Also, in verse 7, Isaiah doesn't just say that this king's dynasty would hold the throne forever, but that He Himself will reign forever.

Jesus' choice of Psalm 110 pointed out yet another indicator that the Messiah was more than a mere descendant of David: David (speaking a prophecy by the Holy Spirit) calls the Messiah "my Lord," a strange turn of phrase to use of one's own descendant. Jesus used this well-known "Messianic Psalm" to show that, even according to David himself, the Messiah was more than a man, more than a king – He is the King of kings and Lord of lords, God in the flesh!

Pray with me:

Father, it is interesting to think about David seeing so clearly the identity of the Messiah nearly a millennium before He was born, and worshiping Him in advance. But through Your Spirit it is no trick to reveal Your future plans to those who love You and follow You whole-heartedly. Help me, Lord, to never rely on my own intelligence or reason to try to understand Your great truths. Instead, help me to turn to You with open ears, open eyes, and an open heart. Amen.

WHEN WE LISTEN

MARK 12:38-40

Read with me:

He also said in his teaching, "Beware of the scribes, who want to go around in long robes and who want greetings in the marketplaces, the best seats in the synagogues, and the places of honor at banquets. They devour widows' houses and say long prayers just for show. These will receive harsher judgment."

Listen with me:

Jesus' condemnation of the teachers of the law was not about what they taught, but about who they were, how they lived, and what was in their hearts. As Jesus pointed out in the parallel passage in Matthew 21:2-7, these men taught the Bible, which is the truth, so people were obligated to obey the truths that they taught. But, by and large, the lives of these men did not meet the requirements that they laid out for others.

The problem was not that they didn't know the requirements of the law – they did, without question. *"This people honors me with their lips, but their heart is far from me."* (Matthew 15:8, quoting Isaiah 29:13) Many of these men had lost their passion for and devotion to God, and had been taken captive by the perks of their position. They enjoyed wearing the long, flowing robes that identified them as experts in the law. They enjoyed it when people recognized them in the marketplaces, greeting them with great respect. They enjoyed being given the best seats in the house for worship services or banquets.

Jesus was warning His followers to not admire these men, or want to be honored and admired like they were. There was a trap in desiring that kind of popularity – a person began to believe that they really were an exceptional person; that they really were especially loved and valued by God; that they really deserved all of the popular acclaim that they were getting. They would cheerfully accept the donation of the last coin from a widow, leaving her nothing to live on, in exchange for a blessing or a prayer that, because of the distance between them and God, had no effect whatever. And the eloquence of their prayers was often so admired that they frequently stretched them out when they prayed in public, adding words and well-turned phrases that were impressive to men, but which impacted God not in the least.

Such men, despite the opinions of those who admired their knowledge and piety, were not worthy of any admiration. They were like whitewashed tombs – beautiful on the outside where people could see, but inside full of all kinds of corruption, hypocrisy, and lawlessness (Matthew 23:27-28). On the Day of Judgment, instead of receiving the honor and accolades that everyone believed were waiting for them, they would end up being condemned and punished severely. The judgment of God is always based on the absolute truth, and is never swayed by public opinion.

Pray with me:

Father, because we can only see the outside, and because we are so easily swayed by glitz, and glamor, and a good PR campaign, we are often persuaded to follow someone who, though they appear good on the outside, are full of rottenness within. And then, when the truth comes out, we find ourselves devastated, and ashamed that we were so easily taken in. Lord, help me to follow You as my guide, my standard, my model. And help us all, as Your people, to be pure and holy on the inside where it counts, so that we demonstrate, not glitz and glamor, but a rock-solid godliness that will never allow us to put ourselves first, and that will never lead others astray. Amen.

MARK 12:41-44

Read with me:

Sitting across from the temple treasury, he watched how the crowd dropped money into the treasury. Many rich people were putting in large sums. Then a poor widow came and dropped in two tiny coins worth very little. Summoning His disciples, he said to them, "Truly I tell you, this poor widow has put in more into the treasury than all the others. For they all gave out of their surplus, but she out of her poverty has put in everything she had — all she had to live on."

Listen with me:

Jesus stunned His disciples when he told them that this widow, who had put two lepta (small copper coins worth a few cents, often derisively called "thin ones") into the offering, had given more than the many wealthy people who had put in gold or silver coins worth many times what she had given. It made no sense to them. How can a two-cent offering be worth more than a hundred-dollar offering?

But Jesus was talking in proportional, not absolute, terms. This widow, out of her gratefulness to God, had given ALL of her money. Those two coins, every last cent that she had, which could have bought her a little food to sustain her, were instead given to God. That giving of her all was not foolish or overzealous as some might think. Instead, it showed great faith. She gave her all to God, and then relied on God to provide for her true needs.

The rich, on the other hand, out of their abundance, had given only a miniscule portion of what God had given them. Out of the thousand silver coins that God had put into their hands, they give back one to Him, and did it in such a way that their gift would be seen and appreciated by those standing nearby (Matthew 6:1-4).

After all, there were many people for whom a silver coin represented a whole day's wages – an impressive sum. When they saw someone give that kind of contribution, they were awed by their assumed generosity.

But, in reality, those rich people were giving God their spare change, what they could easily afford. As good as it looked on the outside, it betrayed a lack of real devotion to God on the inside.

God never gives His people "spare change" of love, or grace, or any other blessing. Instead, He always stands ready to pour into our lives *"a good measure—pressed down, shaken together, and running over..."* (Luke 6:38). God did not even withhold His one and only Son from us, but gave Him completely so that we might be saved – saved from death, saved from an eternity in hell, saved from the power of sin. And it is only reasonable in view of such giving on God's part, for us to give all of ourselves back to Him - all of our energy, all of our resources, all of our time. Not just what we can reasonably or comfortably spare, but ALL. And then we, like that widow, can rely on God to provide for all of our true needs.

Pray with me:

Father, it is so easy for us to think about our giving in absolute terms: giving a check for $1000 is giving a lot. Giving $100 is respectable. Giving $10 is less than we probably should give. But You didn't give us a "respectable amount," and we don't owe you "a lot." You gave Your all, every bit of it. And, because of all that You have given for us to redeem us, we owe You all of ourselves – all we have, all we are, all that we can possibly be. Lord, drive this truth deep into my heart so that I, like that widow, will willingly, joyfully give You all that You deserve, not holding anything back. Then help me to sincerely trust You to provide all that I truly need. Amen.

WHEN WE LISTEN

MARK 13:1-2

Read with me:

As He was going out of the temple, one of his disciples said to him, "Teacher, look! What massive stones! What impressive buildings!"

Jesus said to him, "Do you see these great buildings? Not one stone will be left upon another—all will be thrown down!"

Listen with me:

As Jesus left the temple for the day with His disciples, they were struck afresh by the grandeur and beauty of the temple complex. Even though the original structure of the temple, built after the return from captivity in Babylon, was much less impressive than the one built by Solomon and torn down by the invading Babylonians, the building was still impressive. It had huge stones that made many wonder how they had ever been hoisted into position.

The kings of the Herodian Dynasty had also left their imprint on the temple grounds. Herod the Great, the king who tried to execute the baby Jesus (Matthew 2:13-17), had remodeled much of the temple and the surrounding courtyards and buildings, a work continued by his son, Herod Antipas, and still going on in Jesus' day.

The temple was beautiful, breathtaking even, and the sight of it gladdened the heart of every pilgrim who came within its precincts. But Jesus squashed the disciples' enthusiasm immediately with His terse statement: *"Not one stone will be left upon another—all will be thrown down!"*

Jesus was looking ahead four decades to AD 70, the year that the Romans, led by General Titus, would besiege and conquer Jerusalem, tearing and burning down all of the principal buildings, including the temple itself. The massive stones, fit together with such great skill, were torn apart, huge levers prying each layer off the one below it, until literally one stone was not left on another.

It wasn't that Jesus didn't appreciate the architecture and workmanship of this place. But He clearly could see that all of this beauty and majesty would soon be cast down to earth by mere men. No matter how sublime its original purpose, the temple was earthly, temporary, and able to be destroyed. Jesus had come, not to give credibility to what was temporary, but to establish that which will never be shaken or destroyed. He had come to initiate the kingdom of God, a kingdom with no geographical limits, but composed of people *from every nation, tribe, people, and language* (Revelation 7:9) who have entered through faith in Him. He came to establish the capital of this new kingdom, the New Jerusalem, a city not built by human hands or of earthy materials, but built by God Himself of heavenly, non-perishable stuff. By that one statement, as harsh to our ears as it was to those first disciples, Jesus was turning the disciples' attention away from that which would ultimately fall, so that their eyes could be turned to focus on that which was even then being created, which would last forever.

Pray with me:

Father, we still get overly impressed by things built with human hands, and in the process we lose sight of Your kingdom, which will last forever, and which is grander by far than anything the mind of man can conceive. Lord, give me heavenly eyes that can see Your kingdom clearly, so that the things of this world, no matter how grand and beautiful they are, will never gain a foothold in my heart. Amen.

WHEN WE LISTEN
MARK 13:3-8

Read with me:

While he was sitting on the Mount of Olives across from the temple, Peter, James, John, and Andrew asked him privately, "Tell us, when will these things happen? And what will be the sign when all these things are about to be accomplished?"

Jesus told them: "Watch out that no one deceives you. Many will come in my name, saying, 'I am he,' and they will deceive many. When you hear of wars and rumors of wars, don't be alarmed; these things must take place, but it is not yet the end. For nation will rise up against nation, and kingdom against kingdom. There will be earthquakes in various places, and famines. These are the beginning of birth pains."

Listen with me:

Jesus' brief prophecy about the looming destruction of Jerusalem was nothing short of earth-shattering in the minds of the disciples. They all knew the history of the city and the nation – that six hundred years before their day, God had allowed the city to be destroyed and the people to be carried off into exile in Babylon. But after the exiles returned seventy years later, rebuilt the temple, and reconstructed the walls, popular opinion was that God would never punish His people or reject His temple again. So when Jesus foretold the destruction of the temple (which implied the destruction of the city), the disciples were stunned. Two sets of brothers, Peter and Andrew, James and John, came to Jesus hungry for more information: when would those things happen, and what would be the signs that they could look for that would tell them that it would happen soon?

The first part of Jesus' answer was that many things would happen in the near future: people would appear claiming to be the

Messiah, or even claiming to be Jesus returned, and they would succeed in deceiving a lot of people; wars would come and go; earthquakes and famines would occur. For many people those kinds of confusing and frightening events would make people believe that the world was spinning out of control toward the end of all things. But Jesus cautioned that those things were merely the beginning of the birth pains; much else would happen before Jerusalem fell, let alone before the real end of the world.

Even today many people are looking for signs that the end of the world is near. And they can see plenty of things that convince them that it must be on track to happen very soon. There are still false Messiahs, claiming to be either Jesus or one better than Him. There are still wars and rumors of wars, all piped live into our homes through our televisions and computers. And there are plenty of earthquakes and famines, and all kinds of other natural disasters.

But the fall of Jerusalem and its timing were not dictated by man's wars (even though the Lord used warriors to accomplish it in AD 70), or nature's disasters. The destruction was God's judgment on the people for refusing to receive God's Son when He came. And, in the same way, the end of all things will not come by the decision of people to make war, nor will it come because of the natural occurrence of earthquakes or famines. Instead, Jesus' return and the end of the world will come at a time that God Himself decides, and it will be His final judgment on those who have persisted in their rebellion against Him.

Pray with me:

Father, we do freak out from time to time over the events and disasters that are constantly kept before us on our televisions and radios. But the time of the end will never be determined by those things, but by You alone. Help me, Lord, to never allow myself to get fixated on events, but to keep my eyes steadfastly on You, simply trusting You to choose the absolutely correct time to draw things to a close. Amen.

WHEN WE LISTEN

MARK 13:9-13

Read with me:

"But you, be on your guard! They will hand you over to local courts, and you will be flogged in the synagogues. You will stand before governors and kings because of me, as a witness to them. And it is necessary that the gospel be preached to all nations. So when they arrest you and hand you over, don't worry beforehand what you will say, but say whatever is given to you at that time, for it isn't you speaking, but the Holy Spirit.

"Brother will betray brother to death, and a father his child. Children will rise up against parents and have them put to death. You will be hated by everyone because of my name, but the one who endures to the end will be saved."

Listen with me:

The disciples were consumed with curiosity about the events that would lead up to the destruction of Jerusalem that Jesus had just foretold (v2). They wanted to be told about events that they would be able to see and identify, that would tell them that it was approaching, so that they could be ready. But Jesus began by sharing with them things that would not only happen to them personally, but that would also be true for followers of Jesus all through the ages, far beyond Jerusalem's fall, all the way to the time of Jesus' return.

The "time between" would be a time of great power and victory in the lives of Jesus' followers as the gospel spread out and was preached all over the known world. But it would also be a time of great trial for them as well. They would be handed over to courts and councils, and flogged in the synagogues, treated as blasphemers and renegades. They would even be betrayed by their own family members, and sentenced to death. They would be hated by all people because they bear the name of Jesus.

MARK 13

This is a pretty dark picture. And it is strikingly accurate, as the disciples themselves would be able to attest to. All of the apostles except John suffered death by martyrdom. And even John was persecuted, imprisoned, and exiled. It's accuracy can also be attested to by many modern day disciples, who are persecuted for the sake of the gospel.

But into that dark scene, several rays of bright light shine. Jesus urges all of His followers to not buckle under the pain and stress of persecution. Instead, *"the one who endures to the end will be saved"* (v13b). But the disciples do not have to stand firm in their own strength. Just as Jesus promised that as they go and make disciples of all nations, that *"I am with you always, to the end of the age."* (Matthew 28:20); just as he promised that the Father *"will give you another Counselor to be with you forever."* (John 14:16 NIV); Jesus now promises that even when they are on trial for their lives, they will not be alone: *"don't worry beforehand what you will say, but say whatever is given to you at that time, for it isn't you speaking, but the Holy Spirit."*

Even though the times will appear very dark, Jesus will still be working. Even though it looks like the end of the world is very near, the work of the kingdom must go on in the power of the Holy Spirit until Jesus returns.

Today, as 2000 years ago, it is very tempting for followers of Jesus to take our eyes off of the vital work that He calls us to, and begin to spend time and energy focusing on and discussing the signs of the times, to worry beforehand about what to say, instead of trusting in the Holy Spirit to give us all that we need at the time. God will provide us as His people with all that we need to do the work He has called us to, no matter when we live, no matter where we are, no matter how dark things appear. The vital thing for all of God's people, then and now, is to keep our focus on the work of God's kingdom, and leave the future in His hands.

WHEN WE LISTEN

Pray with me:

Father, it does sometimes feel like things are spinning out of control in our world. We see persecution increasing in other parts of the world, oppression of Christians happening in our own nation, and it is so easy in times like that to get our eyes off of our assigned kingdom work, and to get fixated instead on these events, wondering how they relate to the end of the world. Help me, Lord, to always stay on task for You, to keep Your agenda at the forefront of my life, and to just trust that You are still in control. Amen.

MARK 13:14-20

Read with me:

*"When you see the **abomination of desolation** [Daniel 9:27] standing where it should not be" (let the reader understand), "then those in Judea must flee to the mountains. A man on the housetop must not come down or go in to get anything out of his house, and a man in the field must not go back to get his coat. Woe to pregnant women and nursing mothers in those days!*

"Pray it won't happen in winter. For those will be days of tribulation, the kind that hasn't been from the beginning of creation until now and never will be again. If the Lord had not cut those days short, no one would be saved. But he cut those days short for the sake of the elect, whom he chose."

Listen with me:

Many of the people who read this Scripture today see it as applying solely to the days of Jesus' return. But it, like many other prophecies, is multi-layered, and is relevant to more than one place and time.

In this case, the immediate context of this prophecy is the coming destruction of Jerusalem in AD 70. This was what the disciples had asked most directly about (13:2-4). And this prophecy was amazingly fulfilled in just a few years' time.

According to Eusebius and Josephus, the siege that led to Jerusalem's fall was preceded by a Roman campaign in Judea to put down several rebellions that had sprung up. After a short siege of Jerusalem, the general, Cestius Gallus, inexplicably withdrew. The Jews pursued him, killed some of the retreating soldiers, and captured their weapons. The Emperor Nero then sent another force to crush the rebellion for good.

WHEN WE LISTEN

In AD 66, just after Gallus withdrew from Jerusalem, some of the Christian leadership in the Jerusalem Church saw the siege as a sign from God, a warning shot over the bow. Despite the upbeat message of the Jewish people that they had succeeded in ousting the Romans, the Christian leaders saw this as the beginning of the fulfillment of Jesus' prophecy, and sent word to the Christians to use the opportunity to leave, which they did immediately. They moved across the Jordan to the Decapolis region, to a town called Pella. There they remained, establishing a strong Christian community that lasted for several centuries.

By the time that General Vespasian came along, laying waste to the whole countryside, the Christians were already long gone. This was followed by the disastrous siege of Jerusalem by General Titus which resulted in profound suffering among those trapped in the city, comparable only to the suffering during the Babylonian siege. After the long siege, Titus managed to breach the wall. He burned the city, put the survivors to the sword, and demolished the temple.

The Christians who fled before all of that happened credited God and this prophecy of Jesus with their salvation from this disaster that fell on the city. They were confident of Jesus' ability to know the future, so when the word came that the prophecy was coming true, they immediately obeyed, leaving behind their homes and most of their possessions, being willing to start afresh with God's guidance.

Whether in the days of the Roman Empire, or in the future days before the return of Jesus, the vital thing for God's people is not to spend time compiling and studying charts and graphs detailing what they believe will happen. The vital thing is for us to know God's word, to be about the work of expanding His kingdom through making disciples of all nations, to know God's voice intimately, and be immediately obedient to His leading.

MARK 13

Pray with me:

Father, it is often tempting to get mired in the charts and graphs of end-time prophecies, and in doing so, to neglect the job that You have given us of making disciples. Help me to keep my focus on the things that matter most to You, and then to keep myself unencumbered and light on my feet, so that I can be immediately responsive to Your leading. Amen.

WHEN WE LISTEN

MARK 13:21-23

Read with me:

"Then if anyone tells you, 'See, here is the Messiah! See, there!' do not believe it. For false messiahs and false prophets will arise and will perform signs and wonders to lead astray, if possible, the elect. And you must watch! I have told you everything in advance."

Listen with me:

Whenever there is trouble in the world or in a nation, people are easily drawn to those who claim to have the solution. And the more desperate the trouble, the quicker we are to turn to whoever seems to have the most charisma, the smoothest line, or who tells us what we want to hear in the most convincing tones.

As Gamaliel pointed out to the Sanhedrin (Acts 5:35-39), before the days of Jesus there were leaders who claimed to be the solution to the problems of the people. And some even received these men as their Messiah, their deliverer. But in the end, they proved to be mere men, they were destroyed, and their followers, who put such stock in their promises, were scattered.

Jesus saw that, as the tide turned against the Jews, and as the net closed in around Jerusalem, there would again rise up people who would claim to be the answer, the one, the Messiah Himself. And, because the times would be desperate, many people would turn to them. Some of these men would even seem to do signs and miracles that would deceive many, drawing them into the deception. These miracles would be spectacular enough to draw the attention of even the elect! But, in the end, they will not be able to deceive them. And a key reason why the elect will not be deceived is that Jesus is warning them in advance so that they will be on their guard against these charlatans and pretenders.

294

Modern times are not immune to the same deceptions. When times get hard, people flock to leaders and politicians who promise to lead them to better days, even promising to pull off miracles if only the people will support them or elect them. And, as has always been the case, these men and women never turn out to be the deliverer that they claim to be. Programs fail, problems get worse, or the side-effects of their solutions cause problems of their own.

Only Jesus, the real Messiah, was able to completely deliver what He promised: restoration of relationship between God and whoever is willing to turn away from their sinful lifestyle. And only Jesus is able to save in the day of trouble, the day of disaster.

Pray with me:

Father, sometimes I think that the reason we turn to human "messiahs" for solutions to our problems is that they promise easy solutions, and the cost of following Jesus is too high for many. After all, following Jesus requires us to turn away from sinful behaviors that we have grown to enjoy, to relinquish control of our lives to You, to take up our cross daily, and to take on Your agenda as our own instead of trying to persuade You to bless our agendas. That seems like such a steep price to many. But in the end, we really lose nothing of eternal value when we come to You. Instead we gain an eternal inheritance that thieves cannot steal, and that moth and rust can never destroy. Amen.

MARK 13:24-27

Read with me:

"But in those days, after that tribulation: The sun will be darkened, and the moon will not shed its light; the stars will be falling from the sky, and the powers in the heavens will be shaken. Then they will see the Son of Man coming in clouds with great power and glory. He will send out the angels and gather his elect from the four winds, from the ends of the earth to the ends of heaven."

Listen with me:

Jesus moves back and forth seamlessly between the coming destruction of Jerusalem and His return at the end of all things. He can do this because of the similarities between those times (and between those times and previous instances of God's judging both His people and those of other nations). The details of those times and the time of the end differ primarily in scope.

In the days following the great distress of the siege of Jerusalem, God's judgment was destined to fall on those who rebelled against Him, but who survived the siege. Thus the end of the siege was not going to be relief, but destruction and captivity. It would seem to them that all light had gone from the earth, as if the sun, moon, and stars had all lost their ability to give light.

And then God's judgment would fall on them, all who had rejected Him by rejecting His Messiah. It would be just as it had been during the first fall of Jerusalem. All of those who had rejected God by turning away from Him and His laws to worship idols found themselves captives in the dark of His judgment.

And that is how it will be at the end as well, except that God's judgment will not fall on a single city or land. Instead, all of those who reject God will find themselves terrified by the signs that appear in heaven and on earth, and will feel as if they are running in the dark. The things that they have used for safety and security will prove to be of no use at all on that day. Even bomb shelters and bullet-proof houses and vehicles will provide no safety or shelter at the end of the world.

And then, just when it seems like things could not be more terrifying, all mankind will see Jesus coming in the clouds with great power and glory. Those whose lives have been lived in Jesus will rejoice as they anticipate being caught up with him, but those who have rejected Him, denied Him, and have even convinced themselves that He never existed, will suddenly be overcome with a terror like nothing they had ever known.

At that time it will be too late to turn. Those who have lived their lives apart from Jesus, in rebellion against His salvation and His teachings, will not think of repenting or admitting their error. Instead, they will be completely overwhelmed with terror at the sight of the One they have rejected. They will be consumed by their useless efforts to flee from the presence of the One who fills the universe.

Pray with me:

Father, this is a terrifying picture, especially for those who reject Jesus, those who live carelessly, unheeding of Your warnings that all of this will come to an end when Jesus returns. And it is troubling to those of us who have family and friends who have rejected You. Lord, help me not to be made immobile by this troubling picture. Instead, help it to move me boldly out into the harvest fields, steadfastly doing the work of making disciples of all nations, including my family, friends, neighbors, coworkers, and everybody I care about, so that they will not be on the wrong side when Jesus returns. Amen.

MARK 13:28-31

Read with me:

"Learn this lesson from the fig tree: As soon as its branch becomes tender and sprouts leaves, you know that summer is near. In the same way, when you see these things happening, recognize that he is near — at the door!

Truly I tell you, this generation will certainly not pass away until all these things take place. Heaven and earth will pass away, but my words will never pass away."

Listen with me:

Many have been confused by Jesus' words that *this generation will certainly not pass away until all these things take place.* But the issue that most of them have is that they interpret this prophecy as being solely about the end of time and Jesus' return.

But Jesus' primary context in this whole passage, the one that the disciples were most vitally interested in at that moment, was the coming destruction of Jerusalem which Jesus foretold so matter-of-factly back in verse 2. Of course, the disciples believed that that would also be the time when Jesus returned, but Jesus Himself never said that.

The fall of Jerusalem did indeed happen before that very generation had passed away – in about 40 years. Even the apostle John was still alive at that time.

In the secondary sense of Jesus' prophecy, as He saw through the events of His day to the end of all things, we can understand the words of this prophecy in this way: those of us who follow Jesus, must always be students of the times. Just as people can know that summer is near by seeing a fig tree begin to leaf out, so those of us who keep an eye on what is happening around us will be able to see when things are drawing to a close.

However, that does not mean that we should be straining to sift out obscure clues, or paying attention to all of the people who seem to be constantly calling out that it's the end of the world. There have been countless numbers of these and, to a person, they have all been wrong so far!

Just as God enabled His people in Jerusalem to know that its doom was nearly upon it, and that it was time to leave, giving them settled hearts over the matter so that they simply picked up and left, so He will help His people understand the signs of the times when the end is really drawing near.

In the meantime, the work of the kingdom, the making of disciples of all nations so that the maximum number of people can be saved before the door closes, must go on. Indeed, it must be the primary focus of all of God's people. We can leave the timing of Jesus' return safely in God's hands, just as Jesus Himself did, and focus ourselves wholeheartedly on the work that He has given us to do, just as Jesus did.

Pray with me:

Father, we can so easily let ourselves get trapped into focusing on the day of Jesus' return, and looking for the signs that it might be near. In a way, we can become like a farmer who goes out to his fig tree several times a day to see if the branches might be a little more tender than they were a few hours before, and, in the meantime, lets his crops go unattended. If he would simply go about his farming, focusing on working to make the harvest plentiful, one day he will easily see that the leaves have sprung forth! Help me, Lord, to focus on the vital work that You have left to me, trusting Your timing, and trusting that You will help me to see the signs when the time is really near, just as You did with Your people before Jerusalem fell. Amen.

MARK 13:32-37

Read with me:

"Now concerning that day or hour no one knows—neither the angels in heaven nor the Son—but only the Father.

"Watch! Be alert! For you don't know when the time is coming.

"It is like a man on a journey, who left his house, gave authority to his servants, gave each one his work, and commanded the doorkeeper to be alert. Therefore be alert, since you don't know when the master of the house is coming—whether in the evening or at midnight or at the crowing of the rooster or early in the morning. Otherwise, when he comes suddenly he might find you sleeping. And what I say to you, I say to everyone: Be alert!"

Listen with me:

Many people spend a lot of time and energy studying the Bible trying to figure out when Jesus is going to return. And in every generation, there have been those who profess to have figured out the day and hour of His return.

But Jesus' emphasis, and the emphasis that He tried to instill in His followers, was completely different than that. Jesus knew that God always tells His people everything that we need to know, clearly, and at the precise time that we need to know it. Jesus did not spend His life, or any portion of it, poring over ancient texts, trying to sort out the threads of various prophecies, using numerology and "hidden wisdom" to try to figure out when things were going to happen. He merely pointed out that *"Now concerning that day or hour no one knows—neither the angels in heaven nor the Son—but only the Father."*

This statement has caused impassioned debate among theologians about the nature of the incarnation and the balance between

Jesus' divinity and His humanity, but that wasn't Jesus' point. He was simply stating that, even for Him, knowledge of the day and hour of His return was not need to know information. And He, in His complete submission and obedience to His Father, was fine with that.

Jesus refused to focus on or become obsessed with what the Father had not divulged to Him. Instead, He simply focused on doing the job that He had been given to do, on obeying the Father day by day, hour by hour, moment by moment, and was content to leave all the rest in the hands of the Father.

And that's the approach that He recommended for all of His disciples, as the parable He told clearly shows. When a man goes away and leaves his servants with work to accomplish before his return, he does not want those servants to spend a single moment searching through his papers looking for clues as to how long he might be gone, and arguing among themselves as to when his return might happen. Nor does he want to find them sleeping or goofing off, figuring that they'll get right on the job as soon as they see him coming up the walkway. He wants to return at his own time and find those servants hard at work on the job that he left for them. The work left with the servants is important to the master, more important than anything else that the servants could do in his absence, or he wouldn't have commanded the servants to do it in the first place.

In the same way, Jesus has left a very important job for all of His disciples to do in His absence: to go and make disciples of all nations (Matthew 28:19-20). And He wants us to be focused on that work while He's gone. He wants to find all of those who go by His name hard at work at it when He returns. If someone spends all of their time and energy trying to figure out the day and hour of His return, and neglecting that most important work, even if they get the date and time exactly right, they are most likely to hear from Jesus' lips not "Well done good and faithful servant," but "That's nice, but did you do the work that I commanded you to do? Did you go and make disciples of all nations? Where are the ones who have come to me through your work and your witness?"

WHEN WE LISTEN

Many believe that evangelism is only the work of a few in the Church, the professionals, or those called specifically to be evangelists. But all we need to do is to look at the lives of those first-century disciples to see that the vast majority of them excitedly spread the gospel wherever they went.

Whole communities of believers sprang up all over the Empire (including Rome) from those who received Jesus at Pentecost and carried their faith back to their homes with them. And even after the stoning of Stephen, when persecution broke out, and *all except the apostles were scattered throughout the land of Judea and Samaria* (Acts 8:1), Luke goes on to tell us that *those who were scattered went on their way preaching the word* (Acts 8:4). They understood that the work of making disciples was vital. If people didn't hear about Jesus, they couldn't believe. And if they didn't believe, they would end up separated from God in hell for all eternity.

These believers didn't know when Jesus would return, but that wasn't so important to them. They had been given a job to do, to go and make disciples of all nations, and when Jesus returned, whenever that might be, they were determined that He would find them on the job, with fruit to show from their labors.

Pray with me:

Father, forgive us for letting this job too often fall by the wayside, while we allow ourselves to get pulled aside into other things: our work, our entertainments, our hobbies, and even trying to figure out when Jesus is coming back. Instill in us anew a deep understanding of how vital it is that we be making disciples, each and every one of us. And vital not just for those we help into the kingdom so that they can be saved, but vital to us as well, so that when Jesus comes back, whenever You determine that will be, He finds us faithfully on the job. Amen.

MARK 14:1-2

Read with me:

It was two days before the Passover and the Festival of Unleavened Bread. The chief priests and the scribes were looking for a cunning way to arrest Jesus and kill him. "Not during the festival," they said, "so that there won't be a riot among the people."

Listen with me:

The Passover, one of the three most holy days on the Jewish calendar, was near, only two days away. Even so, the attention of the chief priests and teachers of the law was not on preparing themselves for the celebration, to make sure that they were ceremonially clean beyond question. Instead, they were focused on Jesus – how to arrest Him and kill Him, in order to rid themselves of Him once and for all.

The only indication that that they were even aware of the coming feast was the fact that they discussed that it would be a bad time to arrest Jesus. They feared that the people, many of whom considered Jesus a prophet or more, would riot.

These men who claimed to be among the holiest, most God-fearing people on the planet, had completely lost track of God in their anger and frustration at Jesus (ironically, the one who had been sent by God Himself to show them just how ungodly they really were!) Even on the very eve of their feast that celebrated God freeing their ancestors from bondage, they had no idea that they had allowed themselves to be bound up in chains far stronger and heavier than anything ever worn by those who had gone before them – chains of hatred, anger, pride, judgmentalism, coveting, and even murder. They were oblivious to the state of their own hearts.

WHEN WE LISTEN

It's no wonder that Jesus' primary response to these men was sadness, accurately mirroring God's own broken heart over them. It was just a few days earlier that Jesus had wept over the city of Jerusalem, crying out, *"If you knew this day what would bring peace—but now it is hidden from your eyes. For the days will come on you when your enemies will build a barricade around you, surround you, and hem you in on every side. They will crush you and your children among you to the ground, and they will not leave one stone on another in your midst, because you did not recognize the time when God visited you."* (Luke 19:42-44) It was just hours earlier that He had cried out, *"Jerusalem, Jerusalem, who kills the prophets and stones those who are sent to her. How often I wanted to gather your children together, as a hen gathers her chicks under her wings, but you were not willing! See, your house is left to you desolate. For I tell you, you will not see me again until you say, 'Blessed is he who comes in the name of the Lord.'"* (Matthew 23:37-39)

It was a real tragedy when these same men, after they had beaten Jesus, condemned Him, an innocent man, of blasphemy, and pressured Pilate to condemn Him to death; after they had seen Him hanging on the cross pouring out His lifeblood on the ground; after all that, they went to the temple and sacrificed their Passover lamb, feasting and celebrating, smug in their sureness that God was well pleased with them, and would surely pour out His blessing into their lives.

Pray with me:

Father, it is easy to see the application to our own lives of this chapter from history. Help us to never get so caught up in our religion, our sacred practices and spiritual disciplines, help us to never feel so sure of our own righteousness that we completely miss the point where we have turned off of Your way. Help us to never have our eyes so focused on ourselves and our agendas that we end up actively working against You and Your agenda without even realizing it. Help us instead to walk in step with You, to keep our whole attention and the whole force of our will focused on what You are doing around us. Amen.

MARK 14:3-9

Read with me:

While he was in Bethany at the house of Simon the leper, as he was re-clining at the table, a woman came with an alabaster jar of very expensive perfume of pure nard. She broke the jar and poured it on his head. But some were expressing indignation to one another: "Why has this perfume been wasted? For this perfume might have been sold for more than three hundred denarii and given to the poor." And they began to scold her.

Jesus replied, "Leave her alone. Why are you bothering her? She has done a noble thing for me. You always have the poor with you, and you can do what is good for them whenever you want, but you do not always have me. She has done what she could; she has anointed my body in advance for burial. Truly I tell you, wherever the gospel is proclaimed in the whole world, what she has done will also be told in memory of her."

Listen with me:

On this night, a simple act of devotion quickly turned into an occasion for conflict and a clash of worldviews. The disciples still had no idea what was coming – that in just a couple of days their Lord and Master would be hanging dead on a cross, so badly beaten that He was barely recognizable. All they knew was that things seemed to be going pretty smoothly. Jesus had been hailed as a conquering hero just a few days ago, and he had handily won every debate with the Pharisees, the scribes, and even the chief priests. As they saw it, things were looking up!

They were at the home of Simon the Leper in Bethany having dinner when Mary, the sister of Lazarus, walked in (John 12:1-8). She was carrying a very expensive alabaster jar of pure nard, a distillation from the root of the spikenard plant, but nobody paid much attention to her. That was until she walked over to where Jesus was reclining at the table, pulled out the jar, and broke the wax seal. The strong aroma of the perfume immediately filled the room, drawing the attention of everyone. She then poured the precious perfume on Jesus' head, and on His feet, wiping his feet with her hair (John 12:3), an act of staggering devotion and honor.

It was a precious moment, one that could have served as an immediate object lesson to everyone gathered in the room. But the clash of worldviews erupted almost immediately. Judas (John 12:4) focused on the cost of the perfume – three hundred denarii, or about a year's wages for a common laborer – protested that instead of just being poured out on Jesus, the perfume could have done so much more if it had been sold, and the money given to the poor. And others joined him in his opinion.

But Jesus quickly put a stop to the discussion by His terse, *"Leave her alone. Why are you bothering her?"* Mary knew how much the perfume was worth, how precious it was. In fact, that was precisely the reason that she had chosen to use it as she had. She owed Jesus so much. Jesus had shown her the way of salvation. And just a short time ago He had restored her brother, Lazarus, to life after he had been dead for four days! She was so profoundly grateful that nothing was too precious for Jesus; nothing was too costly. Every drop poured out on Him was a song of thanks to the one who had saved her brother and changed her life.

But in all of this Jesus saw a deeper meaning, one that even Mary was not consciously aware of. Jesus knew that in just a couple of days' time, as the sun was setting on the upcoming Friday, His cold, lifeless body would be taken hurriedly down from the cross, and quickly placed in a borrowed tomb, so as not to extend past sundown, when the Sabbath would begin. Even though Joseph of Arimathea and Nicodemus would quickly pack some spices among the wrappings, there would be no time to properly wash and anoint His body, showing proper respect for the dead. So Jesus accepted this sacrificial outpouring of love, devotion, and fragrant oil as the anointing of His body prior to His burial.

MARK 14

Pray with me:

Father, Jesus told His disciples that those who wanted to follow Him should first count the cost, and make sure that they were willing to pay it: "Every one of you who does not renounce all his possessions cannot be my disciple." (Luke 14:33) Mary understood that. She had committed her whole life to Jesus, and everything that she had, she was willing to lay at his feet, regardless of the cost, regardless of the value. Lord, help me to remember how much I have received from You: blessing upon blessing, Your love, Your presence, and most of all, salvation and eternal life paid for by the precious blood of Jesus. Lord, if that doesn't make my heart as generous toward You as Mary's was toward Jesus, I am in bad shape! Thank You, Father, again, and again, and again for all You have done for me. Amen!

MARK 14:10-11

Read with me:

Then Judas Iscariot, one of the Twelve, went to the chief priests to betray Jesus to them. And when they heard this, they were glad and promised to give him money. So he started looking for a good opportunity to betray him.

Listen with me:

Many kind-hearted souls try to make excuses for Judas, teaching that he was simply misguided, or even that he was someone whose intentions in betraying Jesus were actually honorable – that he was simply trying to force Jesus' hand, encouraging Him to take the strong actions needed for Him to declare Himself king.

But Judas was not an honorable man, let alone an altruistic one. As John pointed out in his gospel, even before the incident at Simon the Leper's house (Mark 14:3-9), which seemed to be a tipping point for him, Judas had been stealing from the bag of money that had been donated to help with the needs of Jesus and His disciples (John 12:6). It was no noble desire that moved him to go to the chief priests with the offer of betrayal, but the desire for money.

Theologians have long debated why Jesus would ever recruit someone like Judas to be His disciple, let alone to be one of His twelve closest followers. And if Jesus had known that Judas would steal from the money bag, why did He entrust it to Him?

The simple answer to both of those is that God the Father told Him to do it, and He simply obeyed (John 5:19). God had always known which of Jesus' followers would ultimately betray Him, so when Judas began to follow Jesus, he was brought all the way into the inner circle. That seems counterintuitive to many, but there were two key reasons that this was the right thing to do. First, by bringing Judas into a close and even trusted relationship with Jesus, he had every possible opportunity to change tracks. If he had opened his heart, he could have grown to love Jesus like the others did, developing a bond and loyalty to Him that would have drawn him toward Jesus and the kingdom that He had come to bring. But even demonstrations of conspicuous trust, such as entrusting him with the money bag, and even giving him power and authority to heal diseases and cast out demons (Matthew 10:1) had failed to melt his hard heart, which was strongly attached not only to money, but to the glory and power that he hoped would come to him through being so closely attached to someone like Jesus. With so much opportunity to change, so many chances to turn away from the pursuit of the world and its riches, Judas' ultimate refusal to change brings his condemnation down on his own head.

Secondly, if Judas had not been in the inner circle, he would not have been in as strong a position to betray Jesus, bringing about everything that was foretold. He would not have had as strong a credibility with the chief priests, and he would not have been as likely to have known where Jesus would be camping that night. He might not have even been with Jesus in Jerusalem during that Passover.

The plain truth is that Judas was a man with a bad heart, a heart that even the unconditional love shown to him by Jesus was not able to touch. His priorities were not those of the kingdom of God, and when he realized that following Jesus was not going to lead to wealth and power, he turned elsewhere, even if it meant betraying the one who had loved him and shown him the light of God's glory.

Pray with me:

Father, this is a sad story. It is hard to imagine how one who had lived with Jesus for years, who had listened to His teaching, seen His mightiest miracles, and even been empowered by Him to do miracles himself, could ever betray Him. But there are still people like that in the world today. Their hearts are hard, their priorities are of this world, and even unconditional love doesn't seem to make a dent. But, Lord, help me to always remember that there are also many with bad hearts, even hearts that are desperately bad, and who have terrible priorities, who CAN be changed by Your love, Your grace, Your salvation. (I myself was one of them!) Help me, like Jesus, to not write people off who seem to be hard cases, but to draw them in, to show them Your love, Your wonders, Your trust, and allow You every chance to work in their lives. Amen.

MARK 14:12-16

Read with me:

On the first day of Unleavened Bread, when they sacrifice the Passover lamb, his disciples asked him, "Where do you want us to go and prepare the Passover so that you may eat it?"

So he sent two of his disciples and told them, "Go into the city, and a man carrying a jar of water will meet you. Follow him. Wherever he enters, tell the owner of the house, 'The Teacher says, "Where is my guest room where I may eat the Passover with my disciples?"' He will show you a large room upstairs, furnished and ready. Make the preparations for us there." So the disciples went out, entered the city, and found it just as he had told them, and they prepared the Passover.

Listen with me:

As God provided everything for Jesus, so He provided even a place in crowded Jerusalem for Him to celebrate this last Passover feast with His disciples. All that was needed was for His followers to go and find it. And Jesus' concise instructions were very easy to follow.

Jesus' death occurring during the Passover had great symbolic meaning. The Passover itself celebrated the Israelites' release from the bondage of slavery in Egypt 1500 years before. Jesus' death provided release from the bondage of sin and death. As the blood of the spotless Passover lamb smeared on the doorposts of the Israelites' houses saved them from death at the hand of the destroying angel, so Jesus' blood, poured out on the cross, saves all who trust in Him from the second death in the lake of fire (Revelation 20:14-15).

The disciples, even after three years with Jesus, were surprised to find everything just the way He had told them it would be. When they entered Jerusalem, teeming with people because of the feast, they quickly saw a man carrying a jar of water – unusual, because women usually did the work of carrying water. When they followed him to his house and asked the owner where the guest room was where the Teacher could eat the Passover with His disciples, they were instantly shown to the large upper room Jesus had told them about. (This room would actually become their headquarters and gathering place over the next several weeks.)

There is some debate as to whether Jesus had pre-arranged all of this, or whether this was an instance of prophecy on His part. But that debate misses the main point, which is that Jesus went through His whole life and ministry trusting that His Father would provide everything that He needed, right when He needed it, and that He would be shown where to find it. Jesus wanted the disciples to develop that same reliance on God and His provision, so that they would know how to rely on their Father in heaven after Jesus had gone.

Pray with me:

Father, I'm afraid that a lot of that discussion and debate comes because we are so used to organizing and orchestrating things for ourselves, that we usually have little opportunity to see You work in these kinds of powerful ways to provide for our needs. Help me, Lord, to look to You more frequently for what I need instead of trying to provide my own security by preparing my own way and doing so much in my own strength, according to my own plans. Amen.

MARK 14:17-21

Read with me:

When evening came, he arrived with the Twelve. While they were reclining and eating, Jesus said, "Truly I tell you, one of you will betray me — one who is eating with me."

They began to be distressed and to say to him one by one, "Surely not I?"

He said to them, "It is one of the Twelve — the one who is dipping bread in the bowl with me. For the Son of Man will go just as it is written about him, but woe to that man by whom the Son of Man is betrayed! It would have been better for him if he had not been born."

Listen with me:

It was the last thing they expected to hear from Jesus' lips. There had been many dinners with Jesus and His twelve closest disciples, but this one was different. Behind the celebration of the Passover, and the prayers, and the ceremony, there was a solemnity, a seriousness, an earnestness in all of Jesus' words and actions that they had not seen before.

He had already startled His disciples by insisting on washing their feet (John 13:3-17), a task usually done by a servant or one of the children of the household. But now, during a lull in the conversation, He shocked them still further by announcing that one of them, one of the twelve people closest to Him, would betray Him.

They could tell from His expression, His whole demeanor, that this was no joke. They all knew that Jesus often knew what was going to happen before it did. Did He know who the betrayer would be? Eleven hearts wondered if they could possibly do such a thing to Jesus, while one heart was filled with sudden dread, dismay that somehow he had been found out.

313

WHEN WE LISTEN

Yes, Jesus knew precisely who would betray Him. He knew, in fact, that the deed had already been done. The money had changed hands, and all that was left was the actual confrontation, which would come in just a couple of hours.

Jesus understood that even this betrayal was part of the ultimate plan, the plan that would lead to His shame and suffering, to the cross and death. But He knew that it also led beyond the cross to resurrection and eternal victory. But for Judas, this path that he had chosen would lead him away from the light he had experienced in Jesus into eternal darkness.

Even though Jesus had seen this coming from the beginning, it still broke His heart that someone He had poured so much of Himself into, someone who had only received love and respect from Him, could betray Him. Even now His heart went out to Judas, the one who would shortly lead a cohort of temple guards to Jesus' camp, and with a kiss would set into motion the events that would ultimately rock the world.

Pray with me:

Father, at first glance, it is inconceivable to me how someone who had experienced so much in Your presence could still turn away from you and betray Jesus like that – throwing all You had done for him back in Your face. But then I look back at my own history, and am shocked to find that I, too, once betrayed You. There was a time as a teen when I turned away from You and sought my own way. I didn't think at the time how much of a betrayal this was, how similar my heart at that time was to the heart of Judas's – cold and hard enough to be able to throw all that You had done for me back in Your face. I thank You, Lord, that in spite of all of that, You didn't give up on me, didn't just throw me on the ash heap and wash Your hands of me. It took more than ten years for my heart to finally break over my betrayal of You; more than ten years wasted in the "far country" before I was willing to really repent. But when I finally heard Your voice, when I turned my tear-stained face upward for the first time in years and cried out, "Save me!" You did.

You forgave even my betrayal of You, and restored "the years that the locust ate." (Joel 2:25) Such love! Such grace! Such unfathomable mercy that You showed to me, Your one-time betrayer! I will love You forever, Lord! Amen.

WHEN WE LISTEN

MARK 14:22-26

Read with me:

As they were eating, he took bread, blessed and broke it, gave it to them, and said, "Take it; this is my body." Then he took a cup, and after giving thanks, he gave it to them, and they all drank from it. He said to them, "This is my blood of the covenant; which is poured out for many. Truly I tell you: I will no longer drink of the fruit of the vine until that day when I drink it new in the kingdom of God."
After singing a hymn, they went out to the Mount of Olives.

Listen with me:

The unleavened bread and wine were a normal part of the Passover meal. But as the meal progressed that night, Jesus began to fill these familiar symbols with new meaning.

The unleavened bread was a symbol of the deliverance of Israel from Egypt. On the night of the first Passover, the Israelites were instructed to make and eat their meal quickly, without even giving the bread time to rise (Exodus 12:11, 39). And the Jewish people ate unleavened bread for a full week starting with the Passover as a remembrance of that event.

Over time, yeast became a kind of symbol for sin, because both yeast and sin multiply quickly and affect everything nearby, spreading until it has affected the whole batch of dough. When Jesus presented the bread to His followers that night, both meanings were very pertinent. The giving of Jesus' body in just a few hours was going to be the mechanism to provide deliverance for the people of the world from their bondage to sin and death. Also, Jesus had lived a completely sinless life, so His body, symbolically given to the disciples in the bread, was pure and holy – without sin. Thus Jesus had no sin of His own that had to be paid for by His death. So

316

His death would be accepted as payment for the sins of all humanity.

The cup symbolized and celebrated the Old Covenant given on Mt. Sinai – a covenant sealed with the blood of bulls, and sheep, and goats. Jesus reinterpreted this cup to symbolize the new covenant, sealed with His own blood that He was preparing to pour out on the cross.

Jesus did not drink the wine that night (Luke 22:17-18). Some have believed that it was because He didn't want the alcohol to dull His senses. But the amount that He would have gotten from that cup that was shared all around would have been very small, and out of His system before His arrest. Right at that moment, Jesus was making the transition Himself from the Old Covenant to the New Covenant. He would drink wine again, but not until that transition had been completed.

This reinterpretation of the Passover meal was a powerful symbol that His disciples never forgot. And these elements have become a central part of Christian worship to this day, reminding all who partake of them that they are part of the holy Body of Christ, the people of the New Covenant that was made once and for all with the blood of the Lamb.

Pray with me:

Father, it always strikes me when we take communion how rich the symbolism is. And the fact that we, as Your people, are joining others all around the world in this same ceremony of remembrance is a powerful reminder of the fact that we are all one in You. Thank you for these symbols, and thank You for the reality that lies behind them. Amen!

MARK 14:27-31

Read with me:

Then Jesus said to them, "All of you will fall away, because it is written: **I will strike the shepherd, and the sheep will be scattered.** *[Zechariah 13:7] But after I have risen, I will go ahead of you to Galilee."*

Peter told Him, "Even if everyone falls away, I will not!"

"Truly I tell you," Jesus said to him, "today, this very night, before the rooster crows twice, you will deny me three times!"

But he kept insisting, "If I have to die with you, I will never deny you!" And they all said the same thing.

Listen with me:

Jesus knew exactly what would happen, because it was all prophesied very clearly. He had already been betrayed for thirty pieces of silver, just as it had been foretold (Zechariah 11:12). And now, as His time grew short, He knew from Zechariah 13:7 that when He was arrested, all of the disciples would flee, leaving Him alone to face all of the suffering and anguish that was in store for Him.

Obviously the twelve protested this. They had faced hard times and conflicts before, and had remained at Jesus' side. They would stand with Him no matter what happened. Peter was especially vocal in His support – even if everybody else fell away, he would stand firm. But Jesus knew Peter better than Peter knew himself. He knew that behind that mask of bravado lay an unsanctified heart, a fleshly heart that, when push came to shove, would seek survival above all else.

But even though Jesus knew that ALL of the disciples would flee at the critical moment (Peter's denial was simply the most tragic of the desertions), He was already looking beyond their failure, beyond their betrayal to His victory and resurrection, and to the time when they would all find restoration, when He would go ahead of them to Galilee (verse 28). There would be failure on a massive scale, but there was restoration waiting just over the horizon.

Pray with me:

Father, it is comforting to our souls to know that our failures do not have to be the end, as long as we seek restoration. That was the main difference between Peter and Judas. Both betrayed Jesus. But Peter's heart was bound to Jesus, and desired above all else to be loyal and faithful, even when his flesh failed him. Judas, on the other hand, had already turned his heart away from Jesus, even before he betrayed Him. And when he was later stricken with pangs of guilt, he did not seek restoration. Instead, he merely sought relief from his guilt, and tried to find it in suicide (Matthew 27:3-5). Father, help me to always have a heart like Peter's; a heart that, in any failure or fault, seeks restoration above all else; a heart that repents powerfully; a heart that can be restored completely. Amen.

WHEN WE LISTEN

MARK 14:32-36, 39

Read with me:

Then they came to a place named Gethsemane, and he told his disciples, "Sit here while I pray." He took Peter, James, and John with him, and he began to be deeply distressed and troubled. He said to them, "I am deeply grieved to the point of death. Remain here and stay awake." He went a little farther, fell to the ground, and prayed that if it were possible, the hour might pass from him. And he said, "Abba, Father! All things are possible for you. Take this cup away from me. Nevertheless, not what I will, but what you will."...Once again he went away and prayed, saying the same thing.

Listen with me:

Jesus was standing right on the cusp of events that would not only challenge Him to His very core, but that would shake history. And what He was seeing ahead was daunting, to say the least. He knew that He had already been betrayed – heartbreaking in itself to think that someone into whom He had poured three years of His life could lift up his heel against Him like that. He also knew that once He had been arrested, the rest of His closest followers would run, leaving Him bereft of any human intimacy.

All of that saddened His heart beyond measure, leaving Him feeling alone even before the events unfolded. But it was what He saw beyond all of that that chilled His soul. He saw the shame and disgrace of being mocked and beaten by the guards of the high priests. He saw the pain and the agony of the lashes He would receive at the hands of the Roman soldiers. He could already hear the jeers of the crowds as He carried the heavy crossbar of the cross through the streets of the city; crowds that just five days earlier had hailed Him as their king. He already felt the agony of the nails being driven through His hands and feet, the shame of hanging

320

helpless and utterly naked along the road into the city, the burning thirst from the profound loss of blood, and even the agony of seeing His own mother on the verge of total collapse from a grief too heavy to bear as she watched Him die.

But all of that was nothing compared to the ultimate horror that loomed before Him. He knew that on the cross He would endure all of the shame, all of the suffering, all of the untold agony that had been earned by the sins of all of the people in the world. And He knew that, in that moment, He would even experience the vast separation from His Father that those sins deserved. The Son of God, who had been one with the Father from all eternity (John 17:5), who, even as a human man, still experienced His presence every moment, would, for the first time, be completely alone.

Jesus could see all of this clearly. He had known that this moment was coming from before the world was created (Revelation 13:8). But now that it was here, now that all of these events would be starting in mere minutes, His human flesh wanted to draw back from pain and suffering that would go far beyond anything physical.

But Jesus, when His flesh was weak and afraid, did not pull away from the Father. Instead, He ran to Him in prayer. His request was basically, "If there is any other way to do this, let's do it that other way. If there is any way to avoid what is coming, I would prefer to avoid it." But, in the end, His prayer was, "Not what I will, but what You will." "If this is the only way to accomplish what you want to do, I'm in."

At that moment, Jesus knew that the events were set, and that, no matter how much His flesh revolted or wanted to pull back, He was committed, and His soul, completely sold out to God and His will, would be in control over His flesh. Jesus came away from those moments of passionate prayer energized, empowered, strengthened, and completely committed to the plan laid out by the Father. From that moment on, there was no fear, no timidity. Instead, there was a firm resolve to accomplish the mission, to gain the victory, even if the way led through the pain of the cross, and the dark chill of the tomb. He knew with all of His knowing that the end would be glory.

WHEN WE LISTEN

Pray with me:

Father, even in His time of greatest challenge, Jesus is our role model. Help me, Lord, when facing my greatest challenges, to run to You, not away from You. Help me to seek You for the strength and resolve that I need to do everything You have called me to do. And help me to do everything with the power and passion that can only come through the heartfelt prayer, "Nevertheless not what I will, but what you will." Amen.

MARK 14:37-42

Read with me:

Then he came and found them sleeping. He said to Peter, "Simon, are you sleeping? Couldn't you stay awake one hour? Stay awake and pray so that you won't enter into temptation. The spirit is willing, but the flesh is weak." Once again he went away and prayed, saying the same thing. And again he came and found them sleeping, because they could not keep their eyes open. They did not know what to say to him. Then he came a third time and said to them, "Are you still sleeping and resting? Enough! The time has come. See, the Son of Man is betrayed into the hands of sinners. Get up; let's go. See, my betrayer is near."

Listen with me:

The disciples had heard Jesus' words at the dinner about being betrayed, but they had no idea what that would look like. They heard the urgency in His voice as He taught them, but they had no idea that this was the night when it would all come down. So when Jesus went off to pray near their campsite, they did not pick up on the fact that their own time of testing was right around the corner.

Even when Peter, James, and John were called to go further with Him, and told about the sorrow and agony that His heart was going through, they were blind to the fact that the betrayer was already on the way, leading a group of armed men to arrest Jesus.

And so their souls were not on the alert. Their bodies were fatigued, and Jesus' warning to "keep watch" found no resting place in their minds. As Jesus agonized with the Father over the terrible things that were already afoot, which would be revealed in mere moments, the disciples fell asleep.

Jesus' rebuke was much gentler than it could have been. Even in the depth of His sorrow, He still loved these clueless men.

His exasperated instruction, urging Peter to "Stay awake and pray so that you won't enter into temptation" was an attempt to clue them all in, Peter especially, that this was a dangerous moment. Peter had sworn only a couple of hours before, "If I have to die with you, I will never deny you." (Mark 14:31) But Jesus understood that though the spirit was willing to die with Him, the flesh was weak. In the moment when he would have to choose, Peter's flesh was going to have the upper hand, because his spirit, though willing, was not on the alert, and was not fortified with prayer.

The disciples were ashamed and embarrassed that they were so weak, that they had fallen asleep not once, but three times, while Jesus was praying in such distress. But after He woke them the third time, it was too late to pray. The time when preparation could be done had passed. Now, whether they were ready or not, the moment was upon them.

We human beings are, by nature, short sighted, much like the sheep that Jesus compared us to. All too often we shrink at shadows in the dark, but utterly fail to see and understand the real spiritual dangers until they are upon us. Jesus could see the danger coming because of His intimate connection with the Father. He was in communion with God, ever listening to His voice, immediately responsive to His every leading. Nothing took Him by surprise. When His betrayer came, He was prayed up. He was on task. He was ready.

Pray with me:

Father, I can absolutely relate to the disciples more than to Jesus on this point. I really am short-sighted when it comes to being able to see what lies ahead. And I can also clearly understand that the reason behind that short-sightedness is primarily that I spend much more time with my focus on the physical realm than on the spiritual. I measure my prayer time with You in minutes, or even moments, and let my mind be taken up with worldly affairs for the hours that are left of each day. No wonder things take me by surprise! Father, help me to keep my communion with You open at all times. Help me, as Paul urged, to pray constantly (1 Thessalonians 5:17), to listen carefully to Your voice in every situation, and to never be caught sleeping when I should be watching and praying. Amen.

WHEN WE LISTEN

MARK 14:43-52

Read with me:

While He was still speaking, Judas, one of the Twelve, suddenly arrived. With him was a mob, with swords and clubs, from the chief priests, the scribes, and the elders. His betrayer had given them a signal. "The one I kiss," he said, "he's the one; arrest him and take him away under guard." So when he came, immediately he went up to Jesus and said, "Rabbi!" and kissed Him. They took hold of him and arrested him. One of those who stood by drew his sword, struck the high priest's servant, and cut off his ear.

Jesus said to them, "Have you come out with swords and clubs, as if I were a criminal, to capture me? Every day I was among you, teaching in the temple, and you didn't arrest me. But the Scriptures must be fulfilled."

Then they all deserted him and ran away. Now a certain young man, wearing nothing but a linen cloth, was following him. They caught hold of him, but he left the linen cloth behind and ran away naked.

Listen with me:

The crowd of men was armed when they came after Jesus because they were afraid of Him. They had never really gotten to know who He was, because they were violently opposed to what He stood for. They saw Him not as a preacher or a teacher, but as an enemy, and that made them fear Him. They also feared His disciples and what they might do when their leader was arrested. (With good reason, it turned out, as Peter sliced off Malchus' ear – John 18:10.)

Judas agreed to the signal of a kiss because in the dim moonlight and shadow of the garden, it would be easy to waste precious moments going after the wrong person. Judas had spent enough time with Jesus that he knew Him even in the dark. With a kiss on the cheek, and a softly spoken "Rabbi" (my teacher), the deed was done, the betrayal was complete, and unstoppable events were set into motion.

Jesus' disciples bravely stood alongside Jesus as long as it looked like He was putting up a fight. They figured that Jesus would give these guards a tongue lashing and that they, like all of Jesus' enemies, would simply slink away with their tails between their legs as they had at other times. But suddenly Jesus simply ended the conversation with "But the Scriptures must be fulfilled," and surrendered to them.

At that moment, all of Jesus' prophecies were fulfilled, both the several times He had told His disciples that He would be handed over to be killed (Mark 8:31-32, 9:30-32 for a couple of examples), and His prophecy that the disciples would all desert Him (Mark 14:27-31). All of them literally did desert Him, leaving Him to face His arrest, trial, and execution alone. It turned out that Peter wasn't the only one with a willing spirit but weak flesh!

Pray with me:

Father, it is easy for us to make all kinds of grandiose promises when things are easy. When the road is level and smooth, it is easy to promise to walk with You a thousand miles. But only You can see the whole road, not just the level path of the present, but also the steep up- and down-grades that lie just around the next bend. Only You see the portions of the road that hug close to sheer cliffs, with terrifying chasms that will make us faint with terror. Only You know the long stretches through deserts where there is no water. In the end, the only way for us to really be able to follow You all the way is to listen when You describe the road ahead, not denying the reality of what You are saying, or trying to argue You out of going that way (as Peter did, and as we are all sometimes guilty of), and then promise that when the road gets scary, we will stand by You and hang on, with Your help. Then, of course, we have to stay prayed up so that we will not fall into the temptation to cut and run when the enemy closes in for the attack. I don't have it in me to stand up for You and for the gospel on my own. And I don't really want to end up like that young man, all of my faith stripped away, retreating in nakedness and shame. Trust and prayer is the only way. Amen.

MARK 14:53-61A

Read with me:

They led Jesus away to the high priest, and all the chief priests, the elders, and the scribes assembled. Peter followed him at a distance, right into the high priest's courtyard. He was sitting with the servants, warming himself by the fire.

The chief priests and the whole Sanhedrin were looking for testimony against Jesus to put him to death, but they could not find any. For many were giving false testimony against him, and the testimonies did not agree. Some stood up and gave false testimony against him, stating, "We heard him say, 'I will destroy this temple made with human hands, and in three days I will build another not made by hands.'" Yet their testimony did not agree even on this.

Then the high priest stood up before them all and questioned Jesus, "Don't you have an answer to what these men are testifying against You?" But He kept silent and did not answer.

Listen with me:

It was very frustrating for the Sanhedrin. There were very few offenses that they could hope to pin on Jesus that would result in the death penalty, but that was the only sentence that they were interested in. So instead of beginning with a crime and evidence, and then figuring out what the sentence should be, they started with the sentence, and then tried to find a crime that would lead to it. A complete inversion of justice. That's how far their hatred of Jesus had taken them.

The easiest death sentence crime to prove (or to trump up) was blasphemy, commonly interpreted as either cursing God, or encouraging the worship of something other than God. But, of course, Jesus had never done either of those things. Even though they were able to recruit a number of false witnesses, people who, for a variety of reasons, were willing to swear that they had heard Jesus say something that He never said, the testimony of two or more of them had to agree, as it did in all death sentence cases. But it never did.

The closest that they could get to a testimony of blasphemy was the man who accurately quoted something Jesus had said some time before, without having a clue as to the context or the meaning of it. Jesus had been asked for a sign to prove that He had authority to throw the money changers and merchants out of the temple courts early in His public ministry. At that time He had said, *"Destroy this temple, and I will raise it up in three days."* (John 2:18-19) But even in this semi-accurate testimony of Jesus' words there were two huge problems. First, even here the testimony of two witnesses did not agree. And second, even if they had agreed, this statement might be written off as the ravings of a lunatic, but it did not in any way rise to the level of blasphemy. Not even close.

They knew that the only way for them to prove blasphemy was if they could somehow get Jesus to make a statement or two in their presence that they could twist in that direction. But their first efforts at this failed miserably. Jesus, challenged to answer the false charges that were being leveled against Him one after another, knew that none of these charges was giving them what they needed to convict Him. So He simply stayed silent.

The chief priest tried to pressure Him based on nothing more than the large number of false witnesses that had testified – surely with this many accusers, even if their stories didn't jibe, Jesus must be doing something wrong. But Jesus refused to play their game. If He tried to defend Himself against these false charges, it would only stoke the fire. Jesus knew how this trial would turn out, but He wasn't going to step deliberately into their trap and give them a chance to put Him on the defensive. He was in control of the whole situation, as they would soon see.

MARK 14

Pray with me:

Father, Jesus' wisdom and intelligence shown here is really mind boggling. How many of us would have the patience (Greek makrothumia, meaning "long-suffering") to listen to person after person making up stories about us, and not rise to the bait and, in the process, by an unfortunate quote, or a slip of the lip, inadvertently give our adversaries enough ammo to sink us. Jesus knew how this would all end, but He wanted it to be clear to everyone that even His worst enemies couldn't find anything that He was doing that was sinful or wrong. He wanted it to be clear that, when He was crucified, He was dying for no sin of His own. Help me to live a life of such holiness that, like Jesus, no charges can stick, except for the charge of being a follower of Jesus. And help me anytime persecution arises, to entrust myself to Your hands, and to answer only as You direct. Amen.

WHEN WE LISTEN

MARK 14:61B-65

Read with me:

Again the high priest questioned him, "Are you the Messiah, the Son of the Blessed One?"

*"I am," said Jesus, "and you will see **the Son of Man seated at the right hand** of Power and **coming with the clouds of heaven."** [Psalm 110:1; Daniel 7:13]*

Then the high priest tore his robes and said, "Why do we still need witnesses? You have heard the blasphemy. What is your decision?" They all condemned him as deserving death.

Then some began to spit on him, to blindfold him, and to beat him, saying, "Prophesy!" The temple servants also took him and slapped him.

Listen with me:

Jesus was not interested in saying a single word to defend Himself against false accusations. But, as He always did, He never hesitated to identify Himself as the Messiah when He was directly asked. So when the chief priest asked, "Are you the Messiah, the Son of the Blessed One?" Jesus would not be silent. His answer was unequivocal: "I am." He was indeed the Messiah, and He was indeed the Son of God Himself.

But this was not an argument about titles or theologies. Those sitting in judgment over Jesus had no idea who was really standing in front of them. They had no conception that the one they had been hating, the one with whom they had been arguing, the one they had been plotting against for years was actually the very God that they claimed to serve, in the flesh. All they saw with their black hearts and their sin-darkened eyes was a man who had annoyed them, who had held up a clear mirror to their sins and spiritual deformity, and who therefore must be done away with.

But Jesus gave them the whole truth. Not only was He the Messiah, but He would sit at God's right hand, making Himself equal to God. And He would come in the clouds of heaven, a reference that all of those scholars would immediately understand as a claim to divinity.

Jesus was speaking the truth, but to the ears of His accusers, this was the blasphemy they had been trying to find. *"We have a law, and according to that law he ought to die, because he made himself the Son of God."* they later told Pilate (John 19:7). To his credit, when Pilate heard that, he had the good sense to be afraid of who might be standing before him.

The Sanhedrin, on the other hand, were simply overcome with glee. They believed that by their great cleverness they had gotten Jesus to slip and expose Himself to the charge of blasphemy. They rejoiced underneath their feigned shock and dismay at the "blasphemy" they had just heard. They smiled as they tore their robes in mock distress. And then they spit on their Messiah; they punched the One who had come to offer them eternal life at His own expense. They believed that they had won a great victory in the moment of their most profound fall.

Pray with me:

Father, sometimes we can be so blinded by our presumptions, our assumptions of what the truth is, and even our prejudices, that we fail to see the truth that is standing right in front of us. Lord, help me to keep my vision clear, so that I can see all that You want to show me. Keep my heart open, so that I will never deny Your truth when it comes. Amen.

WHEN WE LISTEN

MARK 14:66-72

Read with me:

While Peter was in the courtyard below, one of the high priest's maidservants came. When she saw Peter warming himself, she looked at him and said, "You also were with Jesus, the man from Nazareth."

But he denied it: "I don't know or understand what you're talking about!" Then he went out to the entryway, and a rooster crowed.

When the maidservant saw him again, she began to tell those standing nearby, "This man is one of them!"

But again he denied it. After a little while those standing there said to Peter again, "You certainly are one of them, since you're also a Galilean!"

Then he started to curse and to swear, "I don't know this man you're talking about!"

Immediately a rooster crowed a second time, and Peter remembered when Jesus had spoken the word to him, "Before the rooster crows twice, you will deny me three times." And he broke down and wept.

Listen with me:

Peter's devotion to Jesus was unquestionable; it was just imperfect. Peter was devoted with all of the commitment that a human heart could muster up. But his devotion had not yet been transformed by the power of the Holy Spirit into something that was self-sacrificing in its nature.

Peter had followed Jesus at a distance right into the courtyard of the High Priest's house (Mark 14:54), but he went no further. From the courtyard he would be able to hear snatches of what was going on inside at the trial. But at the same time, he figured that he would be safe from being accused of being associated with Jesus. As far as anyone knew, he was just someone warming himself by the fire.

As the night stretched toward the wee morning hours, it happened – he was recognized. Where the servant girl had seen Peter with Jesus was anybody's guess. She had probably been one of the thousands in the crowd as Jesus taught in the temple court. But now she was pointing straight at Peter. She had looked closely, and even in the flickering firelight was sure that Peter was someone whom she had seen with Jesus.

It was more curiosity than threat that was motivating her. Everybody had heard about Jesus; most of them had heard His teachings; and they could all hear the heated conversations going on inside. Who was this Jesus, really? What was His story? Why were the authorities so worked up about Him?

When the woman identified Peter, all eyes moved instantly to him, filled with curiosity. Here was someone who could tell them about this man who was causing such a stir. But in those stares, all that Peter felt was a threat. If they knew that he was one of Jesus' disciples, he could be arrested and taken inside, too! Maybe they would force him to testify against Jesus. He stood and turned away from the fire, not even consciously hearing the rooster crow in the distance as he said, "I don't have any idea what you're talking about. I don't know that man."

He was going to leave, to get away from this woman who knew who he was, but at the entryway he stopped and listened some more to what was happening inside. Things didn't sound like they were going well. He strained his ears for every word. Then suddenly that woman was there again, telling the others nearby, "This fellow is one of them." Again all eyes turned toward him, nailing him down. "Me? The woman is crazy. I don't know the man! I just came in to get warm!"

Peter went back to listening to the conversation from inside the house, but he quickly noticed that several of the people nearby were looking his way and talking in low voices. Finally one of them said, "You have to be one of His followers. We can tell by your accent that you're from Galilee, just like him."

Curious people started to move in his direction. All eyes seemed to be turned toward him, and he was filled with terror.

From inside he could hear the sound of Jesus being slapped, and the loud cries of "Prophesy! Tell us who just hit you!" (Mark 14:65). And he panicked. He swore before God that he didn't know Jesus; called down curses on his head if he was lying.

Just then the sound of a rooster crowing cut through the scene. And with that sound, Jesus' voice came back to Peter, telling him that no matter how much he swore to go even to death for Jesus, before the rooster would crow twice in the morning, Peter would deny three times even knowing Him. Peter had scoffed at the time at the very idea that he would be able to deny Jesus, even swearing that he would die rather than deny Him. (Mark 14:31) But here he was at the cockcrow, and he had done it, just as Jesus had said.

The crowed was astonished as Peter suddenly burst into tears and ran out into the pre-dawn darkness.

Pray with me:

Father, it's easy to pledge allegiance to You when times are easy, and when things are going my way. But the real test is whether I will stand strong for You when times are hard – when people start calling me narrow-minded, or bigoted, or unloving for standing for You and Your word. They might even threaten my home, my business, my family, or my life. Will I stand firm for You then? Or will I deny you to save what is dearer to me than You? Lord, my words, and even my best intentions, mean nothing if they all fade away in the heat of mistreatment or persecution, as Peter found out. Help me to do better now than Peter did then. Help me to stand strong for You, no matter what, so that I can continue to glorify Your name every day of my life. Amen.

MARK 15:1-5

Read with me:

As soon as it was morning, having held a meeting with the elders, scribes, and the whole Sanhedrin, the chief priests tied Jesus up, led him away and handed him over to Pilate.

So Pilate asked him, "Are You the King of the Jews?"

He answered him, "You say so."

And the chief priests accused him of many things. Pilate questioned him again, "Aren't you going to answer? Look how many things they are accusing you of!" But Jesus still did not answer, and so Pilate was amazed.

Listen with me:

Even though the Sanhedrin didn't know it, they were walking right into the path of the prophecy God had given about how the Messiah would die. This was true even to the point that when they found Jesus guilty of supposed blasphemy, they didn't simply take Him out and stone Him to death, according to the law (Leviticus 24:13-17). Instead, He was taken to Pilate so that they could convince him to crucify Him (just as it was prophesied).

One of the first accusations that they brought before Pilate was that Jesus had claimed to be the Messiah, who was also widely believed to be the legitimate king of the Jewish people (Luke 23:2), and who would thus presumably stir up the people to revolt against Roman rule. This stirring up of the people was the crime of sedition, a capital offense. But when Pilate followed up this accusation by asking Jesus directly, "Are You the king of the Jews?" Jesus simply answered, "You say so," which is the Aramaic equivalent of "Yes, it is as you say." The Messiah really was the true King of the Jews, but at the same time, Jesus knew that His kingdom was not an earthly kingdom, but a heavenly one. (John 18:36) Pilate had seen sedition before, and he had seen people trying to stir up rebellion against Rome. But in Jesus' attitude Pilate could see none of that.

When that accusation didn't seem to gain any traction, the chief priests began reeling off other accusations against Jesus, trying to find anything that would lead Pilate to condemn Him. Just as in the Sanhedrin, they hoped to overwhelm the legal system with the sheer volume of the accusations. But, just as He did earlier, Jesus did not answer a single false accusation against Him. That was because at this point in the process, Jesus had placed His entire fate in the hands of His Father. He was now simply going along for the ride as God moved events forward, answering to confirm true statements, but feeling no obligation at all to defend Himself against lies.

This was amazing to Pilate. In any other case like this, the accused would have been struggling to defend himself against every charge, trying to save their own lives. But ever since Gethsemane, Jesus had already surrendered His life – He had nothing to defend except the truth of who He was.

Pray with me:

Father, this is an amazing thought, and very applicable to today. So often we end up allowing ourselves to be put on the defensive over what we believe, and how we apply those beliefs in our lives. We become defensive because we are trying to defend our lives, our lifestyle, our beliefs, or our reputation. But if we have already given ourselves up to You as a living sacrifice, there is nothing for us to defend except the truth. And that frees us up to ignore the many things that the antagonists of the gospel throw at us to try to overwhelm us, and frees us up to simply speak the truth at the appropriate time. Help me, Lord, to make this commitment, this sacrifice, so that I can walk in Jesus' steps, even in this. Amen.

MARK 15:6-15

Read with me:

At the festival Pilate used to release for the people a prisoner whom they requested. There was one named Barabbas, who was in prison with rebels who had committed murder during the rebellion. The crowd came up and began to ask Pilate to do for them as was his custom. Pilate answered them, "Do you want me to release the King of the Jews for you?" For he knew it was because of envy that the chief priests had handed him over. But the chief priests stirred up the crowd so that he would release Barabbas to them instead. Pilate asked them again, "Then what do you want me to do with the one you call the King of the Jews?"

Again they shouted, "Crucify Him!"

Pilate said to them, "Why? What has he done wrong?"

But they shouted all the more, "Crucify Him!"

Wanting to satisfy the crowd, Pilate released Barabbas to them; and after having Jesus flogged, he handed him over to be crucified.

Listen with me:

Pilate was no dummy. He knew that the chief priests had brought Jesus to him, not because He posed any real threat to the authority of Rome (When had the chief priests ever been concerned about challenges to Rome's authority?), but because they wanted Pilate to do their dirty work for them by getting rid of someone that they found a challenge to their own authority.

When the people asked Pilate to continue his annual tradition of releasing one prisoner at the Passover, he figured that this would be the perfect avenue to free Jesus, and to stymie the plans of the Jewish leaders. After all, Pilate didn't live in a box! He had heard of Jesus, and knew that, even though He was hated by the Jewish leaders, he was overwhelmingly popular with the common people.

But the chief priests had already been at work among the crowds, urging them to ask Pilate to release Barabbas (a man who really was guilty of sedition) instead of Jesus. In one of the most stunning turn of events in history, God's people chose a known murderer over the giver of eternal life. They chose a rebel over the Son of the very God that they claimed to serve.

This left Pilate in a quandary. If he released Barabbas, what was he to do with Jesus? He could have simply released Him on the grounds that He had not been proven guilty of anything. But instead, Pilate asked the crowd what should be done. The crowd had already been turned into a mob by the chief priests; a mob that could be easily manipulated. So when Pilate looked to them for reason, he got back manipulated passion instead: "Crucify Him!"

Pilate was stunned. This really put him into a nasty corner. This crowd that had been turned into a mob was quickly threatening to become a riot, and that was the last thing in the world that he wanted. He had already been put on notice by the Emperor for the harsh way in which he had put down a couple of previous insurrections. One more strike, and he was out!

Pilate tried to reason with them. Crucifixion was a terrible thing to do to anyone, the most painful method of execution ever devised by sinful mankind. Pilate's argument to the crowd was that Jesus had not been convicted of any crime, let alone one that deserved death by crucifixion. But the crowd was now beyond the point of logic. The steady chant of "Crucify Him" grew and grew until it overpowered Pilate's voice, and finally overpowered His resolve.

Even though he knew that he was being manipulated, Pilate decided that the easiest path was to placate the crowd. It might be a miscarriage of justice (he could comfort himself by thinking that maybe Jesus really was guilty of something, even if he didn't know what it was), but it was, after all, only one man. And what is one man in the grand scheme of things? So Pilate issued two orders. One released Barabbas from prison, and the other sentenced Jesus to be flogged, and then crucified.

MARK 15

Pray with me:

Father, it is easy to believe that this was a gross miscarriage of justice, when the guilty one was set free and the innocent one was sentenced to death. But isn't that really the gospel in a nutshell? When I receive salvation by receiving Jesus as my Lord and Savior, I am Barabbas, the guilty one who, for no good of my own, suddenly finds that I have been released from my own death sentence, set free from the bondage of sin. And, in my place, Jesus, the spotless, sinless Lamb of God, suffers and dies. So really, Lord, this was not a miscarriage of justice after all. It is instead an amazing picture of Your salvation, painted on the way to the cross. Thank You, Lord, for that amazing love, that amazing grace, that saves a wretch, a Barabbas, like me. Amen.

MARK 15:16-20

Read with me:

The soldiers led him away into the palace (that is, the governor's residence) and called the whole company together. They dressed him in a purple robe, twisted together a crown of thorns, and put it on him. And they began to salute Him, "Hail, King of the Jews!" They were hitting him on the head with a stick and spitting on him. Getting down on their knees, they were paying him homage. After they had mocked him, they stripped him of the purple robe and put his clothes on him.
They led him out to crucify him.

Listen with me:

The mocking of Jesus is difficult to witness. Jesus, flogged horribly, bleeding freely from wounds all over His back, His arms, His legs, is completely helpless and weak. Now He is surrounded by a whole company of soldiers whose job it will be to put Him to death.

These men have heard that Jesus had claimed to be the king of the Jews (Mark 15:2). In fact, the plaque detailing His crime, "Jesus of Nazareth, King of the Jews," which would ultimately be nailed above His head on the cross, was already in their hands. This was way different than the normal type of criminal that they were charged with executing - thieves, murderers, insurrectionists. So they decided to have a little fun with Jesus before they led Him out to the execution site.

They designed their actions to be a farce, a comedy. Only after the fact could the irony of the situation be seen that made it a tragedy instead. They dressed Jesus as a king, draping a royal purple cloak across his torn back and shoulders. A wreath twisted together from thorns served as a makeshift crown. They put a stick in His hand to serve as a staff (Matthew 27:29), and then mockingly bowed down to Him, declaring solemnly, "Hail, King of the Jews!"

But then things turned ugly. They took the stick from His hand, and used it to beat Him over the head. They slapped Him over and over again, and spit in His face. All of this was just as Jesus had predicted (Mark 10:33-34).

In just a few minute's time, they had done their work to degrade and humiliate the "King of the Jews." He had been beaten to a pulp, and was now a mere wreck of a man. The loss of blood and the shock of the beating had left Him so weak that He could barely stand. And that suited His tormentors just fine. That meant that He would die all the quicker, making their job easier.

But it was now time to get on with it. They took off the purple cloak, and draped Jesus own cloak across His shoulders. They then led Him out to start the march out of the city to the execution site.

Pray with me:

Father, to these men the person in front of them was just a man. All that they could see was the outer shell of humanity, already torn and bloodied from the flogging. They had no eyes to see the Son of God inside that human skin, the one whose glory briefly peeking through on the Mount of Transfiguration had filled His disciples with such profound awe. They had no idea that the one that they were mocking as the "King of the Jews" was in fact the King of all kings, and the Lord of all lords; the one before whom every knee will one day bow (Philippians 2:9-11). They had no idea that they were leading to the slaughter the pure, holy Lamb of God, and that through their unwitting participation, they would be helping to bring about the possibility of salvation for all humankind.

But we know those things now, Lord. Help me to never take them for granted; to never minimize what Jesus went through to buy my salvation, suffering all of that torment, humiliation, and pain on my behalf. Help me to always hold Jesus up as my Lord and King, and, as such, to follow Him and obey Him every moment of every day. Amen.

MARK 15:21-32

Read with me:

They forced a man coming in from the country, who was passing by, to carry Jesus' cross. He was Simon of Cyrene, the father of Alexander and Rufus.

They brought Jesus to the place called Golgotha (which means Place of the Skull). They tried to give him wine mixed with myrrh, but he did not take it.

Then they crucified him and divided his clothes, casting lots for them to decide what each would get. Now it was nine in the morning when they crucified him. The inscription of the charge written against him was: **THE KING OF THE JEWS.** *They crucified two criminals with him, one on his right and one on his left.*

Those who passed by were yelling insults at him, shaking their heads, and saying, "Ha! The one who would destroy the temple and rebuild it in three days, save yourself by coming down from the cross!" In the same way, the chief priests with the scribes were mocking him among themselves and saying, "He saved others, but he cannot save himself! Let the Messiah, the King of Israel, come down now from the cross, so that we may see and believe." Even those who were crucified with him taunted him.

Listen with me:

Jesus started out carrying His own cross (actually the heavy crossbeam, which would be attached to the upright at the execution place), but it quickly proved to be more than He could handle in His severely weakened condition. The executioners had no patience to nurse Him along, so they pressed Simon into service to carry the crossbeam for Him.

The simple words, "Then they crucified Him," repeated with only slight variation in all four gospels (Matthew 27:35; Luke 23:33; John 19:18) betrays the disgust that all four writers felt over the very words. For anyone who had ever witnessed a crucifixion, the mere word itself was enough to conjure up in their minds the gut-wrenching reality of the experience. But even for those who hadn't, the word seemed to carry a load of horror that you wanted to stay away from.

After being stripped naked (the loincloths seen in paintings were added to avoid shocking more modern sensibilities), the victim was nailed to the crossbar with large spikes driven through the wrists. This crushed and tore through a major juncture of nerves, causing excruciating pain that radiated through the arms and across the back. (Victims were generally offered wine mixed with myrrh to deaden a bit of the pain, but Jesus refused it when it was offered to Him. His job was to experience every bit of the suffering involved in the process.) The crossbar was then lifted onto the upright post and fastened in place. During this time, all of the weight of the victim was left dangling on the nails through their wrists, frequently dislocating their elbows and shoulders. Their feet were then nailed through with the same kind of large spikes. These lower nails provided a platform for the condemned to use to push themselves up on to temporarily relieve the pressure on their arms.

Despite paintings showing tall crosses, the feet of the condemned were usually only a few inches off the ground. The execution places were chosen for maximum exposure, usually along the main road into the city. The charges for which each person was being executed were written on a board which was then nailed above their heads. Those crucified on either side of Jesus had boards that read "Robber." The one above Jesus' head read "King of the Jews." The whole purpose of those boards was to let people know, "If you do these things, this will be your punishment." It was an effective deterrent.

The humiliation of crucifixion was multi-dimensional. In addition to the shame of hanging there naked and helpless right next to the main road, those passing by often threw insults at the sufferers. Jesus had a special share of those in the form of the Sanhedrin members and chief priests, all of whom came to watch their old nemesis die. They thought that it was doing their hearts good to see the all-powerful, all-wise Jesus hanging there, unable to even save Himself. And they added their jeers to those of the others in the crowd: "He claimed to have saved others, but He can't even save Himself!" "Hey Jesus! Come down off that cross, and we'll believe in You!" And while all of this was going on, just a few yards away, the soldiers in charge of the execution detail were dividing up the clothing of the victims – one of the perks of the job.

Those who were mocking and taunting Jesus for His helplessness and His inability to save Himself had no idea that with a single word He could have changed everything. Jesus knew that if He called on the Father, that He would immediately place at His disposal more than twelve legions of angels to rescue Him (Matthew 26:52-54). But He also knew that going through all of this suffering was the only way that salvation could be purchased for all humanity, and He was absolutely committed to seeing it through. It was not that He was unable to save Himself; He was unwilling to save Himself at the cost of our salvation.

Pray with me:

Father, when I think of all that Jesus went through, all of the pain as well as the humiliation, I am ashamed to remember that I sometimes forget how much He went through for me, and that I sometimes treat His sacrifice lightly. The idea that He could have easily put an end to all of it, but refused for my sake, and for the sake of all humanity, is humbling in the extreme. Help me, Lord, to never forget the cost of the salvation that Jesus bought for me, to never gloss over it, and to never treat it lightly. Amen.

MARK 15:33-37

Read with me:

When it was noon, darkness came over the whole land until three in the afternoon. And at three Jesus cried out with a loud voice, "Eloi, Eloi, lemá sabachtháni?" which is translated, **"My God, my God, why have you abandoned me?"** *[Psalm 22:1]*

When some of those standing there heard this, they said, "See, he's calling for Elijah!"

Someone ran and filled a sponge with sour wine, fixed it on a stick, offered him a drink, and said, "Let's see if Elijah comes to take him down!"

Jesus let out a loud cry and breathed his last.

Listen with me:

Some try to explain the darkness that came over the land through natural phenomena, such as an eclipse. But the crucifixion happened at the Passover, which is always at the time of the full moon when no solar eclipse is possible, since the sun and moon are in opposition. And eclipses don't last for three hours! Instead, this was a decidedly supernatural phenomenon, one that God personally brought about to show those who were witnessing these events that, far from a normal crucifixion, something hair-raising was going on - the people of God killing God's Messiah in cold blood. It was no religious fanatic, no heretic, no criminal hanging on the cross, but God's one and only Son, through whom all things had been created (John 1:3), and by whom all things are sustained (Hebrews 1:3).

The darkness freaked the people out who were gathered by the cross, and some of them left in fear. But others, explaining everything away to their own satisfaction, stayed to taunt Jesus.

347

WHEN WE LISTEN

At the end, Jesus chanted the first line of Psalm 22, a Psalm with deep significance, since God had enabled David to unconsciously extrapolate from his own suffering to describe the sufferings of his descendant, the Messiah, in excruciating detail. Jesus was now living out what David had seen, fulfilling the prophecy to the letter.

But the people gathered there at the cross misunderstood Him, partly because Jesus' swollen lips and tongue made it difficult for Him to enunciate clearly, and partly because they didn't know the Scriptures nearly as well as they should have. They heard in His "Eloi, Eloi" ("My God, my God") a call for Elijah. They gave Jesus a little sour wine to drink, and then taunted Him with, "Now let's see if Elijah comes to take Him down!" But their taunts went unacknowledged by Jesus. Instead, marshalling all of His remaining strength, He shouted out, "Father, into Your hands I commit My spirit" (Luke 23:46), and more softly, "It is finished." (John 19:30) Then He yielded His spirit to the Father, and died.

Pray with me:

Father, it is amazing to see how in-control Jesus stayed this whole time. No last minute ranting, no pleading. He simply walked through the ordeal laid out for Him before the world was made (1 Peter 1:20). His steadfastness, even in the face of nearly continual taunting; the fact that He didn't lash out at those who jeered at Him, but prayed for them instead (Luke 23:34); all of these point us to a life that was infinitely more than it seemed to be. Lord, help me to never minimize what Jesus did, and to never forget the love (both Yours and His) that moved Him to do it. Help me to always stand at the foot of the cross in awe and wonder. Amen.

MARK 15:38-41

Read with me:

Then the curtain of the sanctuary was torn in two from top to bottom. When the centurion, who was standing opposite him, saw the way he breathed his last, he said, "Truly this man was the Son of God!"

There were also women watching from a distance. Among them were Mary Magdalene, Mary the mother of James the younger and of Joses, and Salome. In Galilee, these women followed him and took care of him. Many other women had come up with him to Jerusalem.

Listen with me:

Jesus' death was as supernatural as His life was. The darkness that had fallen over the land (Mark 15:33) ended when He died, but at the same time, the earth shook in a violent earthquake that even broke open some of the tombs in the area (Matthew 27:51-53). It was the conjunction of these terrifying signs that caused the centurion to cry out, *"Truly this man was the Son of God!"* He had seen a lot of crucifixions, a lot of deaths, but he had never seen one accompanied by this kind of cosmic uproar. All of these signs coinciding with the suffering and death of this remarkable man could not be written off as mere chance.

At the moment of Jesus' death the veil in the temple that separated the holy place from the most holy place was torn in two. There were two significant things about this tearing. First, the veil was extremely thick - the rabbis describe it as being as thick as the width of a man's hand. It was composed of multiple layers all woven together into a single mass. Thus it would have been impossible for it to have been torn by a person (or even by many people), even by the shaking of the earthquake.

WHEN WE LISTEN

The second significant thing is that the veil was torn from the top to the bottom. The rip began 30 feet off the ground, clearly disqualifying any human intervention, and showing that this event had originated with God Himself.

This tearing of this dense separator between God's presence and mankind symbolized the fact that, with Jesus' death, God's presence would now be among His people in a new and powerful way. No longer would it just be experienced by the high priests and the prophets; it would be experienced by all of God's people, from the greatest to the least, as prophesied by Joel (Joel 2:28-32; Acts 2:17-21). Jesus' death had made it possible for the sins that had separated people from God to be paid in full, and for full fellowship to be restored.

Verses 40-41 are incidental but important. They point out that there were many of Jesus' followers, faithful women who had served Him during His ministry, who were eyewitnesses to not only His suffering and death, but to all of the miraculous signs that attended them. This lays the ground work for the resurrection to be discovered first by some of these same women.

Pray with me:

Father, even today the death of Jesus is seen by some as merely a tragedy, the undeserved death of a great martyr. Through the ages there have been many deaths of martyrs. But only the death of Jesus was accompanied by these kinds of miraculous signs, showing that this was something more. Your finger prints were all over this, demonstrating that Jesus really was Your Son, just like He had said, and that His death was not only extraordinary, but that it accomplished extraordinary things. Amen.

MARK 15:42-47

Read with me:

When it was already evening, because it was the day of preparation (that is, the day before the Sabbath), Joseph of Arimathea, a prominent member of the Sanhedrin who was himself looking forward to the kingdom of God, came and boldly went to Pilate and asked for Jesus's body. Pilate was surprised that he was already dead. Summoning the centurion, he asked him whether he had already died. When he found out from the centurion, he gave the corpse to Joseph. After he bought some linen cloth, Joseph took him down and wrapped him in the linen. Then he laid him in a tomb cut out of the rock and rolled a stone against the entrance to the tomb. Mary Magdalene and Mary the mother of Joses were watching where he was laid.

Listen with me:

The Sabbath would begin at sundown on Friday, and after that, no work could be done for twenty-four hours, not even preparing a body for burial. So Joseph, who had a new tomb nearby that he had prepared for himself and his family (Matthew 27:60), went to ask Pilate for Jesus' body.

Pilate was surprised that Jesus had already died. He had not suffered as long as many who were crucified - some lasted three or four days before they died. Some have attributed Jesus' relatively quick death to His weakened condition due to the series of severe beatings and whippings that He had received. But Jesus only needed to suffer on the cross until the work there was done. Then He didn't just die, He purposefully "gave up His spirit" (Matthew 27:50).

When Pilate had verified that Jesus was dead, he released the body for burial, and Joseph got to work. Time was passing, and the sun was sinking fast. Normally the bodies of executed criminals received a hasty burial, especially those who had been crucified, and were believed to be cursed by God by being "hung on a tree" (Deuteronomy 21:23; Galatians 3:13). But Joseph, assisted by Nicodemus, who brought along seventy-five pounds of fragrant embalming compounds (John 19:39-40), wrapped the body carefully in a linen cloth, and laid it lovingly in the tomb before rolling the large stone in place across the entrance.

The statement in verse 47 is significant. Some have conjectured that on Sunday morning the women went to the wrong tomb, found it empty, and declared Jesus risen. But there was no mistake. These women to whom Jesus was so dear watched every movement of Joseph and Nicodemus. They saw them roll the stone in place, and they knew that they would be coming back on Sunday morning at first light, after the Sabbath was over, to complete the job of preparing Jesus body for its final rest; a job that had, out of necessity, been hastily done at the time. They knew the place, and noted it well so that there would be no mistake when Sunday morning came.

Pray with me:

Father, these people really put themselves out there. While many of Jesus' closest disciples had fled for fear of being caught up in the snare that had been laid for Jesus, this handful of people had a devotion to Him that overcame any fear, and they bravely identified themselves as being tied to Him, regardless of the possible consequences. Even today, Lord, there are some who hide their faith out of fear of those who oppose them. But there are others, strong witnesses, who stand boldly for Jesus, regardless of the potential consequences. Even in the face of loss of property, imprisonment, suffering, and death, they don't hide, they don't deny, and they don't even remain silent. Help me always to belong to that class of Christian, so that Your name is always glorified in my life. Amen.

MARK 16:1-8

Read with me:

When the Sabbath was over, Mary Magdalene, Mary the mother of James, and Salome bought spices, so they could go and anoint him. Very early in the morning, on the first day of the week, they went to the tomb at sunrise. They were saying to one another, "Who will roll away the stone from the entrance to the tomb for us?" Looking up, they noticed that the stone—which was very large—had been rolled away.

When they entered the tomb, they saw a young man dressed in a white robe sitting on the right side; they were alarmed. "Don't be alarmed," he told them. "You are looking for Jesus of Nazareth, who was crucified. He has risen! He is not here! See the place where they put Him. But go, tell his disciples and Peter, 'He is going ahead of you to Galilee; you will see him there just as He told you.'"

They went out and ran from the tomb, because trembling and astonishment overwhelmed them. And they said nothing to anyone, since they were afraid. (NIV)

Listen with me:

The women had brought with them precious spices and ointments to apply to Jesus' body. These did not "embalm" or preserve the body - that was not their purpose. Their fragrance merely helped to offset the odor of decay. But even more, they hoped to show honor to this man who had meant so much to them. Jesus' body had not been washed and anointed, as was traditional, because the Sabbath had been quickly approaching. They intended to do now what had been left undone two days before.

The biggest issue they believed they would face was the stone that had been rolled in front of the tomb's door to seal it. It was huge, and they had no idea how they would be able to move it so that they could get in.

But that quickly became a moot issue when they got to the tomb and found the stone already pushed to the side. Their first thought was that someone had broken in and had abused or stolen the body. But when they went in, their attention was immediately arrested by the young man dressed in white who was sitting where the body should have been.

The angel's message was short and clear:

- *"Don't be alarmed"* - You can almost hear an echo of Christmas in this: *"Do not be afraid, for look, I proclaim to you good news of great joy that will be for all the people."* (Luke 2:10)

- *"You are looking for Jesus of Nazareth, who was crucified."* - There was no mistake. They had come to the right tomb.

- *"He has risen!"* - The most earthshaking declaration ever pronounced to human ears. The One who was beaten, crucified, and pierced had risen from the dead. He who was certified dead was now alive again!

- *"He is not here. See the place where they put him."* - With one elegant gesture, the angel pointed to the empty slab as proof that his words were true. Jesus' body that had been laid out right there was gone.

- *"But go, tell his disciples and Peter, 'He is going ahead of you to Galilee; you will see him there just as he told you.'"* - The plans that Jesus had laid out before He had been crucified were still in effect. The disciples didn't understand those plans at first, and figured that, since Jesus was dead, they were all useless anyway. But they were planned to be carried out after Jesus rose. (The disciples delayed in going to Galilee while they tried to figure out what had "really" happened. So before Jesus met the disciples in Galilee, He appeared to many of them in and around Jerusalem.)

The women went away trembling with fear and bewilderment. They had heard the words of the angel - clear, concise words. They had seen the empty stone slab where Jesus' body had been laid out. But they couldn't put all of the pieces together in their minds. It was all so far outside of their normal experiences. Sure, Jesus had raised several people from the dead. But who had raised Him?

They didn't speak a word to anyone they met on their way to the upper room where the disciples were gathered. They were not about to sound forth this amazing news until they had time to think it through!

Pray with me:

Father, it strikes me that Jesus had told all of His followers, presumably including these women, that He would rise on the third day, but His words sounded so alien, so out of touch, that they found no resting place in their minds. The disciples were not preparing for the resurrection. They were hiding out in fear that the Jews would come and arrest them, too. (John 20:19) The women weren't preparing for Jesus' resurrection. They had spent their time waiting out the Sabbath and then preparing the spices, so that they could better prepare Jesus' body for the decay that they saw as inevitable. But all of that planning, strategizing, and preparing turned out to be worthless, because Jesus kept His promise and rose from the dead on the third day. Lord, how many of my plans, strategies, and preparations ultimately turn out to be useless, because I have ignored or failed to grasp the amazing promises You have made to me? How much wasted time and energy do I engage in, when all I really have to do is to obey You, and wait for the miracles You have promised? Sometimes Your promises are too amazing for me to believe. Help me to believe them anyway, so that I can see Your power at work in and through my life. Amen.

MARK 16:9-14

Read with me:

Early on the first day of the week, after he had risen, he appeared first to Mary Magdalene, out of whom he had driven seven demons. She went and reported to those who had been with him, as they were mourning and weeping. Yet, when they heard that he was alive and had been seen by her, they did not believe it.

After this, he appeared in a different form to two of them walking on their way into the country. And they went and reported it to the rest, who did not believe them either. Later, he appeared to the Eleven themselves as they were reclining at the table. He rebuked their unbelief and hardness of heart, because they did not believe those who saw him after he had risen.

Listen with me:

Even though this final section is not part of Mark's original gospel, it provides a summary of information condensed from the other gospels and Acts, bringing this gospel to a "neater" finish than it had without it.

Some have wondered why it was to Mary Magdalene that Jesus chose to appear first. The simple answer is that she was the first one who hung around the tomb long enough for Him to make contact. The other women (and Mary) ran to tell the disciples about the open tomb, the missing body, and the angels, immediately after they heard the news. No opportunity there. Peter and John ran into the tomb, followed by Mary, but after they had verified that the body was missing, they immediately walked away (John 20:3-11).

But Mary stayed at the tomb until she became aware of a man standing nearby who she thought was a gardener, and then realized was Jesus (John 20:14-16). If the others had stayed at the tomb for a while, they would have seen Him, too. A lot of the time people miss out on huge blessings because they are far too anxious to move on to the next thing. Their minds and hearts are focused somewhere down the road, and they miss out on what is right next to them, waiting to be revealed.

When Mary reported to the gathered disciples that she had actually seen and spoken to Jesus Himself, they thought that she was crazy, or at best hallucinating. With no frame of reference, no prior similar event in biblical history to point to, they would not believe such an outrageous thing (even though their hearts really wanted to).

Next recalled is Jesus' appearance to Cleopas and another disciple on the road to Emmaus (Luke 14:13-35). Even though Jesus walked with them for some time, talking with them and teaching them, they had no idea it was Him. They didn't believe that He had risen, even though they had heard the testimony of Mary, and they had no expectation that He would suddenly show up next to them on the road, so their eyes were closed to who He really was. It was only when He broke and blessed the bread that their eyes were opened, and they suddenly recognized Him. And then He simply vanished, leaving them with even more questions.

Late that same evening, after Cleopas and the other disciple returned to Jerusalem with their story of seeing Jesus, He suddenly appeared in the midst of their gathering (Luke 24:36-49). Even with Him standing right there, they still had a hard time believing that the resurrection was real. They thought He was a ghost, and it took a while to convince them otherwise.

Jesus rebuked the disciples for not believing those who had already seen Him. No matter how strange His resurrection might have been, no matter how far outside of "normal" experience it was, He had told them clearly that it was going to happen, and that should have been enough for them to be waiting for it, expecting it, and rejoicing greatly when they heard that it had happened.

WHEN WE LISTEN

Pray with me:

Father, we are still so much like those early disciples today. You have made us so many amazing and excellent promises, but we are shocked, and in some cases disbelieving, when You actually make them happen. Father, help me to read and to hear Your promises with new eyes and ears, and with a heart that believes and looks for their fulfillment. Help my first response to be faith every time You speak, so that I don't waste time doubting or trying to explain things away when You act. Amen.

MARK 16:15-20

Read with me:

Then He said to them, "Go into all the world and preach the gospel to all creation. Whoever believes and is baptized will be saved, but whoever does not believe will be condemned. And these signs will accompany those who believe: In my name they will drive out demons; they will speak in new tongues; they will pick up snakes; if they should drink anything deadly, it will not harm them; they will lay hands on the sick, and they will get well."

So the Lord Jesus, after speaking to them, was taken up into heaven and sat down at the right hand of God. And they went out and preached everywhere, while the Lord worked with them and confirmed the word by the accompanying signs.

Listen with me:

This is a summary of Jesus' commands and promises, drawn from several different places in the gospels and the Acts.

•   The commission to "Go into all the world and preach the good news to all creation" is Mark's version of Matthew 28:18-20, the Great Commission, and Acts 1:8. Jesus' ultimate emphasis was on reaching the whole world with the good news (the "gospel"), not just "the lost sheep of Israel," (Matthew 15:24), although His mission while on earth was predominantly to the Jewish people, because they had been prepared more than anyone else to receive Him. But after He had accomplished His work on the cross, the mission for God's people, the Church, was to "preach the good news to all creation," to "make disciples of all nations."

WHEN WE LISTEN

•   The criteria for salvation was (and is) very simple: believe and be baptized. Believing was both belief in who Jesus was (sometimes called "believing in His name – John 1:12-13), and believing that His death and resurrection paid for our sins, and grants us eternal life. This belief is what Jesus was referring to in John 14:6, when He told His disciples, *"I am the way and the truth and the life. No one comes to the Father except through me."* That sounds too narrow and exclusive to many today, but Jesus proved by His resurrection (something no other "religious leader" has ever been able to do) that He was, and is, unique.

•   The list of signs is taken from the list of things that Jesus and the apostles did, both in Scripture, and in tradition. Jesus Himself promised that those who believed in Him *"will also do the works that I do. And he will do even greater works than these, because I am going to the Father."* (John 14:12)

And the early apostles fulfilled that promise:

•   They drove out demons (Acts 5:16, 16:16-18).

•   They spoke in new tongues that enabled them to preach the good news across language barriers (Acts 2:4-12).

•   They were saved from the bites of poisonous snakes (Acts 28:3-6).

•   They placed their hands on sick people and made them well (Acts 2:43, 3:1-8, 5:16, 8:6-7, 9:33-34, and many others).

•   And they did many other miracles, which lent huge credibility to their message.

The sign of not being affected by drinking poison is not attested to specifically in the book of Acts, but is referred to in the traditions of the Church.

Jesus' ascension into heaven to the right hand of the Father is witnessed to in Luke 24:50-51 and Acts 1:9-11, as well as in Stephen's vision of Jesus in Acts 7:55-56. And, of course, the rapid expansion of the gospel, empowered by God's presence and the Holy Spirit, is chronicled throughout the book of Acts and in the epistles.

Pray with me:

Father, it grieves me that there is so little of this power demonstrated among your people today. As a rule, at least in most places in the west, we don't see many Christians doing signs and wonders, healing, casting out demons, and doing "even greater works" than Jesus. Instead, most of Your people seem to be powerless, unable to do what You promised that "anyone who believes in (Jesus)" would be able to do (John 14:12).

Some have taught that miracles like that don't happen anymore; that they were just for New Testament times. But I don't draw any comfort from that, because I don't see it in Your word. And the truth is that we need Your power, Your presence, Your mighty acts working though us today to help us to reach the millions in our own nations who don't know You. I'm not asking this for my glory, but for Yours; not for my own comfort, but so that I can move Your agenda forward in Your power. Lord, visit Your people again with power. Refresh and renew us by the presence and power of Your Holy Spirit flowing through our lives. Help us to do what Jesus did, and even greater things today, so that we can reverse the slide of our cities, our nations, into darkness, and so that we can once again be empowered to bring thousands into Your light. Amen.

ABOUT THE AUTHOR

Will Robertson is the Senior Pastor of Woodburn Fellowship Church of the Nazarene in Woodburn, Oregon. His passion is to help people become active, reproducing, Christlike followers of Jesus, who reflect His glory to the world around them, and who consistently act as salt and light in their communities.

He writes a daily blog, and a column in the local newspaper. He and his wife, Sharla Ann, live in Woodburn, Oregon.

Made in the USA
Columbia, SC
26 September 2024

43103491R00198